MW01519180

The Formation
of Pastoral Counselors:
Challenges and Opportunities

The Formation of Pastoral Counselors: Challenges and Opportunities has been co-published simultaneously as *American Journal of Pastoral Counseling*, Volume 8, Numbers 3/4 2006.

Monographic Separates from the *American Journal of Pastoral Counseling*[TM]

For additional information on these and other Haworth Press titles, including descriptions, tables of contents, reviews, and prices, use the QuickSearch catalog at http://www.HaworthPress.com.

The *American Journal of Pastoral Counseling*[TM] is the successor title to *Journal of Pastoral Psychotherapy* which changed title after Vol. 2, No. 1, 1989. The *American Journal of Pastoral Counseling*[TM], under its new title, begins with Vol. 1, No. 1, 1997.

The Formation of Pastoral Counselors: Challenges and Opportunities, edited by Duane R. Bidwell, PhD, and Joretta L. Marshall, PhD (Volume 8, No. 3/4, 2006). *Two dozen of the most prominent clinicians and scholars in the field reflect on "The Formation of Pastoral Counselors" from clinical, theological, and theoretical perspectives. This unique book explores the challenges to the personal and professional formation of pastoral counselors in a cultural and historic context that's radically different from the era when the profession first emerged as a specialized ministry. Contributors examine formation from a variety of contexts and perspectives, including spirituality and gender, address theological education and intercultural issues, and present emerging models for pastoral counselors.*

The Image of God and the Psychology of Religion, edited by Richard Dayringer, ThD, and David Oler, PhD (Vol. 7, No. 2, 2004). *"It is my hope that this anthology will open the door to further research on God-images, particularly investigating the implications of God-images for issues of race, culture, ethnicity, and racial oppression. It makes new inroads into empirical research about God-images, mental health, and clinical psychotherapy. Multiple religious traditions and perspectives, and the impact of both personified and non-anthropomorphic divine images, are sensitively presented in clients' own words." (Pamela Cooper-White, PhD, Professor of Pastoral Theology, Lutheran Theological Seminary of Philadelphia)*

International Perspectives on Pastoral Counseling, edited by James Reaves Farris, PhD (Vol. 5, No. 1/2, 3/4, 2002). *Explores pastoral care as practiced in Africa, India, Korea, Hong Kong, the Philippines, Central America, South America, Germany, and the United Kingdom.*

Pastoral Care and Counseling in Sexual Diversity, edited by H. Newton Malony, MDiv, PhD (Vol. 3, No. 3/4, 2001). *"A balanced and reasoned presentation of viewpoints." (Orlo Christopher Strunk, Jr., PhD, Professor Emeritus, Boston University; Managing Editor,* The Journal of Pastoral Care)

The Formation
of Pastoral Counselors:
Challenges and Opportunities

Duane R. Bidwell, PhD
Joretta L. Marshall, PhD
Editors

The Formation of Pastoral Counselors: Challenges and Opportunities has been co-published simultaneously as *American Journal of Pastoral Counseling*, Volume 8, Numbers 3/4 2006.

The Haworth Pastoral Press®
An Imprint of The Haworth Press, Inc.

New York • London • Victoria (AU)
www.HaworthPress.com

Published by

The Haworth Pastoral Press, 10 Alice Street, Binghamton, NY 13904-1580 USA

The Haworth Pastoral Press is an imprint of The Haworth Press, Inc., 10 Alice Street, Binghamton, NY 13904-1580 USA.

The Formation of Pastoral Counselors: Challenges and Opportunities has been co-published simultaneously as *American Journal of Pastoral Counseling,* Volume 8, Numbers 3/4 2006.

The development, preparation, and publication of this work has been undertaken with great care. However, the publisher, employees, editors, and agents of The Haworth Press and all imprints of The Haworth Press, Inc., including The Haworth Medical Press® and The Pharmaceutical Products Press®, are not responsible for any errors contained herein or for consequences that may ensue from use of materials or information contained in this work.

The Haworth Press is committed to the dissemination of ideas and information according to the highest standards of intellectual freedom and the free exchange of ideas. Ststements made and opinions expressed in this publication do not necessarily reflect the views of the Publisher, Directors, management, or staff of The Haworth Press, Inc., or an endorsement by them.

Library of Congress Cataloging-in-Publication Data

The formation of pastoral counselors : challenges and opportunities / Duane R. Bidwell, Joretta L. Marshall, editors.
   p. cm.
   "Co-published simultaneously as American Journal of Pastoral Counseling, Volume 8, Numbers (3/4) 2006."
   Includes bibliographical references and index.
   ISBN 13: 978-0-7890-3295-9 (hard cover : alk. paper)
   ISBN 10: 0-7890-3295-3 (hard cover : alk. paper)
   ISBN 13: 978-0-7890-3296-6 (soft cover : alk. paper)
   ISBN 10: 0-7890-3296-1 (soft cover : alk. paper)
  1. Patoral counseling. I. Bidwell, Duane R. II. Marshall, Joretta L.
   BV4012.2 .F67 2007
   253.5–dc21   2006035768

The HAWORTH PRESS *Inc.*
Abstracting, Indexing & Outward Linking
PRINT *and* ELECTRONIC BOOKS & JOURNALS

This section provides you with a list of major indexing & abstracting services and other tools for bibliographic access. That is to say, each service began covering this periodical during the the year noted in the right column. Most Websites which are listed below have indicated that they will either post, disseminate, compile, archive, cite or alert their own Website users with research-based content from this work. (This list is as current as the copyright date of this publication.)

Abstracting, Website/Indexing Coverage . . . . Year When Coverage Began

- *(IBR) International Bibliography of Book Reviews on the Humanities and Social Sciences (Thomson) <http://www.saur.de>* **2006**

- *(IBZ) International Bibliography of Periodical Literature on the Humanities and Social Sciences (Thomson) <http://www.saur.de>* **1997**

- *Academic Search Premier (EBSCO) <http://www.epnet.com/academic/acasearchprem.asp>* **2006**

- *Applied Social Sciences Index & Abstracts (ASSIA) (Cambridge Scientific Abstracts) <http://www.csa.com>* **2006**

- *British Library Inside (The British Library) <http://www.bl.uk/services/current/inside.html>* **2006**

- *CINAHL Plus (EBSCO)* **2006**

- *Current Thoughts & Trends, "Abstracts Section" <http://www.CurrentThoughts.com>* **1999**

- *EBSCOhost Electronic Journals Service (EJS) <http://ejournals.ebsco.com>* **2001**

- *Elsevier Eflow-I* **2006**

- *Elsevier Scopus <http://www.info.scopus.com>* **2005**

- *Family & Society Studies Worldwide (NISC USA) <http://www.nisc.com>* **1998**

- *Family Index Database <http://www.familyscholar.com>* **1995**

(continued)

Bibliographic Access

- ***Cabell's Directory of Publishing Opportunities in Psychology <http://www.cabells.com>***

- ***MediaFinder <http://www.mediafinder.com>***

- ***Ulrich's Periodicals Directory: International Periodicals Information Since 1932 <http://www.Bowkerlink.com>***

Special Bibliographic Notes related to special journal issues (separates) and indexing/abstracting:

- indexing/abstracting services in this list will also cover material in any "separate" that is co-published simultaneously with Haworth's special thematic journal issue or DocuSerial. Indexing/abstracting usually covers material at the article/chapter level.
- monographic co-editions are intended for either non-subscribers or libraries which intend to purchase a second copy for their circulating collections.
- monographic co-editions are reported to all jobbers/wholesalers/approval plans. The source journal is listed as the "series" to assist the prevention of duplicate purchasing in the same manner utilized for books-in-series.
- to facilitate user/access services all indexing/abstracting services are encouraged to utilize the co-indexing entry note indicated at the bottom of the first page of each article/chapter/contribution.
- this is intended to assist a library user of any reference tool (whether print, electronic, online, or CD-ROM) to locate the monographic version if the library has purchased this version but not a subscription to the source journal.
- individual articles/chapters in any Haworth publication are also available through the Haworth Document Delivery Service (HDDS).

As part of Haworth's continuing committment to better serve our library patrons, we are proud to be working with the following electronic services:

AGGREGATOR SERVICES

EBSCOhost

Ingenta

J-Gate

Minerva

OCLC FirstSearch

Oxmill

SwetsWise

FirstSearch

Oxmill Publishing

SwetsWise

LINK RESOLVER SERVICES

1Cate (Openly Informatics)

CrossRef

Gold Rush (Coalliance)

LinkOut (PubMed)

LINKplus (Atypon)

LinkSolver (Ovid)

LinkSource with A-to-Z (EBSCO)

Resource Linker (Ulrich)

SerialsSolutions (ProQuest)

SFX (Ex Libris)

Sirsi Resolver (SirsiDynix)

Tour (TDnet)

Vlink (Extensity, *formerly Geac*)

WebBridge (Innovative Interfaces)

LinkOut.
LINKING TO A WORLD OF RESOURCES

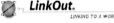

LinkSolver

ULRICH'S RESOURCE LINKER

SerialsSolutions

 WebBridge

The Formation
of Pastoral Counselors:
Challenges and Opportunities

The Formation of Pastoral Counselors: Challenges and Opportunities has been co-published simultaneously as *American Journal of Pastoral Counseling*, Volume 8, Numbers 3/4 2006.

ABOUT THE EDITORS

Duane R. Bidwell, PhD, is Director of the Pastoral Care and Training Center, an AAPC-accredited training and service center at Brite Divinity School at Texas Christian University in Fort Worth, where he aslo teaches pastoral theology, care, and counseling. A certified pastoral counselor since 2000, Dr. Bidwell serves as vice-president of the Southwest Region of the American Association of Pastoral Counselors. He is the author of *Short-Term Spiritual Guidance* and more than a dozen peer-reviewed articles. He is a member of the Society for Pastoral Theology, Spiritual Directors International, and the American Academy of Religion. Ordained in the Presbyterian Church (U.S.), Dr. Bidwell has served rural, urban, and suburban congregations in Texas. His work in pastoral theology, care, and counseling focuses on spirituality, hope, theological anthropology, and the intersection of social constructionist theory with narrative and liberationist theologies and theologies of hope.

Joretta L. Marshall, PhD, is Professor of Pastoral Theology and Care at Eden Theological Seminary in St. Louis, Missouri. Prior to joining the faculty at Eden, Dr. Marshall served on the faculties of Vanderbilt University Divinity School (1989-1993) and Iliff School of Theology (1993-2001). She is an American Association of Pastoral Counselors Fellow and has been a member since of AAPC since 1991. She has been co-editor of the *Journal of Pastoral Theology* and is the author of *Counseling Lesbian Partners*; *How Can I Forgive? A Study of Forgiveness*; and a number of articles in professional and church-related journals. She also co-edited *Forgiveness and Abuse: Jewish and Christian Reflections*. Dr. Marshall's work in pastoral care and counseling focuses on issues of gender, sexuality, developmental theory, forgiveness, pedagogy in theological education, and prophetic pastoral care.

The Formation
of Pastoral Counselors:
Challenges and Opportunities

CONTENTS

About the Contributors

Pamela Cooper-White, PhD, is Professor of Pastoral Theology at the Lutheran Theological Seminary at Philadelphia, an Episcopal priest, and a certified Fellow in the American Association of Pastoral Counselors. Her most recent books are *Many Voices: Pastoral Psychotherapy in Relational and Theological Perspective* (Fortress, forthcoming 2006), and *Shared Wisdom: Use of the Self in Pastoral Care and Counseling* (Fortress, 2004). She received AAPC's award for Distinguished Achievement in Research and Writing in 2005. She can be contacted at Lutheran Theological Seminary, 7301 Germantown Avenue, Philadelphia, PA 19119-1794; pcooper@ltsp.edu.

Joseph D. Driskill, PhD, is Associate Professor of Spirituality and Ronald D. Soucey Lecturer at Pacific School of Religion in Berkely, California, where he also serves as Dean of the Disciples Seminary Foundation. A Christian Church (Disciples of Christ) minister, he practices as a pastoral counselor and spiritual director at the Lloyd Center Pastoral Counseling Service at San Francisco Theological Seminary in San Anselmo, CA. He is the author of *Protestant Spiritual Exercises: Theology, History, and Practice* (Morehouse, 1999) and co-author of *Ethics and Spiritual Care* (Abingdon, 2000). He can be contacted at Pacific School of Religion, 1798 Scenic Avenue, Berkeley, CA 94709-1323; jdriskill@psr.edu.

Alice M. Graham, PhD, is Professor of Pastoral Care and Counseling and Director of the Master of Theological Studies Program at Hood Theological Seminary in Salisbury, North Carolina. An American Baptist minister, she is a Fellow of the American Association of Pastoral Counselors and chair of the leadership development committee for the Southeastern Region of AAPC. She serves on the editorial board of the American Journal of Pastoral Counseling and has published several chapters, journal articles, and audiovisual resources. She can be contacted at Hood Theological Seminary, 1810 Lutheran Synod Drive, Salisbury, NC 28144; agraham@hoodseminary.edu.

Larry Kent Graham, PhD, is Professor of Pastoral Theology and Care at Iliff School of Theology in Denver, Colorado. He is a Diplomate in the American Association of Pastoral Counselors and a minister in the United Church of Christ. His books include *Care of Persons, Care of Worlds: A Psychosystems Approach to Pastoral Care and Counseling* (Abingdon, 1992) and *Discovering Images of God: Narratives of Care Among Lesbians and Gays* (Westminster John Knox Press, 1997). He can be contacted at LGraham@iliff.edu. **Jason C. Whitehead, MDiv, MSW,** is ordained in the Presbyterian Church (USA), a social worker and a pastoral counselor. He is a candidate in the Joint Ph. D. Program in Religious and Theological Studies at Iliff School of Theology and the University of Denver, concentrating in Religious and Psychological Studies. He can be contacted at jwhiteh2@du.edu. Both authors can be contacted via post at Iliff School of Theology, 2201 South University Boulevard, Denver, CO 80210-4798.

Kathleen J. Greider, PhD, is Professor of Pastoral Care and Counseling at Claremont School of Theology in Claremont, California. A United Methodist minister and a Fellow in the American Association of Pastoral Counselors, she is the author of *Reckoning with Aggression: Theology, Violence, and Vitality* (Westminster/John Knox Press, 1997). She can be contacted at kgreider@cst.edu. **William M. Clements, PhD,** is Edna and Lowell Craig Professor of Pastoral Care and Counseling at Claremont School of Theology. He is co-editor of the *Handbook for Basic Types of Pastoral Care and Counseling* (Abingdon, 1991) and author of *Ministry With the Aging: Designs, Challenges, Foundations* (Haworth, 1989) and *Religion, Aging and Health: A Global Perspective* (Haworth, 1989). He can be contacted at wclements@cst.edu. **K. Samuel Lee, PhD,** is Executive Director of The Clinebell Institute for Pastoral Counseling and Psychotherapy in Claremont, California, and Adjunct Associate Professor of Pastoral Care and Counseling at Claremont School of Theology. A United Methodist minister, he is co-author of *Korean Family Devotions* (Upper Room Books, 1995). He can be contacted at slee@cst.edu. Authors can be contacted via post at Claremont School of Theology, 1325 North College Avenue, Claremont, CA 91711-3199.

Hunter R. Hill, DMin, Bonnasue, PhD, Dennett C. Slemp, STM, and W. Victor Maloy, DMin, are members of the clinical staff at the Virginia Institute of Pastoral Care (VIPCare) in Richmond, Virginia. They collaborated in the writing of this article. Hunter R. Hill, a Fellow of the American Association of Pastoral Counselors and a Presbyterian Church (USA) minister, is the Formation Coordinator at VIPCare and a member of the full-time staff. Bonnasue is Associate Professor of Counselor Education and Director of the Pastoral Counselor Training Center at Eastern Mennonite University in Harrisonburg, Virginia, a member of VIPCare's associate staff, and an AAPC Diplomate. Dennett C. Slemp is Coordinator of the Common Life at VIPCare, a member of the associate staff, an Episcopal priest, and an AAPC Diplomate. W. Victor Maloy is Executive Director of VIPCare, an AAPC Diplomate and past President, and a United Methodist minister. They can be contacted at VIPCare, 2000 Bremo Road, Suite 105, Richmond, VA 23226; vip.care@verizon.net.

Zina Jacque, ThD, is the former Director of Pastoral Counseling at Trinity Church in Boston, Massachusetts, and former Executive Director of the Ten Points Coalition in Boston. A Baptist minister, she served in campus and parish ministries after many years in college administration. She has relocated to the Chicago area and awaits placement in a parish or institutional setting. She can be contacted at Zinajacque@aol.com.

Charles Mendenhall, PhD, is Executive Director of the Care and Counseling Center of Georgia, in Decatur, Georgia. He is a Fellow in the American Association of Pastoral Counselors and a Presbyterian Church (USA) minister. He can be contacted at Care and Counseling Center of Georgia, P.O. Box 520, Decatur, GA 30031; cmendenhall@cccgeorgia. org. **Douglas M. Ronsheim, DMin,** is the Executive Director of the American Association of Pastoral Counselors, an AAPC Fellow, and a Presbyterian Church (USA) minister. From 1986-2003, he was Executive Director of the Pittsburgh Pastoral Institute in Pittsburgh, Pennsylvania. He can be contacted at AAPC, 9504A Lee Highway, Fairfax, VA 22031-2303; doug@aapc.org.

Tapiwa Mucherera, PhD, is Associate Professor of Pastoral Counseling at Asbury Theological Seminary in Orlando, Florida. A United Methodist minister, he has served congregations in Iowa, Chicago, Denver, and Zimbabwe. He is author of *Pastoral Care from a Third World Perspective: A Pastoral Theology of Care for the Urban Contemporary Shona in Zimbabwe* (Peter Lang, 2005). He can be contacted at Asbury Theological Seminary, 8401 Valencia College Lane, Orlando, FL 32825; tapiwa_ much erera@asburyseminary.edu.

Rebeca Radillo, DMin, is Professor of Pastoral Care and Community Ministries and Director of Supervised Ministry at New York Theological Seminary in New York, New York. She is also founder of Instituto Latino de Cuidado Pastoral in Bronx, New York. A Fellow of the American Association of Pastoral Counselors, she is a United Methodist pastor. She can be contacted at New York Theological Seminary, 475 Riverside Drive, Suite 500, New York, NY 10115; rradillo@nyts.edu.

Loren L. Townsend, PhD, is Professor of Pastoral Care and Counseling at Louisville Presbyterian Theological Seminary in Louisville, Kentucky. A Diplomate in the American Association of Pastoral Counselors and an American Baptist minister, he is a licensed marriage and family therapist, an AAMFT approved supervisor, and author of *Pastoral Care with Stepfamilies: Mapping the Wilderness* (Chalice Press, 2000). He can be contacted at Louisville Presbyterian Theological Seminary, 1044 Alta Vista Road, Louisville, KY 40205; ltownsend@lpts.edu.

A. J. (Han) van den Blink, PhD, is Diplomate and past President of the American Association of Pastoral Counselors (1998-2000) and Professor Emeritus of Ascetical and Pastoral Theology at Bexley Hall, a seminary of the Episcopal Church in the USA, located in Rochester, New York. He is an Episcopal priest. He can be contacted at AJvdBlink@aol.com. **Margaret Z. Kornfeld, DMin**, is Diplomate and past president of the American Association of Pastoral Counselors (2000-2002), an American Baptist minister, and a pastoral psychotherapist with a private practice in New York City. She is making a transition to the San Francisco Bay area. She can be contacted at Mzkgardens@aol.com.

P. Mark Watts, DMin, is President/CEO of Pastoral Counseling Services (PCS) in Manchester, New Hampshire, a position he has held since 1986. He is a Fellow in the American Association of Pastoral Counselors and a United Methodist minister. He can be contacted at pmw@pcs-nh.org. **David B. Reynolds, DMin**, is Vice President of Community Services at PCS. An AAPC Fellow and Christian Church (Disciples of Christ) minister, he can be contacted at dbr@pcs-nh.org. Both authors can be contacted via post at Pastoral Counseling Services, Manning House, 2nd Floor, 2013 Elm Street, Manchester, New Hampshire 03104-2528.

Foreword

When we were elected in 1998 to positions of leadership in the American Association of Pastoral Counselors (AAPC), we met in New York City at Margaret's office–and at a sunny outdoor Gramercy Park café–for a time of discernment. As we met to address our concerns about the effectiveness of our organization and the future of pastoral counseling, we were given a Zen-like gift, a clarifying question: "What is the soul of AAPC?"

We realized that this question needed to be pondered by our entire membership. And so we "hatched" a plan for corporate discernment: an Association program of Vision and Planning. It was out of this year-long process that members decided (among other things) that the Association must attend to its members' professional formation.

Although that day we did not get *the* answer to the question about AAPC's soul, through our discernment it had become clear that our Association was being called to claim (and reclaim) our work *as ministry*. (Han was already writing and speaking about this.) It also became clear that we must ground our work and ourselves in an intentional spirituality, *and that this was already happening implicitly.*

For a decade we had shared leadership in the Eastern Region and in the national structure of AAPC. We both experienced these ecumenical communities as life giving. We now realized that an implicit but powerful spirituality in our Association had been the source of its differentiated, respectful and supportive collegiality. It was this spirituality that had held us together and empowered us. It had sustained our vision of helping people with the best that therapeutic skill and training have to

---

[Haworth co-indexing entry note]: "Foreword." Van den Blink, A. J. "Han," and Margaret Z. Kornfeld. Co-published simultaneously in *American Journal of Pastoral Counseling* (The Haworth Pastoral Practice Press, an imprint of The Haworth Press, Inc.) Vol. 8, No. 3/4, 2006, pp. xxiii-xxiv; and: *The Formation of Pastoral Counselors: Challenges and Opportunities* (ed: Duane R. Bidwell, and Joretta L. Marshall) The Haworth Pastoral Press, an imprint of The Haworth Press, Inc., 2006, pp. xix-xx. Single or multiple copies of this article are available for a fee from The Haworth Document Delivery Service [1-800-HAWORTH, 9:00 a.m. - 5:00 p.m. (EST). E-mail address: docdelivery@haworthpress.com].

offer, together with the riches of our religious communities and faith traditions. As AAPC's leaders, we were called to make explicit what had been implicit.

Our pastoral counseling profession has been experiencing transformation. It is emerging from a period in which psychotherapeutic theory and practice were kept separate from the formative factors of theological reflection, collegial relationships, professional governance, cross-cultural engagement, and awareness and appreciation of personal and cultural diversity.

In less than a decade, AAPC has come a long way. "Formation" is more than a concept: AAPC has more understanding of pivotal, intentional, life-long formation; association committees support it; training programs include integrative courses and supervision in their curricula; AAPC regions sponsor spiritual retreats, on-going groups and formation forums. Members–at all levels–are beginning to understand the importance of weaving into the theory and practice all the various components that go into the making of pastoral counselors.

This volume is a major contribution to our knowledge of the many and varied aspects of the formation of pastoral counselors. Its appearance is timely, and we are very grateful to Joretta Marshall and Duane Bidwell for shepherding so many excellent and timely contributions into print.

A. J. "Han" van den Blink, PhD
Margaret Z. Kornfeld, DMin

INTRODUCTION

Formation:
Content, Context, Models and Practices

Duane R. Bidwell, PhD
Joretta L. Marshall, PhD

Pastoral care specialists have always been concerned about their professional and ecclesial identity. The pastoral care movement of the twentieth century, growing out of the commitments of churches and synagogues, faith communities, and individual clergy and laity, established legitimacy and accountability through the creation of various organizations, such as the American Association of Pastoral Counselors (AAPC), the Association for Clinical Pastoral Education (ACPE), the Association of Professional Chaplains (APC), the National Association of Catholic Chaplains (NACC), and the Society for Pastoral Theology (SPT). As each area of pastoral care matured, it articulated particular ideas about appropriate content and processes for the formation of pro-

[Haworth co-indexing entry note]: "Formation: Content, Context, Models and Practices." Bidwell, Duane R., and Joretta L. Marshall. Co-published simultaneously in *American Journal of Pastoral Counseling* (The Haworth Pastoral Press, an imprint of The Haworth Press, Inc.) Vol. 8, No. 3/4, 2006, pp. 1-7; and: *The Formation of Pastoral Counselors: Challenges and Opportunities* (ed: Duane R. Bidwell, and Joretta L. Marshall) The Haworth Pastoral Press, an imprint of The Haworth Press, Inc., 2006, pp. 1-7. Single or multiple copies of this article are available for a fee from The Haworth Document Delivery Service [1-800-HAWORTH, 9:00 a.m. - 5:00 p.m. (EST). E-mail address: docdelivery@haworthpress.com].

fessionals. Specialized contextual training models shaped the emerging identities of pastoral care specialists.

Pastoral counselors have been part of this larger movement, concerned about professional identity in ways that are distinct yet related to other pastoral care groups. Drawing upon their theological education and connection to faith communities, pastoral counselors sought to become partners in the mental health community. As the movement gave rise to professional standards and organizational structures, it created a culture of training and certification vested in rituals, language, values, and social structures appropriate to the time (mid-1960s). As the next generations entered this professional community, they brought expectations and experiences different from those that shaped their elders. Pastoral counselors entering the profession today may value the community's commitments and history, but have no memories of the compelling energies that accompanied the formal birth of the field. Tensions arise as traditional understandings are challenged by new insights, experiences, and perspectives. The advent of licensure, diverse psychotherapeutic models, globalization, the marginalization of religious institutions, and the popularity of spirituality has given rise to renewed reflection about what is required to shape and form a community of pastoral counselors.

In this context it is not an overstatement to say that the shared understandings that once unified the work and community of pastoral counselors in North America are no longer adequate to define or prescribe the identity of pastoral counselors or the practices of pastoral counseling. Many are wondering: What makes an "authentic" pastoral counselor? What content is essential for pastoral counselors to master? In what context do we foster a unique and essential professional, ecclesial, and personal identity for the future?

THE TURN TO FORMATION

In response to such questions, AAPC turned to the metaphor of "formation" to describe the processes by which generations–new and old– are shaped into the identity of "pastoral counselor." Formation was chosen as a term, in part, because of its connection to the deeper religious and spiritual heritage of those who self-identify as pastoral counselors. As conceived by AAPC, formation is multi-faceted; it includes elements of self-awareness, faithful spirituality that honors diversity, psychotherapeutic skills and competency, intentional life-long learning, and an understanding of the history and ethos of the pastoral counseling community. Among the first and second generations of pastoral counselors, these elements and their content were institutionalized in formal professional standards for practitioners. These standards included advanced theological degrees, thorough knowledge of psychological theory, and a personhood informed by personal therapy and self-awareness. The contexts and models of formation developed around formal clinical training and supervision. But today, there is no broadly shared understanding of the content of formation, let alone an accepted means by which formation concerns are woven into academic preparation, clinical training, and participation in the changing life and nature of the community.

As the two of us have worked on this volume, we have come to think of formation for pastoral counseling as the life-long, constitutive processes and practices that call forth and shape a person's integrative pastoral identity. Formation creates and clarifies the values, commitments, and habits of the pastoral counselor and gives form to personal, professional, and pastoral identity. Ideally, formation will increase the clinical and relational choices available to a practitioner; encourage clinical, theological and personal flexibility; and acculturate a person to the spiritual and theological norms of at least one faith tradition.

Three layers of formation intersect for pastoral counselors: personal, professional, and pastoral. Personal qualities fostered by formation for pastoral counselors include congruity, warmth, empathy, self-awareness, and a clear sense of identity. Historically, there has been an expectation that clinicians will be engaged in their own therapy, supervision, and spiritual development. The personhood of the pastoral counselor has always been central to pastoral counseling formation.

Professional formation refers to the knowledge and ethos that structure the education, training, identity, practice, and experience of persons who participate in a particular profession. Charles Foster and his colleagues (2006) argue that professional education and formation for the practices of ministry are distinguished by an "emphasis on forming in students the dispositions, habits, knowledge, and skills that cohere in professional identity and practice, commitments and integrity" (p. 100). Every professional formation process is characterized by disciplined reflection on, and intentional integration of, a practitioner's identity; it is contextual, yet features a discourse shared across contexts in ways that hold a profession together; it is constitutive of the profession and of persons; it results in practices and actions that have integrity; and it contributes to a body of scholarship and research that shape the shared discourse of the profession.

It is the *content* of these characteristics that makes formation for pastoral counseling uniquely *pastoral*. Pastoral formation was historically rooted and grounded in the faith experience and ecclesial connection of the pastoral counselor. One of the complexities in our current understanding of formation is the recognition that for many, the ecclesial formation process is no longer as central as it was among the first generations of pastoral counselors. With the growing awareness of spirituality that is not necessarily connected to religious or faith communities, and an increasing move toward post-denominationalism in our culture, identifying precisely what is meant by *pastoral* formation has become one of the challenging dynamics for pastoral counselors.

The formation of pastoral counselors is diverse and dependent on a number of variables, but retains common elements that make our practices distinctively "pastoral counseling." Formation is ultimately contextual and relational. Because it occurs in particular places at particular times through particular relationships, formation is both pursued and received. Keith Beasley-Topliffe (2003), writing about spiritual formation, notes that there are two dimensions to this process: passive and active. Passive formation occurs as the world–through embodiment, finitude, personal experiences, and other means–acts, in this case, on pastoral counselors to shape them in ways they might not have chosen. Active formation occurs intentionally and systemically, allowing pastoral counselors to develop and integrate the knowledges, skills, and experiences required for clinical pastoral practice. Typically, active formation occurs under the guidance and supervision of "elders" recognized by (and accountable to) the professional community; its aims are accomplished through a multitude of practices, including personal therapy, clinical training and supervision, academic study, spiritual direction, and participation in faith communities. From this perspective, formation is communal and holistic; it influences the existential, relational, theological, spiritual, material, and clinical spheres of the pastoral counselor's being, practice, and identity.

CONTRIBUTIONS AND QUESTIONS

We think it is important to keep conversation about the formation of pastoral counselors at the center of the shared, collegial work of pastoral counselors in clinical and academic centers. To that end, we invited a number of persons involved in some aspect of training and education to participate in this collection. These contributions are not exhaustive, but highlight some essential aspects of formation for pastoral counselors.

The volume is divided into two sections. The first frames the conversation by examining the content and contexts of formation. The content includes theological education, psychological theory, pastoral theological reflection, and spiritual and personal development. Understanding and engaging particularities of context have always been part of the formation process for pastoral counselors. In this section, we include attention to racial and ethnic identity, global and intercultural issues, gender and sexual orientation, and the role of socioeconomic factors in the formation of pastoral counselors and pastoral counseling centers.

The second section offers particular models and practices for formation. Practices that can shape formation include supervision that integrates narrative approaches to identity formation and intentionally engages the spirituality of the clinician. Models of formation–illustrated by pastoral care specialist programs that developed in the midst of diverse contexts, as well as by historical developments at specific training programs and centers–provide ongoing conversation about the nature of formation for pastoral counselors. The volume ends with an invitation to expand the horizons of pastoral counseling beyond the primary clinical paradigms.

For more than a year, we have wrestled with the concept of formation in general and with the specific content of the following articles. As we offer the results to the professional community, we want to highlight some patterns in the ways that pastoral counselors think and talk about formation; we also want to signal some questions and concerns for further reflection.

First, although we have suggested that formation requires "disciplined and intentional reflection," it seems that formation is rarely intentionally addressed in the clinic or the academy; it is often assumed to be a by-product of degree programs and training practices. Might formal reflection on formation, as illustrated by some of the practices in the second part of this text, be an emerging standard for training programs and centers?

Second, it is clear that formation for pastoral counseling occurs in context and in community. The best models for formation are intentional about community life and about ongoing education. The tension between the demands and needs of particular contexts and a broader, shared discourse about pastoral counseling requires pragmatic reflexivity; it can also create a generative environment for formation concerns and practices. The question continues to be: What are essential components of formation across contexts, and how do contextual realities change and shift the delivery systems and nature of that content?

Third, despite pastoral counseling's roots in the church and synagogue, the conversation about formation does not rely significantly on the vast literature of spiritual formation or on well-developed traditions of personal formation for ministry and community life. Although AAPC, for example, markets itself as "professionally integrating spirituality and psychotherapy," such integration seems more intuitive than formative. This lacuna seems significant, and we wonder how it might be related to the relatively thin role that formal theological education and spiritual experience seem to assume at the moment.

Fourth, little attention has been given to the epistemological nature of formation, yet formation for pastoral counseling is largely about developing ways of knowing that privilege certain norms and criteria. For example, there is a privileging of Judeo-Christian and psychotherapeutic assumptions and norms while, at the same time, an unwillingness to wrestle with theological and theoretical diversities within the pastoral counseling community that may fundamentally conflict with one another. How do we enhance and foster the diversity of our field while retaining some ability to talk across epistemological and theological differences? What voices are still missing from our discourse and what knowledges would they offer us?

Finally, one of our early goals for this project was to emphasize the counter-cultural nature of formation for pastoral counseling. Yet, we are left with the impression that few formation processes challenge, in public and prophetic ways, the values and assumptions of the dominant culture and its discourses about psychotherapy. The practice of pastoral counseling seems, at times, to lag behind the academic discipline of pastoral theology in emphasizing justice and demonstrating a willingness to participate in public discourse about matters important to the culture. How do we nurture and form pastoral counselors who are willing to engage in the creation and discourse of public theology in ways that honor the work they do with individuals, families, and communities in the context of their pastoral counseling practices?

We believe that intentional reflection on the nature, role, and practices of formation for pastoral counseling can lead to corresponding actions in clinics, faith communities, and training programs. Ultimately this will enhance the vitality of the profession, the unity of our common work as pastoral counselors, and the health of those whom pastoral counseling is called to serve. It is our hope that this volume will broaden and extend conversations about formation in our field by offering rich and rigorous reflections on the challenges and opportunities inherent to the task of formation in this time and place. The perspectives expressed intentionally mirror the theological, social, generational, racial and ethnic, and theoretical diversity of the pastoral counseling community in North America. The essays are intended to engage, challenge, and shape daily life in clinics and training programs.

REFERENCES

Beasley-Topliffe, K. R. (2003). Formation, Spiritual. In K. Beasley-Topliffe (Ed.), *The Upper Room dictionary of Christian spiritual formation* (pp. 107-110). Nashville: Upper Room Books.

Foster, C. R., Dahill, L. E., Goelmon, L. A., & Tolentino, B. W. (2006). *Educating clergy: Teaching practices and pastoral imagination.* San Francisco: Jossey-Bass.

doi:10.1300/J062v08n03_01

SECTION I:
CONTENT AND CONTEXT

The Role of Pastoral Theology in Theological Education for the Formation of Pastoral Counselors

Larry Kent Graham, PhD
Jason C. Whitehead, MDiv, MSW

SUMMARY. Formal theological education, as mediated through degree programs and specialized academic courses of study, provides the foundational outlook and breadth of religious knowledge and practices upon which are built personal beliefs, professional identity and skills, and vocational direction. To be a pastoral counselor, one is expected to be grounded in formal theological education as an essential ongoing resource for forming one's identity and guiding one's practice of counseling. Pastoral theology is the discipline within formal theological education that serves as a bridge between the broader theological milieu and the crucible of pastoral counseling education, supervision and practice in which the more particular elements

[Haworth co-indexing entry note]: "The Role of Pastoral Theology in Theological Education for the Formation of Pastoral Counselors." Graham, Larry Kent, and Jason C. Whitehead. Co-published simultaneously in *American Journal of Pastoral Counseling* (The Haworth Pastoral Press, an imprint of The Haworth Press, Inc.) Vol. 8, No. 3/4, 2006, pp. 9-27; and: *The Formation of Pastoral Counselors: Challenges and Opportunities* (ed: Duane R. Bidwell, and Joretta L. Marshall) The Haworth Pastoral Press, an imprint of The Haworth Press, Inc., 2006, pp. 9-27. Single or multiple copies of this article are available for a fee from The Haworth Document Delivery Service [1-800-HAWORTH, 9:00 a.m. - 5:00 p.m. (EST). E-mail address: docdelivery@haworthpress.com].

of the identity, role, and skills necessary for becoming a pastoral counselor come together. doi:10.1300/J062v08n03_02 *[Article copies available for a fee from The Haworth Document Delivery Service: 1-800-HAWORTH. E-mail address: <docdelivery@haworthpress.com> Website: <http://www.HaworthPress. com> © 2006 by The Haworth Press, Inc. All rights reserved.]*

KEYWORDS. Theological education, pastoral theology identity, integration, context, narrative, relational justice

WHAT IS A PASTORAL COUNSELOR?

A pastoral counselor is a suitably educated and clinically trained practitioner of the ministry of pastoral counseling and psychotherapy. This person operates on behalf of a religious community, providing psychotherapeutic care and religious guidance for those in need. The pastoral counselor utilizes various modes of engagement and reflection in the rigors of psychotherapeutic relationships. These modes of engagement and reflection include: (1) the personal and vocational, through continued pastoral identity development and commitment to one's spiritual and psychological development, (2) the contextual, through careful analysis of the cultural and social milieu, including one's own social location, (3) the theological, through critical, practical, and constructive engagement with the problems and strengths of clients as influenced by the various religious traditions affecting the counseling relationship, and (4) the clinical, in which therapeutic modes of interpretation and intervention are utilized to promote wholeness in personal and relational living. In brief, a pastoral counselor is a person who is involved in a life-long process of ministry in a psychotherapeutic setting on behalf of a religious community, utilizing a variety of complex modes of engagement, interpretation and intervention, in a context of ongoing accountability, education, and formation.

A pastoral counselor is formed out of the creative and constructive interplay of various influences and contexts. The central concern in the formation process for pastoral counselors is the creation of a coherent identity and a viable set of practices from a variety of influences and modes of interpretation. Formation is a complex and ongoing activity, unique for each pastoral counselor. Formation occurs by multiple means. It is never completed.

This chapter explores some of the salient elements in the formation of the pastoral counselor, especially the roles of formal theological education and the manner in which the discipline of pastoral theology links theological education to the formation of the pastoral counselor.[1] We begin our discussion with a brief description of some aspects of Jason's formation as a pastoral counselor.

A PASTORAL COUNSELOR IS FORMED: JASON'S STORY

My journey toward becoming a pastoral counselor began with a sense that ministry was my vocation. However, I wanted my ministry to reflect my interest in psychology and the therapeutic world. As a youth director in a large congregation I found it necessary to utilize my psychological background when meeting with youth in pastoral care situations. I was not theologically trained at the time, but as my work and involvement in the congregation continued I felt pulled to try and connect these theological and pastoral situations with psychology and care. Fortunately, my future mother-in-law had some contacts with the pastoral counseling world and she thought that a dual masters program answered some of the questions I had about how to bring the therapeutic and ecclesial worlds together.

Today, I am dually trained as a Presbyterian minister and a social worker. I worked my way through a Master of Divinity program while concurrently completing the necessary coursework for a Master in Social Work with a specialization in clinical work. This dual masters program provided foundational pieces that helped me connect pastoral care, theology, and psychological sciences. Moreover, it added ongoing resources through which I would later be able to critically, clinically and theologically respond to the problems that clients brought into the room with them. These two programs were the starting points for an organic process of formation that grew from conflicts between my role as a youth director, my psychological understandings, my curiosity about my sense of vocation, and my sense of self. Some of the conflicts I dealt with were issues of ethics and justice as well as the relationship between psychological and theological constructions of the self. Ultimately, I was beginning to work through how I would construct my own sense of identity in relation to theology, pastoral care, and clinical social work understandings.

During my first two years in the Master of Divinity program I was a part of a community that struggled to articulate an interdependent relationship between scripture, theology, pastoral care, preaching, and teaching. The interrelatedness of the coursework, as well as the relationships formed with other struggling students, opened new ways of critically reflecting on what I was learning, and ultimately provided me a new way of viewing the world and my relationship with it. It was more than simple belief or faith; it was a way of constructing and conversing with the world and the situations it presented out of a coherent and dynamic theological framework. I carried this sense of connectedness into my clinical work in the final two years of my program and spent a great deal of time theologically reflecting on the clinical material I was learning. Without my time in seminary, in that crucible of theological construction, I wonder if I would have been able to build the necessary framework for sustained theological reflection needed when working as a pastoral counselor. For example, the case studies we presented during our training often involved theological reflection concerning a particular client. In order to fully engage in this process I had to have a working knowledge of theological themes and a sense of where I stood in relation to the themes as they were presented during case conferences. Without the sustained experience of theological reflection during seminary I would have been unable to productively reflect on these themes and how they might affect the worldview of the client and inform a therapeutic response to the client.

I joined the associate staff at the Virginia Institute of Pastoral Care (VIPCare) in 2002. I was a 30-year-old therapist and the youngest member of the staff by about 20 years. My early time on the staff was marked by my sense of feeling paralyzed. It took about two years before my supervisor found the right moment to rip me from a rigid yet comfortable therapeutic existence and reignite my malleability. I remember the event to this day. I left her a voice mail that offered some excuse as to why I could not make it to supervision that week. I don't remember her reply; I only remember that her words circumnavigated whatever depressive defense structure I had erected and made me angry. Instead of neglecting supervision that morning, I arose ready for a fight. When I arrived we didn't fight; instead we processed my reaction and worked on ways to combat a depression that I had not acknowledged or addressed. Following that hour we began to focus more on my theological and psychological integration and formation. I entered into a therapeutic relationship to work on my depressive features. Finally, I began to intentionally reflect on where I was and the experiences that brought me to that point in my life.

Looking back, I realize my formation as a pastoral counselor began in two relatively safe places where people were valued, challenged, and accepted. They were patient atmospheres that sought to nurture me through constant attention and unrelenting care for the development of my pastoral identity. Union-Presbyterian School of Christian Eductaion (PSCE) and Virginia Commonwealth University were the places where I first tested the boundaries of faith, theology, and pastoral care. VIP-Care was the place where stories came alive as staff members shared their own struggles and growth throughout their years together. The staff members at VIPCare used their individual and relational histories to propel them into a continual state of incompleteness, seeking opportunities for growth that stretched their imaginations and experiences of life.

In the end, my formation process was one of self-discovery and awareness in the context of three particular communities attuned to the struggles and hopes of any growth process, but intensely focusing on the unique particularities of each person. I was nurtured by stories of success and failure and given the space to try new things and develop my own sense of creativity. The more I discovered about myself, the more open I became to the lives of the clients I saw.

Out of these experiences the concept of formation has come to have an organic feel. For me, it recalls visions of potters stretching their clay-crusted fingers over a lump of clay. My spouse and I spent one Saturday afternoon driving the Blue Ridge Parkway in western Virginia. Moments after we left the parkway, we happened upon a large house set off of the road with a large sign reading, "Pottery." Having a soft spot for pottery we pulled off the road to take a look. After examining the polished pieces in the shop we ventured into a workshop where we found a man in his sixties sitting at a manual potting wheel. A moment after we entered he grabbed a lump of clay and slammed it into the smooth surface of the wheel. The wheel began to spin and his clay-crusted fingers moved knowingly over the lump, adding gentle pressure as if listening to what the clay wanted to become. I sensed that there was a moment when his mind and the clay decided what would be formed and he seized it, adding pressure and introducing shape. As clay walls began to form the potter spoke absent-mindedly about the different forms of clay, and the mishmash of soil, chemicals and water that went into the lump that sat before him. Clay is carefully crafted for the purpose of creating pottery. Pastoral counselors are not that different; we have carefully poured the right amount of chemicals and water into the soil of our lives, developing a mass of potential awaiting a potter to begin their work.

When I look back at the formative events from church work to seminary, and social work to supervision, I can see that there was a necessary willingness on my part to want to be more than just proficient. I had to claim who I was pastorally and embrace my strengths and weaknesses in order to ground who I was, where I was. I had already developed all of the language and reflective skills of a counselor, but formation meant utilizing myself–who I was and how I thought, felt and acted–as a partner with what I had learned through my theological and clinical training.

As I think further about my journey the elements necessary for the formation of a pastoral counselor come into focus. Many elements had to be pressed together and carefully crafted to form a pastoral counselor into something of beauty and usability. They include formal academic programs, clinical service and education, the supervisory context, and the pastoral counselor's unique psycho-spiritual processes. In my case these coalesced creatively at a significant point in my life under the hands of a very astute supervisor. This event was one of many that helped me to expand and achieve a viable pastoral counselor identity and practice that was firmly integrated into my faith commitments and personal developmental history.

THE GOALS OF THEOLOGICAL EDUCATION

Theological education today has many expressions, especially in the context of the theological school. The Association of Theological Schools (ATS) in the United States and Canada lists over two hundred degree-granting institutions as accredited member institutions. Some form of ministerial education comprises the lion's share of the degrees offered by ATS member schools. For the purpose of this discussion, we take the general goals of ministerial education as our guide to interpreting formal theological education as a foundation for forming pastoral counselors. These goals are well described by the ATS (2005):

> Curricula for programs oriented toward ministerial leadership have certain closely integrated, common features. *First*, they provide a structured opportunity to develop a thorough, discriminating understanding and personal appropriation of the heritage of the community of faith (e.g., its Scripture, tradition, doctrines, and practices) in its historical and contemporary expressions. *Second*, they assist students in understanding the cultural realities and social settings within which religious communities live and carry out their missions, as well as the institutional life of those communities themselves. The insights of cognate disciplines such as the social sciences, the natural sciences, philosophy, and the arts enable

a knowledge and appreciation of the broader context of the religious tradition, including cross-cultural and global aspects. *Third*, they provide opportunities for formational experiences through which students may grow in those personal qualities essential for the practice of ministry, namely, emotional maturity, personal faith, moral integrity, and social concern. *Fourth*, they assist students to gain the capacities for entry into and growth in the practice of the particular form of ministry to which the program is oriented. Instruction in these various areas of theological study should be so conducted as to demonstrate their interdependence, their theological character, and their common orientation toward the goals of the degree program. The educational program in all its dimensions should be designed and carried out in such a way as to enable students to function constructively as ministerial leaders in the particular communities in which they intend to work, and to foster an awareness of the need for continuing education.

The curricula for preparing ministerial leadership in the context of formal theological education have many interlocking features. They emphasize critical thinking and personal appropriation of historical, contemporary, religious, and secular knowledges. They foreground contextual analysis and global perspectives. They provide occasion for interfaith and other forms of cross-cultural and intercultural exposure. They are concerned with practical skills for particular ministries and they place a large emphasis upon the way all of these elements come together in the spiritual and personal formation of the student. It is not possible to gain a formal theological education without some sustained and accountable exposure to all of these elements within a program designed to critically integrate them into one's own personhood and to help students live out of them in the practices of their life and ministry.

We believe that two special characteristics necessary for the formation of ministerial leadership in general, and pastoral counselor formation in particular, result from the kind of comprehensive and integrated theological education available in seminaries and accredited programs. These characteristics are theological fluency and traveling theological knowledges.

The term, "theological fluency" was articulated by our colleague, Carrie Doehring, Associate Professor of Pastoral Care and Counseling at the Iliff School of Theology in Denver, Colorado. Doehring makes a distinction between "theological literacy (being able to read and write about theological ideas) and theological fluency (using theological ideals as a basis for practice)," noting that, ". . . we become fluent when we 'inhabit' our theology as a faith perspective that we use to understand and respond to spiritual and psychological needs. Whereas becoming theologically literate is part of learning how to think critically, becoming theologically fluent involves formation" (Petersen & Rourke, 2002, 311). As we use the term, theological fluency refers to the manner in which a pastoral counselor is able to internalize modes of thinking and relating derived from her formal theological education in such a manner that it becomes available for informing her pastoral counseling identity and practice.

The idea of "traveling theological knowledges," was coined by Professor Sheila Greeve Davaney in a discussion of curriculum review at Iliff School of Theology in Denver, Colorado. The concept of traveling theological knowledges refers to the manner in which the skills, capacities, and bodies of knowledge learned in one area of theological curriculum would be carried into other areas of the curriculum and eventually into the practice of ministry, continued academic and professional work, or other forms of religious leadership. For example, one question might concern how the capacity to examine a biblical, historical or theological text in its context might travel to a pastoral care class in which persons are learning to listen to a "living human document" in its multiple contexts. Further, it may be that listening skills necessary for the pastoral care of individuals might provide clues about how to engage the "otherness" of a biblical, theological, or other historical text and to more fully understand what goes on when one's own life is interrogated by the process of engagement and interpretation.

The benefit of formal theological education for the formation of the pastoral counselor, therefore, is that it cultivates a form of theological fluency on the part of the graduate. Such theological fluency is the means by which a variety of theological knowledges might travel from place to place with the student during the classroom phase of his or her formation, and beyond that into a variety of ministerial contexts and settings. When knowledge travels in this manner, it has the potential of becoming a strategic resource for ministry. It also becomes exposed to contexts where its limits are disclosed and occasions for new understandings and practices are discerned. Furthermore, these new understandings may lead to novel theological insights that can in turn inform theological education. As we use the term, therefore, traveling theological knowledge refers to the pastoral counselor's ability efficaciously to relate skills, information, and perspectives gained in formal theological education to the clinical context as a whole, and to the particular dynamics of specific clinical situations. In turn, theological insights are generated or reinterpreted in clinical practices that have critical and constructive implications for what is taught in formal theological education.[2]

We are aware as we write that the American Association of Pastoral Counselors (AAPC) has developed membership standards for pastoral counselors that include a "Body of Knowledge." This Body of Knowledge is a set of core courses that comprise the range of academic subjects indigenous to the work of the pastoral counselor. This information may be gained in two ways. First, it is available in a variety of institutional and clinical settings accredited by one or more mental health or pastoral counseling organizations. Second, the Body of Knowledge may be gained through an accredited academic program, such as those offered in specialized degree programs in a theological school or university. It is our view that the AAPC Body of Knowledge provides a certain degree of formal theological education, but that the curricular requirements of the Master of Divinity Degree offer a more comprehensive measure of what comprises a formal theological education for ministerial leadership (AAPC, 2006). Taken together, formal theological education as embodied in degree programs and the AAPC Body of Knowledge are essential elements comprising the rich mix of ingredients necessary for forming a pastoral counselor. They provide a basis for theological fluency and a means for that fluency to travel in a variety of directions in relation to pastoral counseling.

PASTORAL THEOLOGY AS A POTTER'S WHEEL

Jason's vignette earlier demonstrated how the crucible of the pastoral counseling context pressed him to bring together in a new way his formal education, his vocational destiny, his personal dynamics, and his counseling practice. Many forms of knowledge, practice, skills, and habits of mind were shaped into new configurations as his life and ministry began to spin, much like the potter shapes an item of art spinning on a device designed to bring creative beauty out of a multiplicity of materials. As the potter's wheel is the device to bring clay into art, we want to suggest that pastoral theology is the means by which the theological fluency and theological knowledges gained in formal theological education travel to the counselor and the clinic, and back again to the school and beyond. Pastoral theology is the potter's wheel upon which the various ingredients necessary to the formation of a pastoral counselor come together and are shaped into a usable *objet d'art*.

There are many views of pastoral theology. Our use derives from Seward Hiltner's classic, *Preface to Pastoral Theology* (Hiltner, 1958). Pastoral theology is the branch of theological inquiry that draws theological conclusions and fashions guidelines for pastoral care and counseling from reflection on the religious tradition in which care occurs in the light of the specific concerns arising in the caregiving relationship. Pastoral theology includes the constructive appropriation of cognate secular resources bearing on the issues at hand. The caregiver becomes the pastoral theologian and ventures new understandings of self, care, vocation, and theology from his or her immersion in the dilemmas faced by those with whom they minister. More extensive elaborations of pastoral theology can be found in Graham (1992), Graham (2000) and Ramsay (2004).

It has not been central to pastoral theology to focus on the formation of the pastoral caregiver. The focus of pastoral theology has been on responding to the needs of the careseeker, interpreting the nature of healing, sustaining, guiding, reconciling, and liberating indigenous to pastoral care and counseling, and to constructing adequate theological interpretations. However, the person and creative engagement of the caregiver-as-pastoral-theologian is assumed in this view of pastoral theology. It is the pastoral caregiver who is on the "potter's wheel" in which all of these elements are spinning and who is trying to make something novel and usable from them. It is the pastoral caregiver who is pressed to form all these elements into something new, and in so doing to become something different as well. In forming others and reforming one's religious tradition, one is formed.

Our central claim, then, is that pastoral theology is the academic discipline and personal habit of mind that provides the conceptual and procedural methodology by which a pastoral counselor may develop all the elements connected with his or her professional identity and function into a coherent, effective, and creatively generative whole, while keeping oneself always open to revision and new possibilities. Pastoral theology is an academic discipline which has emerged in Protestant theological education, but it is non-sectarian and has utility for a variety of religious communities within and beyond Christianity. As we understand it, pastoral theology is the means by which formal theological knowledge travels beyond the classroom. It is a method by which pastoral counselors become formed into theologically fluent practitioners.

The process of forming a pastoral counselor is a pastoral theological process. It allows formal theological education, personal identity, the exigencies of caregiving, and conflicting or contending values and orienting systems, both religious and secular, to come together in an efficacious manner. Whether the pastoral counselor begins with a personal crisis, as reported by Jason above, or with an impasse in caregiving, or a theological conundrum arising in practice, the responses to these challenges are central to what takes place in the process of forming a pastoral counselor. Theological fluency gained in formal theological education sometimes clashes with questions not previously addressed. Pastoral theology provides a way to engage these questions. The struggle between the old and the new promotes depth of engagement. The outcome of the engagement forms a novel identity and engenders more precise understandings. These products of the formative process then stand in place to inform new meanings and guide new practices. For us, this interaction is the heart of pastoral theology and offers an indispensable resource for the formation of a pastoral counselor.

PASTORAL THEOLOGY
IN PASTORAL COUNSELOR FORMATION:
LARRY'S STORY

When I was in Clinical Pastoral Education (CPE) during my MDiv degree, some core tenets of my formal theological education clashed with the ethos and mindset of the clinical setting. In my Lutheran theological context in the 1960s, I was learning that Christian love required one to be a "man for others," as interpreted by Dietrich Bonhoeffer, and to promote self-giving Agape as a higher theological ethic than the more self-regarding loves thematized as Eros.[3] Further, we were taught that pastoral care should not impose any agenda on the care-receiver because that would be self-regarding, moralistic, and invasive. The norms for pastoral care were derived from theology, especially as interpreted through Scriptures and church teachings, with psychology and social analysis regarded as appropriate only to the degree that they corroborated or provided the technical means to fulfill theological and religious goals. In contrast, my CPE program was asking us to claim our authority as persons, to find ways to be more congruent and expressive in relation to our personal identities, and to see ourselves as embodied agents of care and grace. Rather than being a "man for others" we were learning to be "persons with others," sharing our health as well as our brokenness in an accountable manner. The metaphor, "use of self," struggled against the metaphor "denial of self" at this point in my formative development. Further, secular resources for interpreting human need and the requirements of care dominated the clinical environment, and theological language was either non-existent or reinterpreted in psychological terms. The support for self-awareness and self-engagement found in the clinical setting and its secular theories clashed with formulations about self-denial and self-sacrifice mediated through norms arising in the formal theological education that I brought to the pastoral care context.

This situation pertained through several units of Clinical Pastoral Education and into the pastoral counseling context in which I received training as a part of my doctoral studies. I was increasingly troubled by a sense that the theological and the clinical were irrelevant to one another, or were irrevocably conflicted. I felt caught between two masters and could relinquish neither. This conflict became exacerbated as I was working as a pastoral counselor with women whose internalized view of self-sacrificial love, valorized by notions of Christian Agape and the high values Christianity places on being "men and women for others," functioned to keep them depressed, divided, and trapped in abusive situations. How could I help trapped women work against a normative theology and ethics that participated in creating and maintaining their difficulties when these were my belief systems too? How could I represent as a pastoral counselor a faith tradition that stood against the freedom and healing that I was trying to promote in the clinical context in the name of that faith and tradition? I had either to resolve this theologically or leave ministry as a vocation.

Though I did not fully realize it at the time, pastoral theology provided the means to be faithful to my religious tradition while revising and advancing my relation to it in the context of the ministry of pastoral counseling. Pastoral theology argues for a "two-way street" between theological and psychological perspectives in the context of care, meaning that insights about healing in the clinic carry theological freight in relation to the religious tradition in which healing occurs. The religious tradition in which I work recognizes that all our truth claims are provisional and that the "church is always under reformation," meaning that we must always be under judgment and open to new truths in the light of what it means to increase love, justice and freedom from bondage. For these female clients to be free from bondage, love had to be understood as involving human agency and limit-setting, and holding others accountable for their actions. Self-sacrificing to the abuse of others could be regarded as neither ethical nor psychologically healthy. An ethic of mutuality began to replace in my mind an ethic of Agape, with Agape being regarded as an element of mutuality rather than cut off from it.

Pastoral theology was for me a means to resolve a theological dilemma in the practice of pastoral counseling. But it was more. It was a means by which I developed a mindset as a pastoral counselor that went beyond issues of clinically astute pastoral practice. It was a way of forming a consciousness toward my faith and its orienting traditions of meaning, and of incorporating secular knowledge and pastoral practice into my identity and function as a pastoral counselor. It was the means by which I could form or construct my identity. Pastoral theology continues to guide how I live out my identity and role as a pastoral counselor. And it has been an instrument of ongoing formation and reformation as a pastoral counselor. For me, pastoral theology has increased theological fluency and has been the bridge on which theological knowledge has traveled between the classroom and clinical, and beyond.[4]

CORE ELEMENTS IN PASTORAL THEOLOGY FOR THE FORMATION OF PASTORAL COUNSELORS

In more specific terms, what elements of pastoral theology are central to the formation of the pastoral counselor? What takes place on the potter's wheel where theological education, the clinic, and one's psycho-spiritual history of faith and understanding spin and come together? How might these be employed intentionally in the formation of the pastoral counselor, especially in helping knowledge travel between formal theological education and the other dimensions of formation? We identify five intersecting elements

1. The pastoral counselor is formed through a contextually creative engagement of the past with the inescapable dilemmas emerging in the contemporary clinical setting. Contextual creativity refers to the pastoral counselor's capacity to be knowledgeable about a variety of traditions of meaning and practice in a manner that makes them relevant and efficacious in the particularities and novelties of clinical practice (Graham, 1992). Formal theological education travels to the clinical through a process of contextually creative analysis and application. The formative process in becoming a pastoral counselor involves the capacity to create new meanings and self-understandings by a novel use of the materials at hand, including the materials gained in formal theological education. Contextual creativity usually results from response to a crisis of self-understanding, meaning, or practice. For Jason, contextual creativity meant attending to ideas and constructions concerning himself in relationship with his identity as a minister and social worker in order to better integrate the novel possibilities held within each of these two disciplines. For Larry, it involved constructing a whole new way of thinking about how secular and religious resources could be positively related in creating novel theological understandings and new interpretations of the love-ethic in the therapeutic context.

2. *The pastoral counselor is formed through an envisioning process that engenders imaginative possibilities for arranging life and interpreting its significance.* Envisioning is a practical pastoral process closely related to healing, guiding, sustaining and liberating which functions as a guide to these acts of pastoral care and counseling. In order to heal, guide, sustain, or liberate the pastoral counselor must have an idea of what health, a destination, rest, or freedom looks like in a particular situation or context. Otherwise, the pastoral counselor functions without meaning or direction. Likewise, the pastoral counselor must also envision possibilities of formation for themselves and the communities in which they provide counsel. On the personal level, envisioning takes on the idea of an "incomplete living human document" who dreams, hopes, or visualizes the next step in his or her development. This intentional process of envisioning provides possibilities for both a destination and path for the journey the pastoral counselor is taking. Moreover, because envisioning involves the future, the destinations and pathways are always in flux given the ever-changing landscapes in which we live. On the social level, envisioning offers the pastoral counselor the opportunity to hope or dream about the alleviation of conditions that cause anxiety and distress in their clients. Additionally, through envisioning the pastoral counselor might find paths or causes that can help diminish the injustices and systems that provide the fertile grounds for dysfunction. Finally, theological envisioning involves opportunities of engaging grace and hope in the midst of a broken world. Thus conceived, envisioning imagines new uses to which formal theological education may be put, and new ways of blending formal theological education with the other elements on the potter's wheel of pastoral theological formation of the pastoral counselor. Jason envisioned new ways of relating parish ministry, theological education, social work, and self-understanding in the practice of pastoral counseling in the clinic. Larry used pastoral theology to envision new ways of interpreting Christian views of love and relating them to clinical practice and social justice.

3. The pastoral counselor is formed by re-authoring narratives of interpretation and meaning that provide possibilities for empowered and hopeful living. One of the key recent insights from pastoral theology and counseling is that human beings are literally formed by our stories, and our relation to what we regard as sacred or ultimate stories. Pastoral counseling is about helping our clients deconstruct internalized personal and social narratives that bind and destroy, and discover or author stories that give power and healing in their lives.[5] To be formed as a pastoral counselor is to be theologically fluent about the multiplicity of sacred stories available to our work and to our clients, and to envision contextually creative ways in which these stories might become resources for healing and transformation. For Larry, this meant a re-appropriation of the Protestant Reformation story of the church always breaking out of legalisms to freedom. For Jason, it meant accepting his strengths and weaknesses and trusting his theological and therapeutic instincts for the benefit of his clients.

4. The pastoral counselor is formed to live out of the ethical norm of relational justice as the basic structure and central outcome of care-giving. To be formed as a pastoral counselor requires critical judgments about the moral context of our work. Pastoral counseling assumes a moral context of law, ethics, and social good. We are required to be knowledgeable and fluent about professional ethics and trained to establish appropriate pastoral relationships. At times we are required as a part of our work to assist clients in the process of making difficult moral decisions and to live with the consequences. A central moral norm that has emerged in pastoral theology that links formal theological education to the clinical practice of counseling is that of relational justice. By relational justice is meant a quality of personal and social life characterized by "right relationship" in which mutuality, shared power, shared responsibility, and equitable access to resources are available without respect to sexuality, social status, or political identification.[6] Larry found that his work with abused women disclosed the way Christian views of Agape and sacrificial love were employed to perpetuate injustice for women. Pastoral theology helped him to reformulate his pastoral identity in such as way that his tradition became available to him and to his clients as a resource for relational justice in the counseling relationship. He became more theologically and ethically fluent through this formative process, and the ethical and theological knowledge gained and created has traveled back to the theological school by means of books and articles, and into the large public through the lives of people attempting to construct relationally just communities.

5. The pastoral counselor is formed by expectant adventuring in a world of surprise and novelty. "Adventure" is a central concept in process theology that points to the gifts of unexpected beauty and relational advances arising in every detail of living (Jackson, 1981, 99-121). Adventure is the capacity of the power of the past and the intense moment of present possibility to synthesize into unprecedented patterns of vitality. Adventure is viewed here as God's way of engaging the world. God's envisioning presence stimulates and lures each of us to new depths of experience, including new ways of appropriating the past for the richness of life today. The concept of adventure recognizes that the past is tenacious, the present is tensive, and the future tentative. Adventure in the formation of a pastoral counselor is a unique coming forth, based on struggle and possibility, in response to the pull of the past and the possibilities in the present. Each pastoral counselor appropriates a unique past. Each has internalized a unique interpretation of the theological and religious tradition in which they are gaining fluency. Each is situated in multiple social locations and negotiates multiple identities. Each faces unique possibilities for the future in the context of pastoral caregiving. Knowledge does not travel easily or predictably between the theological school, the clinic, the pastoral psychotherapy relationship, and the pastoral counselor. Each pastoral counseling situation is novel, and requires new ways of envisioning, creating, authoring, and relating materials from the past to the intensity of the present. This adventurous engagement is complex and sometimes costly, yet often exhilarating. Its outcomes are unpredictable and fluid. But when done faithfully and well, "a new thing of beauty" is brought forth to stand before us on the potter's wheel, offering itself as a usable vehicle for life's healing, sustaining, guiding, liberating, and envisioning.

CONCLUSION

Pastoral theology is a two-way street on which knowledge travels between formal theological education and the practice of pastoral counseling in the formation of the identity and skill of the pastoral counselor. The formation process mediated by pastoral theology is complex and ongoing. It provides a means to synthesize with integrity and coherence personal identity, therapeutic practice, contextual analysis, vocational self-understanding, and traditions of religious belief and practice. A pastoral theological interpretation of the formation of pastoral counselors emphasizes contextual creativity, imaginative envisioning, narratival plotting, relational justice, and novel adventuring as the core elements of the formative process.

POSTSCRIPT

The editors asked us to include a brief reflection upon how our collaboration in co-authorship provided an opportunity for continued formation as pastoral counselors and pastoral theologians.

Larry's story: Without Jason I would not have accepted the invitation to write this article. I had no energy for the topic, and I could not conceive of a way of contributing to it. Jason was in a PhD seminar I was leading on pastoral theology. It was his first seminar in his PhD program. As I shared with the class the invitation to write this article, Jason disclosed that he was in an independent study with my colleague Carrie Doehring on the topic of formation in pastoral counseling. We reflected as a seminar on the role that pastoral theology might play in the formation of pastoral counselors. Jason's ideas about envisioning pastoral theology in a new way, along with his work on formation, generated a desire to participate in this volume. It occurred to me that we could productively blend our competencies: his in pastoral counseling as identity formation and mine in pastoral theology. The editors accepted our proposal to co-author the chapter, and we began to work on it.

We each contributed to the final product. We listened to one another's ideas, shared assignments for drafting various portions, and each reviewed and revised the work. For me, the work was made easier by sharing it with Jason. I benefited from our conversations and his insights. Jason expanded my view of pastoral theology through his work on envisioning, and he was broadening my appreciation for all that goes into the formation of a pastoral counselor. In turn, I felt that I was helping to form a pastoral counselor into a pastoral theologian! Working with an established pastoral theologian gave Jason a leg up as new pastoral theologian; working with Jason gave me a sense of creating something new and being a part of assisting a new generation of pastoral counselors and pastoral theologians to emerge. I am glad we did it!

Jason's story: Before entering Iliff and Denver University, I believed that my role as a doctoral student was to endure the program while displaying an appropriate amount of fear and awe toward the professors who would govern my life. Working with Larry over the past few months on this article has caused me to rethink that assessment. Certainly, there is a power differential between those who know and teach and those who are learning. However, while writing this article I felt as though I was treated like a colleague and a burgeoning pastoral theologian who had something valuable to offer. Being formed means being shaped, in part, by the context that surrounds you. Through the give and take that created this article, I began to feel like I belonged in the doctoral and pastoral theological communities. The power that Larry held in the process was used to empower me, enabling me to seek out and speak the thoughts and ideas that crossed the landscape of my mind. This process, which reminded me of a supervisor/colleague relationship, enabled me to begin to accept the idea that I might belong in the academic world of pastoral theologians. I can sense that this collaborative project will enrich my studies in the short and long-term, which makes me proud to be a part of it.

NOTES

1. We are venturing a pastoral-theological interpretation of the formation of pastoral counselors. We recognize there is a great deal of literature from psychology and sociology of professional development interpreting formation (e.g., Marshall, 1994; Wimberly, 1980; Wolfe, 2003).

2. There is considerable attention to the ways the elements of theological education relate to one another and to the practices of ministry. One influential approach is found in studies conducted by Carnegie Foundation for The Advancement of Teaching: Preparing for The Professions. The volume prepared for educating clergy identifies three intersecting "formative apprenticeships": cognitive, practical and identity (Foster, Dahill, Goelmon, & Tolentino, 2006).

3. One of the foundational texts in my theological education articulating this viewpoint was Nygren, 1953.

4. Space does not permit the elaboration of other dimensions of the dilemma I faced between my received theological tradition and the requirements of clinical practice. Another framework for interpretation can be found in John Patton's (1993) discussion of a transition from a classical to clinical paradigm in pastoral theology and care. The Nygren material represented my education and formation in a "classical paradigm" in which the message was central to care. The crisis emerged for me because I was being formed as a pastoral counselor in a "clinical paradigm" in which the personhood and the relational humanness of the caregiver is central. Pastoral theology was the means by which I could adjudicate the tensions between these paradigms.

5. We are indebted to our colleagues, Christie Neuger (2003) and Andrew Lester (1995) for their work on the power of narrative in forming and transforming identities and challenging unjust social arrangements.

6. Nancy Ramsay (2004) clearly articulates the central norm of "relational justice" that has emerged in pastoral theology since 1980.

REFERENCES

American Association of Pastoral Counselors. (2006). *Fellow body of knowledge requirements* (April 24, 2006). Available: http://www.aapc.org/FellowBOKRequirements.pdf

American Theological Schools. (2005). *General institutional standards*, 4.2.1.1. (April 24, 2006). Available: http://www.ats.edu/accrediting/standards/05GeneralStandards.pdf

Foster, C. R., Dahill, L. E., Goelmon, L. A. & Tolentino, B. W. (2006). *Educating clergy: Teaching practices and pastoral imagination.* San Francisco: Jossey-Bass.

Graham, L. K. (1992). *Care of persons, care of worlds: A psychosystems approach to pastoral care and counseling.* Nashville: Abingdon Press.

Graham, L. K. (2000). Pastoral theology as public theology in relation to the clinic. *Journal of pastoral theology, IX*, 1- 17.

Hiltner, S. (1958). *Preface to pastoral theology: The ministry of theory and shepherding.* Nashville: Abingdon Press.

Jackson, G. E. (1981). *Pastoral care and process theology.* Lanham, MD: University Press of America.

Lester, A. D. (1995). *Hope in pastoral care and counseling.* Louisville: Westminster/John Knox Press.

Marshall, J. L. (1994). Toward the development of a pastoral soul: Reflections on identity and theological education. *Pastoral psychology*, 43, 11-28.

Neuger, C. C. (2003). *Counseling women: A narrative, pastoral approach.* Minneapolis: Fortress Press.

Nygren, A. (1953). *Agape and eros* (P. S. Watson, Trans.). Philadelphia: Westminster Press.

Patton, J. (1993). *Pastoral care in context: An introduction to pastoral care.* Louisville, KY: Westminster/John Knox Press.

Petersen, R. L. & Rourke, N. M. (Eds.). (2002). Theological literacy and fluency in a new millennium: A pastoral theological perspective. In *Theological literacy for the twenty-first century* (p. 311). Grand Rapids: Eerdmans.

Ramsay, N. J. (2004). *Pastoral care and counseling: Redefining the paradigms.* Nashville: Abingdon Press.

Wimberly, E. P. (1980). The pastor's theological identity formation. *Journal of the interdenominational theological center, 7* (2), 144-156.

Wolfe, B. E. (2003). Knowing the self: Building a bridge from basic research to clinical practice. *Journal of psychotherapy integration, 13* (1), 83-95.

doi:10.1300/J062v08n03_02

Theological Reflection
and the Formation of Pastoral Counselors

Loren Townsend, PhD

SUMMARY. Data gathered as part of a grounded theory study of pastoral counselor practices suggests an interactive relationship between pastoral counselor formation, models of theological reflection, and psychotherapeutic theory. Four models of theological reflection are identified and described, drawn from coded counselor interviews and pastoral statements. Analysis and conclusions offer a preliminary model illustrating how specific values and philosophical commitments active in pastoral counselor training shape interactions between formation, model of reflection, and psychotherapeutic theory. doi:10.1300/J062v08n03_03 *[Article copies available for a fee from The Haworth Document Delivery Service: 1-800-HAWORTH. E-mail address: <docdelivery@haworthpress.com> Website: <http://www.HaworthPress.com> © 2006 by The Haworth Press, Inc. All rights reserved.]*

KEYWORDS. Theological reflection, research methodology, contextual theories, correlation, diagnosis, integration

The purpose of this essay is to offer a preliminary empirical description of how theological reflection interacts with pastoral counselor formation. I approach this from my experience as an educator and observations emerg-

[Haworth co-indexing entry note]: "Theological Reflection and the Formation of Pastoral Counselors." Townsend, Loren. Co-published simultaneously in *American Journal of Pastoral Counseling* (The Haworth Pastoral Press, an imprint of The Haworth Press, Inc.) Vol. 8, No. 3/4, 2006, pp. 29-46; and: *The Formation of Pastoral Counselors:Challenges and Opportunities* (ed: Duane R. Bidwell, and Joretta L. Marshall) The Haworth Pastoral Press, an imprint of The Haworth Press, Inc., 2006, pp. 29-46. Single or multiple copies of this article are available for a fee from The Haworth Document Delivery Service [1-800-HAWORTH, 9:00 a.m. - 5:00 p.m. (EST). E-mail address: docdelivery@haworthpress.com].

ing from an ongoing qualitative study of pastoral counselors. Qualitative research methods assume it is impossible for any observer to take a position of genuine objectivity, so my first task is to name the experience, beliefs, and social location that influence my observations. I will do this by: (1) describing the vantage point from which I observe the interaction between theological reflection and formation, (2) offering working definitions of both "formation" and "models of theological reflection," and (3) describing the research methodology that structures my observation, provides an interpretive framework, and organizes observation into meaningful conclusions.

VANTAGE, DEFINITIONS, AND METHODS

I am a pastoral counselor. I have lived my own formation. On one hand, I am a stereotypical white, male, Baby Boomer, seminary educated, ordained Protestant clergy (American Baptist Churches, USA), who has been an AAPC Fellow or Diplomate for nearly thirty years. Another part of my formation begs exception from this stereotype. I was not trained in a traditional AAPC context. I was a licensed marriage and family therapist in active practice before discovering pastoral counseling just after seminary. I entered pastoral counseling "sideways" without the benefit or constriction of supervisors who modeled or taught a method of theological reflection through years of formative training. Instead, my personal reflective practice grew from curiosity about (and graduate study of) how religious commitments and theological belief systems interact with the everyday practice of psychotherapy. Out of this grew research questions about how pastoral counselors reflect theologically and how they learn to do this.

My vantage point is influenced by the fact that my seminary training was preceded by and followed by graduate study in research-strong universities. Consequently, I tend to value an empirical approach to investigating the relationship between theology, psychotherapeutic theory, and pastoral counselor formation. Furthermore, my particular educational experience predisposes me toward specific theological and theoretical commitments. These affect how I observe and interpret formation and reflection. It is significant that my own formation is rooted more clearly in liberation theologies and process theism than in orthodox, neo-orthodox, evangelical, or existential theologies. As a therapist, I am more at home with Bateson, Goolishian, White, Foucault, and Friere than with Freud, Winnecott, Rogers, or Bowen. I am likely to attend to how meaning (and theory) is socially constructed in particular social locations and to be skeptical of invariant, universal claims made by either theology or psychotherapeutic theory. This means that I am concerned here with describing how theological reflection and pastoral formation interact in specific contexts and not with uncovering universal realities that could be defined as normative.

Defining "formation" in the context of pastoral counseling is tricky. It is one of our few near-sacred terms, tied as it is to ancient religious metaphors of transformation into a vocation in response to divine call. I leave depth analysis of historical meanings to others in this volume. For this essay, I will explore formation primarily as an epistemological event. That is, it can be observed as a set of experiences that act to structure knowledge by shaping a perceptual field and cognitive-emotional interpretive frameworks. I find contextual developmental theory particularly helpful for understanding this process.

Contextual theorists such as Vygotsky, Bronfenbrenn and Rogoff have demonstrated that knowledge and meaning are constructed within social environments. More precisely, the values expressed by a specific context guide interactions that shapes both an individual's cognitive apparatus (i.e., those neural processes and schemata that structure thought) and the content of thought. This is a recursive process. Individuals do not simply internalize the social world. Instead, they appropriate the social world into their "intramental" reality in unique ways that in turn shape interactions in the "intermental" world. The intermental and intramental never mirror each other exactly, but they are so intertwined that it is functionally impossible to distinguish between individual and interpersonal aspects of cognitive functioning (Rogoff, 1990). Consequently, individuals' internal lives and the social context in which they exist are continuously forming and reforming, weaving a near-seamless fabric of shared meaning. This forming and transforming process produces quantitative and qualitative results. Quantitatively, both the community and individuals increase their repertoire of useful knowledge. Qualitatively, interactions produce shifts in cognitive schemata (those frameworks of mind that organize perception, memory, language, and affect) that are best described as an individual's psychological system reorganizing itself (Vygotsky, 1978; Cole & Cole, 1993; Gagne, Yekovich & Yekovich, 1993). What emerges is an active-person-in-cultural-context that organizes reality "through a system of meaning and its psychological tools–a culturally constructed system of knowledge" (Miller, 1993, 409). This system of knowledge is maintained through inner speech and practical skills, which stimulate advanced thinking, innovative thought, and new behavior through peer collaboration.

Contextual developmental theory is particularly useful for exploring pastoral formation. First, it is one of the few developmental approaches grounded in cross-cultural research in Eastern Europe, Asia, Africa, Oceania, Native American tribes, Latin America, and North America. These studies help us understand how formation is specific to particular social locations. They help us avoid a universal normative vision of formation limited by North American, patriarchal, heterosexual, and individualistic understandings of human development. Second, contextual theory provides a corrective to the near-exclusive emphasis on a philosophy of subjective individual consciousness (Habermas, 1987) that frames most discussion of pastoral formation. Contextual theories help us see formation from the perspective of intersubjective, collaborative construction of meaning shaped by and shaping the values of the community in which it takes place. Third, these theories show us that formation is transformation–it reorganizes both the behavior and the psychological world of those who participate. Formation constructs a consistent cognitive-emotional framework to guide perception, organize what is known, and determine how knowledge is used. Finally, these theories offer a practical conceptual frame to observe the dynamics of formation in various communities of pastoral counselors.

For this essay, "model of theological reflection" is defined as the formal and informal procedures pastoral counselors use: (1) to organize perception of religious and spiritual factors in psychotherapy, (2) to organize therapists' thought and behavior in relationship to clients (including theory selection), and (3) to judge the outcome of therapeutic intervention. It is not my agenda here to review reflective models offered in the pastoral theological literature. Rather, my intent is to explore how front-line pastoral counselors organize their daily practice and how these procedures translate into functional models of theological reflection in particular contexts of pastoral practice.

This essay is part of an ongoing research project directed by the author and entitled "What's Pastoral About Pastoral Counseling: A Grounded Theory Study." (Funding is partially provided by an Association of Theological Schools/Lilly Research Costs Grant. Complete results will be published in 2007.) Grounded theory is a qualitative research strategy designed to study people and processes in their natural context (Glazer & Strauss, 1967; Strauss & Corbin, 1998). It is a method capable of investigating how meanings, such as "formation" and "theological reflection" are created, understood, and used. As a research strategy, it uses constant-comparison to examine raw data and discover concepts and relationships that can be organized into a theoretical explanatory framework.

To date, data for this study consists of interviews and written pastoral statements of 70 pastoral counselors. The sample was selected for maximum diversity in denominational endorsement, location of training, race, gender, and geographic location of current practice. It was limited to AAPC certified Fellows or Certified Pastoral Counselors in at least half-time clinical practice. Counselors who primarily teach or supervise were excluded. Microanalysis of transcripts and statements was organized using open and axial coding assisted by *NVIVO*, a computer assisted qualitative data analysis software program. Constant-comparative evaluation produced an emerging model of the relationship between theological reflection and formation. Readers familiar with grounded theory will recognize the following as an expanded memo describing axial coding and movement toward the first stages of theory building.

OBSERVATIONS

Data from the study highlight two predominant themes in pastoral counselor self-identification. Therapists in the sample almost universally state that they work at the intersection of psychotherapy and religion (or spirituality) and that their practice represents not so much a set of skills as an identity. "Pastoral counselor is who I am, it's not what I do." (Sources of quotations from data are not cited to protect confidentiality.) Most participants referred to a process of "formation" that structured their sense of self as a therapist and use of self in therapy. While the meaning of these statements varied according to where and how a particular clinician was trained, the statements revealed almost universal agreement that pastoral therapists "think theologically about clients and therapy." According to respondents, the purpose of theological reflection in pastoral counseling is to:

- Increase knowledge of one's self and client,
- Link ministry with the practice of counseling,
- Bring spiritual and religious resources to bear on a client's treatment,
- Help identify the 'big questions' of life important to clients,
- Act as an evangelistic influence through therapy,
- Join therapist and client together as co-pilgrims on a spiritual journey,
- Guide religious rituals in therapy, and/or
- Develop a special treatment relationship in (therapeutic) "holy space."

Counselors interviewed generally struggled to describe the process of theological reflection in their own work. More than half were confused by questions about models of theological reflection. In the entire sample (interviews and statements), only five therapists named a model of theological reflection or spontaneously described a specific approach to reflective practice. However, microanalysis and coding of data revealed several distinct approaches. These appear to correspond broadly to specific locations of professional formation.

"Formational" Approach

By far, the majority of counselors participating in the study described a "formational" model of reflection. That is, their ability to "do theological reflection" was an artifact of their formation as a pastoral counselor—"It's just part of who I am"; "it comes from within me in my relationship with the client." For the most part, "reflection" meant intuitive perception about the client and client's situation. This intuition was grounded in the counselor's own emotional life, most often described as "the spirit" working in a particular session (or episode of case review) that led intuitively toward an intervention that was spiritually inspired or religiously grounded. Frequently, counselors regarded this intuition as "mystery" unrelated to a particular methodology of reflection. One cannot anticipate when it will happen, but counselors repeatedly commented: "I know it when it is happening." This experience is described as "holy space." Several therapists reported that this special relationship was more important than counseling skills.

Counselors claiming this intuitive "formational" framework for reflection almost universally describe it as a condition of training. "You couldn't get out of that program if you couldn't connect with clients this way" was one representative statement. How do pastoral counselors learn to intuit and access "holy space"? Most spoke of "internalizing a way of being" that was grounded in self-awareness, personal therapy, and "work with my own issues" in supervision. Frequently, therapists recalled a supervisor's deep insight into key issues of the student's emotional life, which merged into parallel discussions of spiritual dynamics with specific client cases. By exploring their own formation, supervisees made an intuitive transfer to clinical cases. It is striking that this intuitive transfer was consistently described as a function of the *therapist's* internal life and independent of any statements clients made about their own spiritual life. Intuition belongs primarily to the therapist, though client self-disclosures often coalesce with therapist intuitions. The therapist's understanding of their own formative journey organized how clients were met, what theories of therapy were selected, what client issues attracted therapeutic attention, and how spiritual-religious issues were framed in therapy. For most respondents, formation as a pastoral counselor was seen as an extension of a life-long process of self-discovery. This usually included healing of past personal and family wounds through personal therapy and religious transformation. Almost all of these therapists believed that their own history in Clinical Pastoral Education (CPE) or a training center's heritage in CPE was a critical factor in their own formation.

Pastoral counselors claiming a "formational" approach largely believed that psychoanalytic theory or depth psychology was a necessary element in both formation and reflection. One therapist concluded that theological reflection could be dangerous without psychoanalytic theory to center reflection in the therapist's own emotional life. Self-awareness gained through therapy provided protection against therapists being misled by their own unfinished psychological issues. Most respondents stated that they saw no distinction between their use of psychodynamic theory and theological reflection. Both were anchored in the self of the therapist in the formation process. Psychodynamic theory provided a comfortable language to translate theological reflection into clinical practice. Most pastoral counselors claiming this model reported that they were more at home with psychotherapeutic language than theological or religious language. An ethnographic study of pastoral counselors in Canada by O'Connor and Meakes (2006) showed a similar dynamic. When pastoral counselors were asked to reflect theologically, they repeatedly gravitated toward psychotherapeutic rather than theological language.

"Correlational" Approach

Several participants in the study described a correlational approach to theological reflection. In most cases, this was a refinement of the "formational model." Information gathered from clinical experience with clients was compared directly and intentionally to scriptural metaphors, theological themes (such as grace, love, hope), and defining dramas of religious history. Correlation appeared to augment intuitive processes by providing a set of concrete theological and religious lenses to interpret the "living human document." Seward Hiltner, Charles Gerkin, Merle Jordan, and William Oglesby were cited as authorities for this approach. These counselors saw correlation as a direct way to integrate their theological education into clinical work. Most were articulate about how correlation fit with their Reformed, neo-orthodox, evangelical, or liberal protestant theological foundations. All of these therapists had completed graduate study in pastoral counseling (DMin or PhD) or were graduates of an AAPC approved training program. Like "formational model" colleagues, they learned correlation from supervisors who helped them integrate formal theological education and clinical observations. These pastoral counselors generally saw correlation as a value added to transferential intuition.

Four pastoral counselors described approaches to correlation that were not anchored in a transferential-intuitive frame. Rather than arising from the internal life of the therapist, theological reflection was grounded in the therapist's education as a minister. These therapists began in theology, scripture, and religious ritual, asking how these related to the therapist or client's experience. This was not divorced from the person of the therapist or empathic connection, but was a distinct (and less intuitive) process independent of transference phenomenon. These therapists were more likely to ask clients direct questions about their spiritual experience and routinely completed a spiritual history. Formation as a pastoral counselor was not a central category for these counselors. Instead, they recalled supervision that focused on skill with less attention to the therapist's use of self. Clinical supervision stressed attention to integrity with the *client's* experience rather the therapist's internal life. When specifically considering formation, these counselors spoke of their religious heritage, entry into ministry through forms of apprenticeship, and their experience in theological education. Only one of these counselors was trained in an historic AAPC context.

A very small minority of sampled pastoral counselors used a form of correlation to guide clients toward religious or scriptural claims on their life. One respondent stated that the purpose of reflection in pastoral counseling was to bring together "fidelity to the teaching of the inerrant Biblical Word of God" with "rigorous, responsible inquiry" about problems in living, methods of counseling, and client outcomes. Those who see reflection in this way expect to bring the "essentials of conservative, evangelical faith" together with the facts of clients' lives in a way that allows the pastoral counselor to "be a disciple of Christ and make disciples of Christ." Theological reflection helps the therapist sort the "essentials of God's claim" on a client's life from "non-essentials." In practice, this allows the therapist to help the client with spiritual discernment and invite the client into behavior that reflects the "truth of God's written Word and the centrality of Christ's saving work." This form of correlation is a limited dialogue that compares authoritative scripture and normative doctrine with client lives, counseling theory, and counseling action. Theological reflection is a corrective that makes pastoral counseling "an avenue of grace leading to union with God, self, and others, not as an end in and of itself. Thus it falls in line with Jesus' greatest command (to make disciples, teaching them to observe all things I have commanded [sic], Matthew 28: 19-20)." These counselors attributed their correlational frame to their formation as pastoral counselors. Like those describing an intuitive-transferential approach, this frame of reflection and action was "who I am." However, unlike other pastoral counselors, clinical supervisors did not appear as a central element in counselor formation. Instead, formation was related to a specific understanding of ministerial call, past religious history, and the counselor's "mission in the modern world" as defined by their community of faith. These therapists did not report strong ties with traditional AAPC training programs.

Diagnostic Models

One distinct minority of pastoral counselors described a diagnostic approach. This is a refinement of both the "formation model" and correlational model. It offers a conceptual anchor to compare theological resources with client experience and clinical diagnostic categories. These counselors describe matching religious/spiritual issues with problems in living or psycho-religious problems with recommended clinical intervention. One pastoral counselor expressed the desire for a "religious DSM" to help with this process. Though this approach was a desirable method of reflection, most who named it denied competence in its practice. "It's a place I really need to grow" was a frequent comment. Most felt pastoral counseling lacked an adequate diagnostic language to make seamless connections between observed problems in living and categories of religious pathology. Diagnostic practices included: (1) taking a routine religious history and relating personal history themes to psychological and religious pathology; (2) applying specific diagnostic models (respondents referred to Paul Pruyser (1976), Wayne Oates (1987), Merle Jordan (1986), and Donald Denton (1998); and (3) juxtaposing DSM categories with religious metaphors observed in the client's life (described by one therapist as "baptizing the DSM-IV").

Pastoral counselors using this model reported two distinct influences on their formation. First, "pastoral diagnosis" was usually learned from a supervisor operating from an intuitive-transferential framework. However, this supervisor "pushed" students to conceptualize the connections between clinical material and observed patterns in clients' religious or spiritual lives. Respondents referred to this as "learning to think" in particular categories that gave specific diagnostic content to transferential intuition. Second, these therapists were driven by a need for clinical parity with other professionals. They believed they needed religious diagnosis to justify pastoral-specific intervention in an inter-disciplinary context. Formation for these therapists appears to include a recursive exchange between the clinical demands of traditional medical psychotherapy and pastoral counselors' need to establish a unique reli-gious contribution to this community. The diagnostic model appears to provide specific competencies that build a bridge for this transaction. At the same time those respondents who used it fully embraced the intu-itive-transferential theme that "pastoral counselor is an identity, not a skill." Consequently, pastoral diagnosis relies more on intuitive transfer than empirically established criteria.

Feminist and Liberative Models

A minority of respondents (less than 10%) looked to feminist and lib-eration theologies to frame reflective practice. These pastoral counselors spoke of reflection as a critical engagement with the social contexts of therapy and specific forms of gendered, racial, or cultural oppression. This was strikingly different than those claiming "formational," correla-tional, or diagnostic models. In fact, these therapists generally rejected the intuitive-transferential and hierarchical assumptions of these models as culturally captive values and patriarchal artifacts. (Here, "hierarchical assumption" is used to describe an approach to training that privileges the therapist with special knowledge of the client's internal world, behavior, or relational life; this practice seems prominent in clinical intuition in-formed by personal pastoral formation.) Several respondents believed that male, heterosexual, and white privilege is reinforced when theologi-cal reflection is anchored in the language of patriarchal psychotherapeu-tic theories, diagnostic schemas, or in the therapist's internal life. This becomes an issue of justice when clients (particularly women, non-het-erosexual, non-Euro American, and disabled clients) become the *object* of reflection rather than participants in reflection.

Like other pastoral counselors, theological reflection for these thera-pists arises from questions raised by the client/therapist relational field or the professional practice of counseling. However, instead of relying on knowledge based in the person of the therapist (intuitive-transferential connection or a set of guiding diagnostic categories) these therapists turn first to social analysis. Problems are defined by social location and not personal pathology. Consequently, therapists "need questions more than answers" and favor "discovering with" the client the sets of social contexts that frame therapeutic problems and their embedded meanings. Reflection is a joint venture to identify dominant cultural, family, and religious narratives that structure oppressive meaning and behavior in the client's life. Typical themes include issues of women's embodiment, racial and ethnic location, social class, and disability. Reflection usually includes a community of colleagues to stretch the therapist's imagination, propose new questions, or question how psychotherapeutic models and theology participate in oppression. In general, these therapists were articulate about feminist and womanist critique and liberation methods that guided their reflective process.

One subtle distinction was evident in the research data. Pastoral counselors using intuitive-transferential approaches often spoke of feminist commitments and the need to reflect on issues of social location. However, this concern operated as a function of the therapist's own internal world. That is, reflection was a personal activity to increase the *therapist's* knowledge and gain a deeper intuitive understanding of the client's internal life. This knowledge may or may not be shared with the client, be instrumental in guiding therapy, or become an agenda for advocacy or social action. For therapists working from a feminist or liberative model, reflection was a form of interpersonal dialogue to produce personal and social change for both the client and the therapist. These pastoral counselors, saw little distinction between theological reflection, intervention, or social action (thus, theological reflection *is* therapy and social action), and were more concerned with change than increasing therapist knowledge. Therapists using this model reported commitments to feminist and post-modern psychotherapeutic theories (such as narrative, feminist, and collaborative systemic therapies).

Both male and female respondents using these methods were trained almost exclusively in AAPC contexts and were ambivalent about their own process of formation. While they valued their training deeply, most felt they were forced either to resist (and be named as resistant) or to accommodate to "traditional AAPC" approaches (usually described as formational) that did not match their personal feminist-liberative commitments. Two pastoral counselors reported moving to feminist-liberative approach in reaction to supervisors operating from a "formational" frame. These therapists experienced their supervisors' methods as objectifying, intrusive, and oppressive.

Most counselors claiming this model reported that their feminist-liberative values existed prior to training. Usually, these were grounded in personal experiences of oppression, seminary education, past participation in social action, or undergraduate study. None of the sample to date reported finding pastoral supervision that modeled this form of therapy or reflection. However, respondents repeatedly recalled "good supervisors" who tolerated their position or helped them articulate it more clearly. This was important to their formation and their ability to stay connected with AAPC and other pastoral counselors, though nearly all reported feeling somewhat marginalized as pastoral counselors. Most important for several respondents were non-pastoral counselor supervisors who valued their religious commitments and modeled methods of social analysis, less subject-centered visions of the human person, and therapy consistent with social constructivist values. One pastoral counselor suggested that the most powerful interaction between her formation and theological reflection was the continuous (and tiring) necessity of resisting the dominant formational, intutitive-transferential approach of pastoral counseling in favor of her own values. This forced her to be clear with her own commitments and to interpret conflict with colleagues in creative and redemptive ways. Like her colleagues, she claimed that pastoral counselor is "who she is," though from her own account this is more a function of specific social and theological commitments than clinical training. Consequently, she sees her identity as a pastoral counselor expressed quite differently from "traditionally trained" pastoral counselors.

CONCLUSIONS AND IMPLICATIONS

A Model of Interaction

By definition (van den Blink, 2004), pastoral counselor formation is a life-long process. At the same time, therapists responding to this study repeatedly turned to training as a powerful factor defining their identity, methods of therapy, and reflective practice. For that reason, I will focus here on formation as observed through the training process. Any assumption that these observations hold true through a lifetime of formation will need to be tested.

Data suggests that there is a mutually influential interaction between pastoral counselor formation and models of theological reflection. However, it is clear that this interaction is complex and involves multiple variables. At the very least, these include a therapist's past personal and religious history, supervisors' favored psychotherapeutic theories, the community in which training is located, a counselor's community "fit," and personally transforming experience apart from professional life. These require additional investigation before drawing firm conclusions. However, it is possible to observe one basic set of interactions: Pastoral counselor formation appears to take shape conditioned partly by how theological reflection is defined and practiced. This appears to be a reciprocal interaction–theological reflection practiced and understood in certain ways shapes attitudes and expectations about formation. Conversely, attitudes about formation also shape the nature and expectations of theological reflection. Supervisors' and trainees' preferred psychotherapeutic theory appears to act as a controlling variable in this interaction.

Figure 1 represents one beginning empirical model. The shape of formation (A) is influenced by reciprocal interactions of two conditions of formation–psychotherapeutic theory privileged by the training/forming context (B) and a specific (if often ill-defined) model of theological reflection (C). These are held together by philosophical congruence between psychotherapeutic theory, theological reflective method, and expected outcomes of formation. Personal history and religious history play an indefinite role in the process by establishing values and attitudes that predispose a therapist toward one kind of formative process rather than another. Specific dynamics and outcomes of formation will vary depending on the particular location of training and the philosophical commitments of the supervisor or program. Choosing a place to train (or a supervisor) is equivalent to committing to a particular philosophy of formation guided by specific models of therapy and theological reflection. Through the lens of contextual developmental theory, this process of formation will result in a culturally constructed system of knowledge expressed through a system of meaning and its particular psychological tools.

Illustration

Most of the pastoral counselors sampled fit strongly in the "formational" model of reflection. The training they described highlighted a strong commitment to theologies and psychotherapies grounded in "philosophies of the subject" (Habermas, 1987). Put very simply, these philosophies assume an experiencing subject/self capable of taking an objective attitude toward the world. This attitude then produces knowl-

FIGURE 1

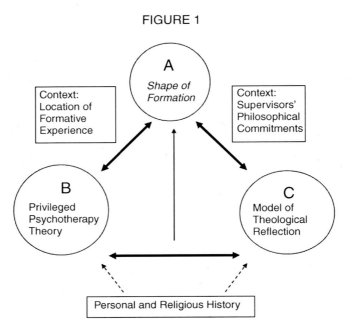

edge of objects and others as they actually are (here, "object" refers to anything, including persons, that can be said to exist). By using one's subjective resources (such as diagnostic categories or transferential intuition), it is possible to perceive what lies below the surface of objects/others and disclose "what causes what." Through discovering these subterranean causal links, one can intervene in these causal connections and create change. The subject's primary interest is self-formation as expressed through self-expression and self-actualization (Simpson, 2002). This position is observed clearly in Cartesian, Kantian, and existential philosophies that ground psychodynamic and humanistic psychotherapies taught in most traditional pastoral counselor training programs. This is matched by commitments to modern (in distinction to post- or pre-modern) mainline Protestant theologies that emphasize the subjectivity of the human person. For instance, therapists trained in the "formational model" recalled similar experience: Supervisors described the goal of formation as "personal integration." This meant that a supervisee should use personal therapy, supervision, and theological reflection to explore the depths of their own motivation and gain insight into the personal issues that impact their ability to see others or themselves in relationship to others. This is the most valued task in training. It is accomplished in constant interaction with theologies and psychotherapies that value the human self as the center of meaning and insight as the primary avenue to meaningful experience. Theological reflection was described as the activity that confirmed congruence between personally integrated theology, psychotherapy, and vision of one's self as a pastoral counselor.

Two selection dynamics appear to support formation in the "formational model." First, those embracing this model reported a personal history, history of personal psychotherapy, CPE, or course of theological study that predisposed them toward such "formational" training. Second, selection appears also to rely on attrition or eliminating pastoral counselors who do not share philosophy of subject values. Students who shared these values upon entering training reported good experience in supervision and spoke of their supervisors as "mentors." However, supervisors quickly identified incongruence between a student's values and a program's (or supervisor's) philosophy of subject values. Incongruous values usually resulted in supervision problems. In these cases, mandatory personal psychotherapy often became the gatekeeper of formation. Students were given the option of pursuing personal change that would produce congruence with the expectations and philosophy of training. When this failed or was rejected, students either chose to leave or were asked to leave that context of training. These two elements of selection assure that a coherent community of formation is created that shares: (1) a common understanding of what theological reflection looks like and means, (2) a shared philosophical paradigm, and (3) a schema for procedures to guide the action of pastoral counseling.

Similar interactions are observed for those reporting a feminist-liberative model of reflection. Again, there is congruence between guiding theologies, privileged psychotherapies, and expected outcomes of formation held together by post-modern and social constructivist philosophies. These philosophies take a stance toward personal formation and therapy that shifts attention away from individual, subjective formation and approaches that seek to "uncover" hidden dynamics and information. Rather, these philosophies focus attention on how social reality is co-constructed through intersubjective interchange and languaged into meaning for particular times and places. Instead of plumbing the depths of enduring psychological structures (which themselves are social constructions), reflection reveals processes that create and maintain specific socially located meanings. Formation, then, is not an individually owned subjective experience that prepares one to act upon other persons/objects through therapy. It is a set of community-grounded language-meanings (or narrative-meanings) that structure personal experience and one's interactions in the world. Therapists claiming this position tend to reject psychodynamic and humanistic therapies in favor of systemic, narrative, and collaborative language therapies that share a constructivist paradigm.

It is important to note that pastoral counselors described by this model, like those in the "formational model," do not represent a pure type. In this small sample there were therapists who described thoroughgoing constructivist commitments. There were also therapists who retained subjectivist philosophical assumptions (along with commitments to depth and humanistic psychologies), but were committed to social analysis characteristic of feminist-liberative reflection. (This is reminiscent of Hegel and Marx, who worked within a subject/object paradigm but also accounted for social conditioning in the self-forming interaction between subject and object.)

Unlike therapists represented by the "formational model," none of the counselors describing strong feminist or liberative models viewed their training program as organized around these values. Instead, they described important formative influences coming from the margins of traditional training through a supervisor or subgroup that nourished feminist-liberative values.

It is important to note that the interaction between formation, model of theological reflection, and privileged psychotherapy seemed to shift for counselors who embraced strongly evangelical or conservative theologies. For these therapists, personal and religious history appears to determine both the expected outcome of formation and the model of reflection. Formation is interpreted first as a condition of Christian ministry (to date, all counselors responding in this way have claimed evan- gelical Christian ecclesiastical connections). Instead of "pastoral counselor is who I am," these respondents claimed, "I am first a Christian and a minister and a pastoral counselor because of this." In these cases, pre-modern expressions of evangelical theology appear to organize formation, theological reflection, and therapy around a common purpose: To interpret Christ's claims on human life, to be a disciple, and to make disciples. Respondents claiming this position often interpreted their own formation as a result of a very specific call to ministry and congregational apprenticeships. Those who completed pastoral counselor training valued it primarily as a location of skill acquisition and not formation. These few individuals felt it was necessary to protect their Christian and ministerial formation from values and philosophies embedded in training programs.

IMPLICATIONS

These empirical observations have several limitations and implications. First, this study is in the early stages of extensive data collection and analysis. Categories have not yet been saturated and additional observations about important interactions may yet emerge. Second, the study is not at the stage where racial, ethnic, class, and sexual orientation differences can be reliably observed or evaluated. Third, qualitative studies must not be generalized to populations. That is, it is would be inappropriate to say that these observations represent the whole population of pastoral counselors. They describe only pastoral counselors in specific locations. Nonetheless, these observations can be used to generate a theory of the relationship between formation, model of theological reflection, and psychotherapeutic theory which can then be tested. This essay is but a first step in that process. Consequently, only a few broad conclusions can be offered.

First, pastoral counselors represent a rather homogenous group. What little diversity exists derives primarily from variations in pre-training value commitments and where people trained or with whom. Those whose values do not fit easily into "traditional" training contexts reported experiences of marginalization. This suggests that those who organize training could benefit from clearer analysis of the philosophical and value context of training and how this affects attitudes about diversity of students, models of formation, theological reflection, and psychotherapy. This will be increasingly important as more people from diverse ethnic identities and faith traditions other than Christian enter training.

Second, pastoral counselors interviewed were largely inarticulate when describing their method of theological reflection. Most claimed procedures modeled by supervisors. However, these same counselors could not easily talk about their method, clearly describe its procedures, or articulate its philosophical foundations. This has important implications for supervision and training. Pastoral counselors' literacy and public theological voice may be improved through supervision that both models and openly articulates connections between formation, theological reflection, and the practice of psychotherapy. This is especially true for those embracing a "formational" model of reflection. Likewise, new generations of pastoral counselors may benefit from supervisors who articulate the philosophical foundations that ground the interaction between formation and psychotherapeutic models.

Finally, it is important to recognize that "pastoral formation" as a category may best be seen as "pastoral formations" that manifest particular contextual values. Any normative vision of pastoral counselor identity is likely to reflect dominant, white, Protestant Christian values. Rather than focusing on such a normative notion, it may be more important to train pastoral counselors who can give coherent voice to their own process of formation, value a diversity of formations and theological reflective practices, and find language to express how these relate to outcomes in training and therapy.

REFERENCES

Cole, M. & Cole, S. R. (1993). *The development of children* (2nd ed). New York: W.H. Freeman and Company.

Denton, D. D. (1998). Religious diagnosis in a secular society: A staff for the journey. Lanham, MD: University Press of America.

Gagne, E. D., Yekovich, C. W. & Yekovich, F. R. (1993). *The cognitive psychology of school learning* (2nd ed). New York: Harper Collins.

Glaser, B. & Strauss, A. (1967). *Discovery of grounded theory*. Chicago: Aldine.

Habermas, J. (1987). *The philosophical discourse of modernity* (F. Lawrence, trans). Cambridge, MA: The MIT Press.

Jordan, M. R. (1986). *Taking on the Gods: The task of the pastoral counselor*. Nashville: Parthenon Press.

Miller, P. (1993). *Theories of developmental psychology* (3rd ed.). New York: W. H. Freeman and Company.

Oates, W. E. (1987). *Behind the masks: Personality disorders in religious behavior*. Philadelphia: Westminster Press.

O'Connor, T. & Meakes, E. (2006). Expected publication 2007. The Praxis of Theological Reflection in Pastoral Care and Counselling: An Ethnographic Study. Conducted in association with Waterloo Theological Seminary, Waterloo, Ontario and partly funded by ATS/Lilly research grant.

Pruyser, P. (1976). *The minister as diagnostician*. Philadelphia: Westminster.

Rogoff, B. (1990). *Apprenticeship in thinking: Cognitive development in social context*. New York: Oxford University Press.

Simpson, G. (2002). *Critical social theory: Prophetic reason, civil society, and Christian imagination*. Minneapolis: Fortress Press.

Strauss, A. & Corbin, J. (1998) *Basics of qualitative research: Techniques and rocedures for developing grounded theory*. Thousand Oaks, CA: Sage Publications.

van den Blink, H. (2001). *Thoughts on formation*. Essay presented to the American Association of Pastoral Counselors. Available: http://www.aapc.org

Vygotsky, L. (1978) (and M. Cole, John-Steiner, V., Scribner, S., & Souberman, E. Eds.). *Mind in society*. Cambridge, MA: Harvard University Press.

doi:10.1300/J062v08n03_03

Thick Theory:
Psychology, Theoretical Models,
and the Formation
of Pastoral Counselors

Pamela Cooper-White, PhD

SUMMARY. Pastoral counselor formation encourages the articulation of a psychological theory one uses in pastoral counseling. It is not important simply to have a theory and to be able to articulate it. Formation ought also to assist clinicians in adopting a theoretical framework that is useful to therapy and, in dialogue with pastoral theology, has the power to generate more and better questions and to develop multiple meanings for a situation. Good theory also has the power to critique itself and to search for assumptions and biases. Theory is used in pastoral counseling to develop diagnostic sensitivity, empathic anticipation, and play and imagination. doi:10.1300/J062v08n03_04 *[Article copies available for a fee from The Haworth Document Delivery Service: 1-800-HAWORTH. E-mail address: <docdelivery@haworthpress.com> Website: <http://www.HaworthPress.com> © 2006 by The Haworth Press, Inc. All rights reserved.]*

KEYWORDS. Psychological theory, countertransference, diagnosis, empathy, play and imagination

---

[Haworth co-indexing entry note]: "Thick Theory: Psychology, Theoretical Models, and the Formation of Pastoral Counselors." Cooper-White, Pamela. Co-published simultaneously in *American Journal of Pastoral Counseling* (The Haworth Pastoral Press, an imprint of The Haworth Press, Inc.) Vol. 8, No. 3/4, 2006, pp. 47-67; and: *The Formation of Pastoral Counselors: Challenges and Opportunities* (ed: Duane R. Bidwell, and Joretta L. Marshall) The Haworth Pastoral Press, an imprint of The Haworth Press, Inc., 2006, pp. 47-67. Single or multiple copies of this article are available for a fee from The Haworth Document Delivery Service [1-800-HAWORTH, 9:00 a.m. - 5:00 p.m. (EST). E-mail address: docdelivery@haworthpress.com].

The head of music at my daughter's school emailed me with a request: "As the chair of the performing arts committee, could you find me a volunteer to accompany the middle school select chorus? And actually, I was hoping it would be you." Daunted, I replied, "I'm a singer, not a pianist. How hard is the repertoire?" She wrote back within the hour, "You're on! Hey, it's middle school, how hard can it be?" My daughter brought the music home to me a week later, and my worst fears were realized. There was one piece in particular that snagged me every time I attempted it. A wonderful "Gospel swing" piece with a heavy stride base and large chords in the right hand, this song featured a sudden key change midstream from G (one sharp) to A^b (four flats). It was like rafting down a calm river and suddenly hitting the rapids!

Feeling dutiful, and being somewhat obsessional in character, I had no choice but to soldier on. Chord sequences in the second half of the piece kept tripping me up every day. Finally, I took a mental step back from my finger-fumbling and growing panic, and put on my musicology "hat" to think about the piece. What was its history: who would have performed it originally? What was the theoretical analysis: what were the harmonic progressions, and why did certain chords change as they did? The answers helped me immediately. The piece was, of course, never meant originally to be learned or performed off a written page. It would have been improvised at first, and then handed on from performer to performer by ear. A Gospel pianist would know instinctively how to move from chord to chord, because the harmonies followed certain formal patterns, and the creative departures from those patterns still belonged within the tonal universe of the style of music being presented. I needed to get my nose away from the sheet music in order to begin to feel my own way almost improvisationally, guided by the theory, into the movements of the melody, the chords, and the song's rolling rhythms.

WHY PASTORAL COUNSELORS NEED THEORY

Some students and some experienced therapists resist the need for theory, stating that they do not want to force individual clients with their unique issues into some kind of artificial or preconceived framework. Some practitioners believe that theory is too abstract, too removed from the flesh-and-blood realities of human thought, feeling, and behavior. While it may be true that some colleagues seem to treat their theoretical models like a procrustean bed, forcing every client to fit their theory, and disregarding aspects of clients' lives that are not explained by their conceptual frame, this is not the fault of theory *per se*, but rather a faulty use of it. As Patrick Casement has warned from his psychoanalytic framework, "There is a temptation, rooted in the acquired knowledge of psychoanalytic theory, for analysts and therapists to try to mastermind the analytic process rather than to follow it" (Casement, 1985, p. 183). This applies to all counselors' premature or over-zealous applications of theory. But as Casement (1985) continues,

> Patients will . . . often resist a therapist's premature application of theoretical knowledge, and preconceived ideas about them in order to reinstate the necessary 'period of hesitation' [citing Winnicott]. Without the space created by this hesitation there can be no room for analytic discovery or play. With it there is room, in every analysis and therapy treatment, for theory to be rediscovered and renewed. (p. 53)

Rather than resisting theory as the culprit, then, it is perhaps more accurate to recognize that in fact, *every practitioner has a theory*, whether it is articulated or not. The Greek word θεωρια (*"theoría"*) literally means a looking at, viewing, or contemplation, as well as speculation or *theory* in the sense we understand it. Our theory is, at its most basic meaning, our *viewpoint* as we enter into the work we do with clients.

Theory is classically defined as follows:

> A scheme or system of ideas or statements held as an explanation or account of a group of facts or phenomena; a hypothesis that has been confirmed or established by observation or experience, and is propounded or accepted as accounting for the known facts; a statement of what are held to be the general laws, principles, or causes of something known or observed. (OED, 3284)

As it functions in the context of counseling and psychotherapy, theory encompasses two domains. It represents a set of governing concepts about human behavior ("psychological theory")–encompassing explanations for human motivation, personality formation, emotional and cognitive development, and causes of pathology. And it also represents a framework for practice ("practice theory")–a rationale for using certain methods for both diagnosis and treatment. Various schools of thought within the vast range of contemporary counseling practice may place more emphasis on either the psychological or the practice domain. The most comprehensive theoretical frameworks encompass both, since a particular conceptualization of the human psyche would be expected to have implications for approaches to care.

Unarticulated theories, I would argue, can be as harmful to clients as rigidly guarded conscious formulations. An unarticulated practice theory might be an unconscious conviction that "It is my job to be nice to everyone." Under the powerful sway of this unarticulated conviction, a therapist might end up avoiding exploring painful material with a client, steering away from conflicts arising in the therapeutic relationship, fostering emotional dependency, and even crossing boundaries under the rubric of being a "special carer."[1] A corollary psychological theory might be that "all people are essentially good," and if given sufficient nurture, will naturally grow toward their highest potential. The pitfalls of this general theory include a failure to examine culturally and socially laden assumptions (including racial and gender constructions) about what constitutes "goodness," resulting in an empathic failure to recognize aspects of the client's aggression, sexual desire, greed, hunger, or hate.

Here, of course, I am already showing my own theoretical cards. Even one's approach to theory is already theory-laden. My theoretical home is, broadly speaking, psychoanalytic, and within the ever-expanding range of psychoanalytic models, I have pitched my tent with the "relational" school[2]—a contemporary movement within psychoanalysis that follows postmodern, constructivist concepts of psychological reality as socially or interpersonally constructed, and regards "self" as a more multiply constituted subject than a unified or integrated core of identity or being. Its corresponding practice theory emphasizes the fluid interplay of self and other, and attention to countertransference as a primary tool for empathically identifying the thoughts, feelings, sensations, and enactments that continually bubble up in the "intersubjective" or shared area of consciousness/unconsciousness between therapist and client (Cooper-White, 2004). Because this school of thought has evolved out of earlier object relations models, I also continue to find guidance and wisdom in its forebears, for example, the writings of D.W. Winnicott (1965), Harry Guntrip (1961), Melanie Klein (2002), and of Freud himself (1961a)—whose multiply layered and ever-developing thought continues to be a rich resource.

Given my own theoretical biases about theory, then, I am prone to believe that we are drawn to our favored psychological and practice theories (conscious and unconscious) by our own personal histories, experiences with people we are close to, and professional experiences—in other words, our countertransference. For example, I am gravitationally pulled toward Guntrip's (1975) and André Green's (1986) writings about the dead (depressive) mother, Freud's (1961b) explanations of neurotic symptoms as an outbreaking of repressed sexual and aggressive desires, Klein's unflinching descriptions of biting, guilt, and reparation, and Jane Flax's (1993) and Jodie Messler Davies' (1998) theories about the emancipatory qualities of multiplicity, because they resonate symphonically with my own inner experience. I am drawn to Winnicott's (1965) descriptions of practice because they speak to the kind of "good-enough" care that touch my own yearnings to be cared for and understood.

The role of countertransference in the development, conscious and unconscious, of our psychological viewpoint, our theory, points to the need for self-knowledge, and personal therapy, as part of both the theoretical formation and the overall professional formation of pastoral counselors. As others in this symposium will have pointed out, formation involves not only training in skills–perhaps the most rudimentary part of formation–but a knowledge base from which to draw about the human psyche, the causes of dysfunction, effective modes of healing, and as pastoral counselors, the spiritual dimensions of human growth and living. Moreover, formation suggests growth in the area of identity–both in terms of personal maturity and an understanding of one's role as a professional helper.

The work of therapy calls especially for self-awareness as a person, because the knowledge of one's own wounds is a prerequisite both for avoiding the pitfalls of bias and projection, and for being open and available to the subjective experience of the other who comes to us for care. The hypothetical counselor above, whose unarticulated theory is to be nice at all times, has no less inward predilection toward his or her theory than I have toward mine. We cannot escape the force of our own internal landscape. But to the extent that we can come to recognize some of the elements within it, we can make choices about what makes the most sense to us, how to conduct ourselves as professionals, and what is most likely to be genuinely therapeutic in our work with clients–putting their emotional and developmental needs above our own during the time we spend with them. Learning from the highly developed and carefully articulated theories of those who have gone before us gives us a richer repertoire from which to form our own models of psychology and therapeutic practice.

WHAT MAKES A "GOOD" THEORY?

Not all theories are created equal. I like mine, and you like yours, but we need better reasons for these inclinations than that they "ring true" somehow, or even that we can identify how they resonate with our personal experience, as I described above. What is good theory, and how can we tell?

Good theory, first of all, should be useful to the healing work of therapy. A theory should be internally consistent, and may even be brilliant or fascinating in its speculations about the motives and meanings of human behavior, but if it does not connect to the struggles of real human persons, it is not enough. A theory should have sufficient explanatory power to help illuminate both *what* is happening to the client internally and in his or her relationship to others in the world, in terms of some larger patterns that are common to human behavior, and *why*.

Second, as pastoral counseling belongs under the larger umbrella of disciplines of ministry, or practical theology, good pastoral counseling theory must also be in dialogue with pastoral theology, in which theory, theology, and practice are seamlessly interwoven. As postmodern philosophers such as Foucault and Derrida have pointed out, the separation of theory and practice is actually an artificial dichotomy. Don Browning (1991) and Edward Farley (1990) have both argued that all authentic theology is at heart "practical in its import." (See also Ramsay, 2004.) Browning advocates for an inductive "practice-theory-practice" orientation in which practice is recognized both as implicitly theory-laden, and offering a rich source, via "thick description" (Geertz, 1973), for building theory.

Further, the claims human beings make *ethically* upon one another–each encounter with difference, each encounter with the unique face of the other (to borrow from the philosopher Emanuel Lévinas, e.g., 1969)–call us continually to draw from, and at the same time to reappraise and revise, our theological premises in light of whatever new form of love and justice this new "I-Thou" (Buber, 1970, as elaborated and contested in Levinas, 1969) encounter demands. As David Tracy (1973) has argued (drawing also from Tillich, 1951, esp. 40-47), there must be, indeed, a mutual dialogue or "critical correlation" back and forth between theology and the human situation. Pastoral theology always takes suffering as its starting place[3]–in Jürgen Moltmann's (1993) words, "the open wound of life in this world" (p. 49). The classic pastoral functions, as articulated in the mid-20th century (and amplified in recent decades), immerse the pastoral theologian directly in this open wound, through a commitment to ministries of healing, sustaining, guiding, reconciling, liberating, and empowering (Clebsch and Jaekle, elaborated by Watkins Ali, 1999, p. 9).

In order to serve this purpose well, theory needs to be *thick theory*, borrowing from anthropologist Clifford Geertz's (1973) term for good ethnographic observation, "thick description." The goal of good theory is, to quote Geertz, "not an experimental science in search of law but an interpretative one in search of meaning. It is explication I am after, construing social expression on their surface enigmatical" (p. 5). As Geertz continues,

> What generality it [theory] contrives to achieve grows out of the delicacy of its distinctions, not the sweep of its abstractions . . . [T]he essential task of theory building here is not to codify abstract regularities but to make thick description possible, not to generalize across cases but to generalize within them. (25-26)

A thin theory, like thin description, imagines far fewer questions. A theory is a paradigm (Kuhn, 1996),[4] which can only explore the questions its adherents can imagine. Thus thick theory is marked not by its factual *accuracy*, but by its power to generate more and better *questions*.[5] Pastoral psychological theory must be "thick": layered and detailed enough to take into consideration the complexity and multifariousness of human living and its many modes of symbolization, together with the vicissitudes of psychological unfolding over time.

Finally, following Derrida, I would argue that "good theory" is theory that also has the capacity not only to interrogate its subject of inquiry, but to interrogate itself. Thick theory raises questions about its own presuppositions and biases, thus generating both more rigorous and more creative possibilities for understanding. As such, a "good theory" is one that continually breaks itself open. In the words of one scholar of postmodernism (Lemke, 1998):

> Derrida in particular mounted a radical philosophical critique in which he pointed out that the very act of meaning making always presupposes an unanalyzable ground of the possibility of meaning and of sign systems, and that the dialectic of sign and ground produces an inherent instability or indefiniteness in any meaning.

To the extent that theory is itself a practice of naming, Derrida's (1978) reflections about the slipperiness of words caution us that there is an irreducible gap between the act of naming and whatever may exist as actual reality: "It is . . . simultaneously true that things come into existence and lose existence by being named" (p. 70). The reality of our clients' subjective experience can never be fully known, even as its contours may be traced and given meanings in the ongoing dialectic between the therapist's and client's respective theoretical knowledge/speculations, and the narrative they construct together, more and more with each successive therapy session. What I am calling "thick theory," then, grows out of an ongoing dialectical relationship between each moment of engagement in the therapeutic encounter (including its symbolic representation in words), and our contemplation of the relationship (also interpretation, also symbolic, but at another level of remove[6])–especially before and after each session.

This approach has emancipatory implications. Rather than using theory as a tool by which to measure or evaluate clients, which is a unilateral act of power on the part of the therapist as expert, theory is fluid and malleable as it passes through the ongoing floes of the therapeutic relationship (both conscious and unconscious). Michel Foucault wrote in detail about the intrinsic link between knowledge and power, and in particular the use of theoretical knowledge to set the medical, psychiatric, or other professional in a position of superior political power by virtue of the expertise accorded. We hold legitimate power that we cannot shed, in the form of responsibility and trust based on a non-reciprocal ethical duty to care for our clients. Our use of theory involves serving this trust faithfully–using our analytical abilities and therapeutic skills to empower rather than disempower our clients, as we engage in mutual rather than unilateral practices of exploration, interpretation, and meaning-making. We bring a fund of theoretical knowledge with us as part of our training, and then our theory, in turn, is shaped and challenged by each new encounter. Thick theory, to borrow words from Foucault (1977),

> . . . does not express, translate, or serve to apply practice: It is practice. But it is local and regional . . . and not totalizing. This is a struggle against power, a struggle aimed at revealing and undermining power when it is most invisible and insidious. (p. 208)[7]

To bring this abstract theorizing about theory down to earth, let me offer an example. I once had a client in California, "Britt," a former competitively ranked figure skater, who was involved in self-injury. Britt was pushed early and hard by her parents to perform. As an adult, her perfectionism and related self-punishment for imperfection were unrelenting. Initially, my theoretical understanding was a fairly standard conceptualization of self-injury: that her cutting was an externalization of inner pain, and also that there was a physiological addiction, related to the endorphins released by cutting. This was a supportive understanding that corresponded well to Britt's own conscious understanding of her motives for cutting, her inability to stop it, and the relief it provided her.

That year, during the winter Olympics, I saw an advertisement by a knife company with a full-page photograph of the legs of a female figure skater with knives for skate blades. The ad jolted me, both because of the violent and sexual fetishization implicit in the image, and because of my immediate association to Britt. I realized that my theory had been too thin. It had not allowed into my reverie about the client the possibilities either of the erotic or the violent, aggressive aspects of her self-harm. I went back to my theoretical resources and began to consider more widely some of the possible unconscious meanings that had eluded me before–partly in unconscious collusion with the client's own need to be seen only as victimized and pure in motive. I thought from a self-psychological perspective about skates and knives as selfobjects. I thought from a Kleinian perspective about themes of eroticism fused with aggression, guilt, and reparation. I thought about gender theory and the female figure skating world, its sexual performativity,[8] and its enforcement of a certain paradoxical image of child-woman femininity (think of star performers being pelted by fans with both flowers and teddy bears). More associations came to me, but suffice it to say that suddenly my theory was now thick with multiple associations having to do with both the erotic and the aggressive dimensions of Britt's cutting. Issues that had previously seemed unrelated came into focus in a new way–body image, desire and inhibition, bravado, rage, and revenge.

Note that my "aha!" moment of viewing the knife ad did not suddenly lead me to make ham-handed interpretations, catalyzing a clichéd cathartic, cure-all moment for Britt. Rather, my inner shift from thin to thick theory *sensitized* me to the many more possible meanings of Britt's cutting that had previously been opaque to me, so that over time I could hear more, explore more, and empathically understand more. My new openness helped make a space for Britt to verbalize more–thoughts, feelings and fantasies she previously had kept both unconsciously repressed and consciously suppressed out of shame and fear of judgment. Thick theory thus facilitated a form of "hearing into speech" (Morton, 1985). Britt experienced this as empowering and freeing for

her, and as less consciously acceptable aspects of her motives and behavior became more tolerable to her, her crises of self-injury finally
ceased.

THREE IMPORTANT USES OF THEORY

There are many ways in which theory can be helpful, and many theories about theory itself. I will highlight three that I believe to be particularly important: (1) diagnostic sensitivity, (2) empathic anticipation,
and (3) play and imagination.

Diagnostic Sensitivity

Diagnosis, like theory itself, has fallen on hard times in some therapeutic quarters. *Pastoral* diagnosis in particular has seldom been addressed as a topic *per se*. The two major exceptions to this are Paul
Pruyser's (1976) now classic text, *The Minister as Diagnostician*, and
Nancy Ramsay's (1998) recent important contribution, *Pastoral Diagnosis: A Resource for Ministries of Care and Counseling*. Because of
reductionistic and sometimes sexist misuses of diagnosis to label, (mis)
define and pathologize clients, some therapists are wary of diagnosis.[9]
Resistance against intrusive oversight by managed care and third-party
payers can also play into this distrust. Some therapists therefore prefer
to take a more intuitive approach to assessment, allowing the therapeutic process to unfold without formal evaluations or case formulations.
Implicit in this resistance sometimes is a parallel resistance to the notion
of pathology itself, with some therapists feeling that to identify problems with living as pathology is automatically to assume a superior position to the client and to patholog*ize*.

I agree that concepts of pathology, diagnosis, and a medical or "disease" model of psychology and psychotherapy have rightly become
suspect in recent decades, to the extent that they set up an expert thera-
pist/passive client dynamic, in which clients come to be identified glob-
ally and impersonally with their suffering and impairments, or labeled
as "problems" in order to impose political and social conformity. However, I believe that to do away with all forms of assessment or diagnosis
would be to pretend that various recognizable forms of illness and pain
did not exist (Cooper-White, 2006).

I would argue on the contrary that *pathology* does not have to be understood as a pejorative term, by which individuals may be labeled and

thereby dismissed, but rather as a means of naming a quality of suffering. The root of the word pathology is not sickness but παθεμα/παθs? ("*pathéma*"/"*páthos*")– suffering or passion. *Pathology* is the study of suffering and passion: παθso-ολογos ("*pathos-logos*"). Understanding pathology in all its nuances requires diagnosis or assessment, in order to have some means of categorizing the shapes that mental and emotional suffering tend to take, at least in any given cultural location. Consensus about these categories and specific terminology evolves and changes over time as different theories hold sway, but there is a shared language and at least a broadly consensual conceptualization in the field of psychology, without which professional communication and consultation regarding practice, research and training would be very limited. *Diagnosis*, from the Greek word διαγνωσκω?("*diagnósko*"), simply means to distinguish or inquire, to make a decision, or make something known. In this regard, pathology and diagnosis belong to the practice of pastoral psychotherapy, as one area of disciplined focus, in order to shape the care given and receiving with a thoughtful assessment of "what ails" (Yalom, 1989, pp. 89, 232).

The reigning understanding of diagnosis taught in pastoral clinical training programs is codified in the United States in the *Diagnostic and Statistical Manual of Mental Disorders* ("DSM"). The DSM offers descriptive classifications, and does not refer to etiology (the study of causation).[10] While the "reliability" of its classifications continues to be a subject of some controversy and even diatribes against the DSM (e.g., Kirk and Kutchins, 1997), the utility of having some common clinical vocabulary is valued by most professional therapists. But it should be noted that the DSM is not in and of itself a *theory*, although its categories were originally developed with underlying theoretical biases (often functioning invisibly, like all effective ideologies). Sophisticated readings of the DSM and other diagnostic manuals require the clinician to pay attention to their ever-changing and evolving definitions and underlying theoretical constructs. The *Introduction* to the DSM itself includes cautions on the limitations of a categorical approach, and the still-fledgling efforts of the DSM task force to incorporate "ethnic and cultural considerations" (p. xxii, xxiv; see also Lukoff and Turner, 1992). Very different constructions of mental health and spiritual wellbeing are authoritative in non-western cultures.

As Nancy Ramsay (1998) has written,

> Diagnosis is not a neutral process; it has both interpretive and con-
> structive functions. Diagnosis reiterates the anthropological and
> philosophical assumptions of the practitioner and validates the
> usefulness of those assumptions for naming reality. (p. 9)

Optimally, therefore, diagnosis should be self-reflective and self-criti-
cal, watchful for biases and gaps in one's own understanding, and above
all, engaged in collaboration with the client, in an ongoing process of
shared reflection, dialogue, and continual revision as the client's suffer-
ings come to evolve, change, and carry different meanings over time.

The value of theory for diagnosis lies beyond–often far beyond–the
descriptive shells of DSM categories. Fluency in psychological theory
helps the clinician to move beyond such quantitative measures toward a
more subtle and nuanced, empathic interpretation of the causes of an individual's distress. Such an interpretation (which must always be acknowledged as such, and not as a factual account) may be summarized
as *case formulation*. Such a formulation is a working sketch of a client's
inner world and external relations, for the purpose of offering the best,
most sensitive therapeutic response. As such, it is always provisional,
and subject to ongoing revision. As psychoanalytic supervisor Nancy
McWilliams (1999) has written,

> [I]t is a more inferential, subjective, and artistic process than diag-
> nosis by matching observable behaviors to lists of symptoms. . . .
> [A] good tentative formulation . . . attends to the following areas:
> temperament and fixed attributes, maturational themes, defensive
> patterns, central affects, identifications, relational schemas, self-
> esteem regulation, and pathogenic beliefs. (p. 11, see also 208-9)

Case formulation, while often associated with psychoanalytic therapy, is a valuable tool for counselors practicing from variety of theoretical orientations, ranging from family systems to cognitive-behavioral
therapies. A good formulation, regardless of the practitioner's theoretical orientation, is one that begins with a nuanced and detailed understanding of the client's concerns, in the client's own language, and connected to the client's own sensibilities.

Only a thick theory aids the pastoral counselor in thick description
(encompassing what is observed in fine detail both about the other, and
about one's own affective experience within the flow of the therapeutic
relationship). Only such a thick description, in turn, can sensitize the
counselor to the minute, specific and detailed vicissitudes of the client's

speech, behavior, affect, and communication–expressing the delicate
turns of his or her life, both inner and outer. And as observations are
shared and explored with the client, the formulation of "what ails," and
why, is mutually constructed. Diagnosis becomes a relational process
rather than a product created by an expert solely for communication
with other experts. This leads naturally from diagnosis to treatment as
therapeutic relationship–and theory becomes helpful once again as an
empathic tool.

Empathic Anticipation

   While theory may be most obviously associated with initial diagnosis
and case formulation, it is also invaluable in the continuing pastoral assessment that flows inseparably with ongoing practice in the therapeutic
relationship, as discussed above. Casement (1985) describes this con-
templative turn within the therapeutic work in terms of an "internal supervisor" (esp. pp. 29ff). The "internal supervisor" is a composite
metaphor for the therapist's internalization of his or her own supervision, personal therapy, and clinical experience. This internal supervisor
functions, at least in part, as a metaphor for the way theory continues to
function, sometimes subliminally, as an internal compass when in the
midst of working with a client.
   Part of the way in which this internal supervisor functions is to facilitate
a variety of different imagined empathic connections with the client's material, beyond what occurs in session. In my experience, allowing for an as-
sociative process of making such "trial identifications," including a
free-floating consideration of transference-countertransference dynamics
and enactments as they have begun to bubble up in the therapeutic relationship, helps the therapist to be more nimble and sensitive when actually in
session with the client. Drawing on a musical analogy, Casement writes:

   In order that we can develop a more subliminal use of the internal
   supervisor when we are with a patient, it is valuable to use (or in a
   Winnicott sense, to 'play' with) clinical material outside of the
   session. A musician plays scales, or technical studies, in order that
   these can become a natural part of his [or her] technique. So too in
   psychotherapy: When a therapist is 'making music' with a patient
   [s/]he should not be preoccupied with issues of technique. That
   technique can be developed by taking time, away from the consulting room, for practicing with clinical material. Then, when in the
   presence of a patient, the process of internal supervision is more

readily available when it is most needed. (p. 38, also citing Winnicott, 1971)

Theory thus enhances our ability to be truly, empathically present with a client from moment to moment. The work we do in actual therapy sessions has a performative dimension–it is an enacted narrative, constructed by both therapist and client, that operates simultaneously at a verbal and an embodied level. As such, the work and the *play* (Winnicott, 1971) of therapy is akin to improvisation, rather than to the production of a scripted drama. Thick theory requires a multi-dimensional capacity to enter vicariously into the worldview and affective life of the client, and to be open, as well, to the subtleties of feeling and fantasy arising spontaneously within one's own frame of reference, one's own counter-transference.

Heinz Kohut (1959) defined empathy as "vicarious introspection," (p. 459) and contended that sustained empathy, or "empathic-introspective inquiry" is the primary tool of therapeutic observation and insight (e.g., Stolorow et al., 1987). Empathy works primarily through the medium of the therapist's own subjectivity or countertransference, as the therapist experiences affects, resonances, fantasies, and images that are drawn from the pool of unconscious material and "shared wisdom" in the intersubjective dynamic of the therapy. We ourselves are the most sensitive instruments to "catch" the vibrations of the music that is occurring between the client and ourselves, especially at the level of unconscious relationship. At first we may not even be able to sing the melody back, i.e., verbalize in our own minds what is happening. But as the therapy progresses, and we consider the interactions between our clients and ourselves–particularly moments that seem deeply affect-laden or powered by nonverbal enactment–both our personal self-awareness and theoretical knowledge can aid us in our understanding of the client, and of the therapeutic relationship. As Christopher Bollas (1987) wrote in *The Shadow of the Object*:

> . . . [I]in order to find the patient, we must look for him[/her] within ourselves . . . By establishing a countertransference readiness I am creating an internal space which allows for a more complete and articulate expression of the patient's transference speech than if I were to close down this internal space and replace it with some ideal notion of absolute mental neutrality or scientific detachment . . . What the [therapist] feels, imagines, and thinks to himself while with the patient may at any one moment be a specific element of the patient's

projectively-identified psychic life . . . that creation of a total environment in which both patient and [therapist] pursue a 'life' together. (pp. 201-202)

Such readiness, I would suggest, is enabled and facilitated by a combination of a discipline of introspection, and an ongoing engagement with the best theoretical thinking available, both historically and in the present. Finally, this readiness requires a willingness on our part to *play*.

PLAY AND IMAGINATION

Scripture scholar Frances Young uses the metaphor of a concerto performer's virtuosic cadenza for preaching and teaching, but this analogy could just as easily be extended to the improvisational virtuosity of the pastoral counselor in session with a client: "The performer of a cadenza keeps to the style and themes of the concerto" [here, we might substitute *psychological and practice theory* for "the style and themes of the concerto"], "but also shows virtuosity and inspiration in adapting and continuing in keeping with the setting and form" (Wells, 2004, p. 60, citing Young, 1990). All the technical training, all the theory and analysis, all the historical study that a musician or a therapist has incorporated becomes crystallized in a moment of creative imagination in the irreducible present moment of performance or therapeutic encounter. This creativity is not constrained but rather is carried by the boundaries of setting, and it is resourced by the received theoretical structure and its theoretical underpinnings. In this way each therapeutic session becomes a duet, in which the harmonic resolution desired is healing, growth, or revitalization for the client.

Paradoxically, given the reams of psychotherapeutic publications over the last one hundred years, and the tooth-and-claw fights among therapists of differing theoretical persuasions, perhaps the most important capacity of a therapist is "the moral courage not to understand" (Reik, 1948, as cited in McWilliams, 2004, p. 21). A favorite quote among relational analysts is Wilfred Bion's (1970) statement that therapists should approach the work of therapy "without memory or desire" (pp. 32, 41-54). The therapist, like the poet, should be "capable of being in uncertainties, mysteries, doubts, without any irritable reaching after fact and reason" (ibid.). It is ironic that Bion, of all possible theorists, wrote so much toward the end of his life about therapy as an "act of faith" (pp. 32, 41), when one of his greatest concerns was laboriously categorizing modes of cognition, including an elaborate grid of algebraic symbols. Yet, Bion's (1965) own symbol for the ineffable, "O," literally went "off the charts"–it does not appear on Bion's complicated grid (1965, frontispiece). "O" referred to a reality beyond what can be grasped, like Derrida's ineffable "ground" that lies as a trace in the gaps between sense and representation.

This is perhaps the paradoxical value of deeply critical, theoretical thinking–that it finally leads to the recognition of its own limits, and a lifting of one's gaze past books and papers and theories toward the horizon of that which, inevitably, appears in the distance as a shimmering Unknown. Bion's (1970, 26) own slipping into theological language show how thin the membrane finally is between the "faith" of secular therapy and a religious sensibility:

> O . . . can 'become,' but it cannot be 'known.' It is darkness and formlessness, but it enters the domain K [knowledge] when it has evolved to a point where it can be known, through knowledge gained by experience, and formulated in terms derived from sensuous experience; its existence is conjured phenomenologically. (p. 41)

Finally, the knowledge of theory and practical skills must dissolve into the immediacy of the therapeutic encounter. One does not theorize as a primary activity in the presence of a client. But one must first *have* a theoretical foundation in order to suspend it. It is perhaps only once one is secure in one's capacity to play theoretically, based on a thoroughgoing acquaintance with respected theoretical models, that one is freed to hold such "knowledge" lightly. We suspend it within the practice of "evenly hovering attention" (Freud, 1961c) to all the registers of the therapeutic encounter–affective, cognitive, sensory, and in the realms of nonverbal enactment and unconscious/semi-conscious fantasy. Theoretical speculations are precisely that–they are *speculi*, mirrors, or more aptly, prisms, by which one facet of theory after another can be held up to our experience with a client, to see what lights and patterns may be reflected–always with the benefit of the client and not merely the brilliance of the therapist as the aim. Theory ultimately does not provide us with "information" about the client, but rather, a sensitivity to multiple meanings that arise in the intersubjective matrix of the therapeutic relationship. It does not provide us with answers, but over time it may provide us with more complex and sophisticated questions.

SUMMARY RECOMMENDATIONS

To bring all this again back to concrete training and practice, how can therapists, supervisors, and training programs foster "thick theory"?

1. Both beginning and experienced therapists should make it a life-long habit to read widely in clinical, theoretical literature, both contemporary and historical. Just as a musician can learn new pieces more readily when s/he has already learned an extensive repertoire, therapists gain in theoretical sensitivity and a capacity for vicarious introspection by assimilating a broad range of theoretical ideas.
2. Practitioners should foster a capacity for critical reflection on their theoretical resources. Questions to ask include: What is the underlying paradigm being presented? Who is served, and who is left out in this paradigm? What are the cultural, social, and political biases behind this theoretical formulation, and how is power being mediated?
3. Practitioners should also reflect on their countertransference reactions to theoretical formulations. What in the theory excites, disturbs, attracts or repels me? What might be the inner sources of such reactions, and how might such self-awareness enhance the use of this theory for the benefit of clients?
4. Finally, practitioners should foster an awareness of desires on their own part either to resist theoretical play and reverie about a given client, or to fall too rigidly into a fixed formulation. What might such resistances to imaginative speculation and improvisation mean in the ongoing dynamic of a particular case? And what does the particular interplay of the therapist's desire to know, desire not-to-know, and the "negative capacity" for suspending knowledge, suggest empathically about the client's own subjective life and experience?

I have had three rehearsals with the middle school chorus so far. I am never going to be an exceptional pianist, but I have come a long way since the first day of practicing that challenging music. Practicing has strengthened my skill, and I am more fluent with all the pieces that at first I stumbled my way through. But especially by taking a step back and thinking about the theory and the history of the notes on the printed page, I have been able to let go and recapture just a bit of the improvisational genius behind the written composition. Paradoxically, it was connecting to the theory behind the notes that allowed me to really play the music.

NOTES

1. I have described the pitfalls of the need to be a "special carer" based on my empirical research in Cooper-White, 2004, esp. 155-80, and in Cooper-White, 2001, 5-35.

2. The foundational text for this school of thought is Mitchell (1988); see also Greenberg (1991) and Aron (1996). The development of relational theory can be traced through the journal *Psychoanalytic Dialogues* beginning with Vol. 1 in 1991, and in Mitchell and Aron, Eds., 1999. For more on the history of relational psychoanalysis, see Mitchell and Aron, 1999, Preface, *Relational Psychoanalysis*, ix ff; Greenberg and Mitchell (1983), esp. pp. 9-20 and Mitchell (2004).

3. This method is characterized by Anton Boisen's foundational concept of the "living human document" as a corrective for approaching pastoral care and therapy with human subjects through the lens of theory first rather than examining the client's experience as the primary "text" to guide assessment and care, in Boisen, 1971. This expression was further developed by Charles Gerkin, (1973). See also Bonnie Miller-McLemore's (1996) further creative and feminist elaboration as the "living human web."

4. Cf., Geertz (1973), 27, on the process by which unproductive theories are retained beyond their usefulness.

5. Geertz similarly evaluates his "interpretive anthropology" as "a science whose progress is marked less by a perfection of consensus than by a refinement of date. What gets better is the precision with which we vex each other" (p. 29).

6. For a further discussion of heremeutics and theory, see Geertz, (1973) esp. pp. 24-30.

7. See also Foucault (1980), p. 145. For a good discussion of Foucault's writings on social theory, see also Lemert and Gillan (1982).

8. At the time, I had not yet read Judith Butler's *Gender Trouble* (1990), but it is relevant to this discussion.

9. Largely driven by managed care, a trend has arisen in the last decade or so, variously called outcome-based practice or EVT (empirically validated treatment) (see, for example, Seligman, 1998). It is a pragmatically oriented practice theory of sorts, a teleological theory in which the ends-as defined by the interests of insurers as much as by clients-not only justify but dictate the means. This is the approach adopted by the National Board for Certified Counselors, and by extension, most state licensure requirements. It appeals to the desire of legislators and the medical establishment to validate counseling practices from a positivist scientific model, and to regulate practice from a risk-management perspective, i.e., to minimize malpractice liability. In large part, however, it is a practice theory without a psychology, so in its worst manifestations, an EVT approach would suggest that the same therapist, based on quantitative outcome research, should be a cognitive-behaviorist with depressed clients, a behaviorist with anxious ones, a family systems therapist with couples in conflict, a psychopharmacologist with psychotic clients, and perhaps-only after cognitive methods have been tried

first—a psychodynamic therapist working with traumatized clients. The inherent bias of this research is toward short-term interventions that restore a baseline of functioning but rarely focus on helping a client to reach any deeper understanding of the root causes of his or her problems.

10. The one obvious exception to this is Post-Tramatic Stress Disorder and its related brief form Acute Stress Disorder, which by definition require a trauma to have occurred as the origin of the disorder.

REFERENCES

American Psychiatric Association. (2000). *Diagnostic and statistical manual of mental disorders (4th ed., text revision)* ("DSM-IV-TR"). Washington, DC: Author.

Aron, L. (1996). *A meeting of minds: Mutuality in psychoanalysis.* Hillsdale, NJ: Analytic Press.

Bion, W. (1965). *Transformations.* London: Heinemann.

Bion, W. (1970). *Attention and interpretation.* London: Tavistock.

Boisen, A. (1971). *Exploration of the inner world: A study of mental disorder and religious experience.* Philadelphia: University of Philadelphia Press (Original work published 1936).

Bollas, C. (1987). *The shadow of the object: Psychoanalysis of the unthought known.* New York: Columbia University Press.

Browning, D. (1991). A *fundamental practical theology: Descriptive and strategic proposals.* Minneapolis: Fortress Press.

Buber, M. (1970). *I and Thou* (W. Kaufman, Trans.) New York: Scribner.

Butler, J. (1990). *Gender trouble: Feminism and the subversion of identity.* New York: Routledge.

Casement, P (1985). *Learning from the patient.* New York: Guilford Press.

Clebsch, W. and Jaekle, C. (1964). *Pastoral care in historical perspective.* Englewood Cliffs, NJ: Prentice-Hall.

Cooper-White, P. (2001). The use of the self in psychotherapy: A comparative study of pastoral counselors and clinical social workers. *American Journal of Pastoral Counseling, 4* (4), 5-35.

Cooper-White, P. (2004). *Shared wisdom: Use of the self in pastoral care and counseling.* Minneapolis: Fortress Press.

Cooper-White, P. (2006). *Many voices: Pastoral psychotherapy in relational and theological perspective.* Minneapolis: Fortress Press, in press.

Davies, J.M. (1998). Multiple perspectives on multiplicity. *Psychoanalytic Dialogues, 8* (2), 195-206.

Derrida, J. (1978). *Writing and difference,* (A. Bass, Trans.) Chicago: University of Chicago Press.

Farley, E. (1990). Practical theology. In R. Hunter, (Ed.), *Dictionary of pastoral care and counseling* (pp. 934-936). Nashville: Abingdon Press.

Flax, J. (1993). *Disputed subjects: Essays on psychoanalysis, politics and philosophy.* New York: Routledge.

Foucault, M. (1977). Intellectuals and power (discussion with Gilles Deleuze). (M. Seem, Trans.) In D. Bouchard, (Ed.), *Language, counter-memory, and practice: Selected essays and interviews by Michel Foucault.* Ithaca: Cornell University Press.

Foucault, M. (1980). Power and strategies. In Foucault, M., *Power/knowledge: Selected interviews and other writings, 1972-1977*. New York: Pantheon.

Freud, S. (1961a). *The standard edition of the complete psychological works of Sigmund Freud*, 24 vols. (J. Strachey, Ed. and Trans.), (Hereafter cited as *SE*.) London: Hogarth.

Freud, S. (1961b). *Three essays on the theory of sexuality*. SE, 7: 125-245. Original work published 1905.)

Freud, S. (1961c). *Recommendations to physicians practicing psycho-analysis*. *SE, 12*: 111-120. (Original work published 1912).

Geertz, C. (1973). Thick description: Toward an interpretative theory of culture. In Geertz, C., *The interpretation of cultures* (pp. 3-32). New York: Basic Books.

Gerkin, C. (1973). *The living human document: Revisioning pastoral counseling in a hermeneutical mode*. Nashville: Abingdon Press.

Green, A. (1986). The dead mother. In Green, A., *On private madness* (pp. 142-173). New York: International Universities Press. (Original work published 1980).

Greenberg, J. R. (1991). *Oedipus and beyond: A clinical theory*. Cambridge, MA: Harvard University Press.

Greenberg, J. R. and Mitchell, S. A., (1983). Object relations and psychoanalytic models. *In Greenberg, J.R. and Mitchell, S.A. (Eds.), Object relations in psychoanalytic theory* (pp. 9-20). Cambridge, MA: Harvard University Press.

Guntrip, H. (1961). *Schizoid phenomena, Object-relations, and the self*. New York: International Universities Press.

Guntrip, H. (1975). My experience of analysis with Fairbairn and Winnicott (How complete a result does psychoanalytic therapy achieve?) *International Review of Psycho-Analysis*, 2, 145-56.

Kirk, S. and Kutchins, H. (1997). *Making us crazy: DSM–The psychiatric bible and the creation of mental disorders*. New York: Free Press.

Klein, M. (2002). Love, guilt, and reparation, and other works 1921-1945, and Envy and gratitude and other works 1946-1963. In R. Money-Kyrle, (Ed.,) *The writings of Melanie Klein* (Vols. 1 and 3). New York: Free Press.

Kohut, H. (1959). Introspection, empathy, and psychoanalysis: An examination of the relationship between mode of observation and theory. *Journal of the American Psychoanalytic Association*, 7, 459-483.

Kuhn, T. (1996). *The structure of scientific revolutions* (3rd ed). Chicago: University of Chicago Press.

Lemert, C. and Gillan, G. (1982). *Michel Foucault: Social theory and transgression*. New York: Columbia University Press.

Lemke, J. (1998). Postmodernism and critical theory. [On-line]. Available: http://academic.brooklyn.cuny.edu/education/jlemke/theories.htm

Lévinas, E. (1969). *Totality and infinity* (A. Lingis, Trans.) Pittsburgh, PA: Duquesne University Press.

Lukoff, D., Lu, F., and Turner, R. (1992). Toward a More culturally sensitive DSM-IV: Psychoreligious and psychospiritual Problems. *Journal of Nervous and Mental Disease, 180* (11), 673-82.

McWilliams, N. (1999). *Psychoanalytic case formulation*. New York: Guilford Press.

McWilliams, N. (2004). *Psychoanalytic pychotherapy: A practitioner's guide*. New York: Guilford Press.

Miller-McLemore, B. (1996). The living human web: Pastoral theology at the turn of the century. In J.S. Moessner, (Ed.). *Through the eyes of women: Insights for pastoral care* (pp. 9-26). Minneapolis: Fortress Press.

Mitchell, S.A. (1988). *Relational concepts in psychoanalysis: An integration*. Cambridge, MA: Harvard University Press.

Mitchell, S.A. (2004). *Relationality: From attachment to subjectivity*. Hillsdale, NJ: Analytic Press.

Mitchell, S. A. and Aron, L. (Eds.). (1999). *Relational psychoanalysis: The emergence of a tradition*. Hillsdale, NJ: Analytic Press.

Moltmann, J. (1993). *The trinity and the kingdom*. Minneapolis: Fortress Press.

Morton, N. (1985). *The journey is home*. Boston: Beacon Press.

Oxford University Press. (1971). Theory. In *The compact edition of the Oxford English dictionary, complete text reproduced micrographically* (cited as "OED"), (Vol. 2, p. 3284). Oxford: Author.

Paul Pruyser, P. (1976). *The minister as diagnostician*. Philadelphia: Westminster.

Psychoanalytic Dialogues 1 (1) (serial beginning 1991).

Ramsay, N. (1998). *Pastoral diagnosis: A resource for ministries of care and counseling*. Minneapolis: Fortress Press.

Ramsay, N. (Ed.). (2004). *Pastoral care and counseling: Redefining the paradigms*. Nashville: Abingdon Press.

Reik, T. (1948). *Listening with the third ear: The inner experience of a psychoanalyst*. New York: Farrar, Straus.

Seligman, L. (1998). *Selecting effective treatments: A comprehensive, systematic guide to treating mental disorders* (rev. ed.). San Francisco: Jossey-Bass.

Stolorow, R., Brandchft, B., and Atwood, G. (1987). *Psychoanalytic treatment: An intersubjective approach*. Hillsdale, NJ: Analytic Press.

Tillich, P. (1951). *Systematic theology* Vol. 1. Chicago: University of Chicago Press.

Tracy, D. (1975). *Blessed rage for order*. New York: Seabury.

Watkins Ali, C. (1999). *Survival and liberation: Pastoral theology in African American context*. St. Louis: Chalice Press.

Wells, S. (2004). *Improvisation: The drama of Christian ethics*. Grand Rapids: Brazos Press.

Winnicott, D.W. (1965). *The maturational processes and the facilitating environment*. London: Hogarth.

Winnicott, D.W. (1971). *Playing and reality*. London: Tavistock/New York: Basic Books.

Yalom, I. (1989). *Love's executioner and other tales of psychotherapy*. New York: Basic Books.

Young, F. (1990). *The art of performance: Towards a theology of holy scripture*. London: Darton, Longman and Todd.

doi:10.1300/J062v08n03_04

Spirituality and the Formation
of Pastoral Counselors

Joseph D. Driskill, PhD

SUMMARY. As part of the interdisciplinary nature of pastoral counseling, the formation of pastoral counselors needs to tend to issues of spirituality. Recognizing that all truth and meaning is socially located and constructed, spiritual practices can open the pastoral counselor to diverse understandings and experiences of God. Developing spiritual practices is integral to formation and might be enhanced by spiritual direction. Ultimately, spirituality contributes to the healing and wholeness of clients, therapists, and communities. doi:10.1300/J062v08n03_05 *[Article copies available for a fee from The Haworth Document Delivery Service: 1-800-HAWORTH. E-mail address: <docdelivery@haworthpress.com> Website: <http://www. HaworthPress.com>* © 2006 by The Haworth Press, Inc. All rights reserved.]*

KEYWORDS. Spirituality, spiritual practices, training, diversity, healing, prayer

As the clinical paradigm of pastoral counseling was being critiqued and challenged from within the field, a broad interest in spirituality emerged in North American culture. The rise of popular interest in spirituality, initially viewed by many as a fad, was soon followed by the for-

---

[Haworth co-indexing entry note]: "Spirituality and the Formation of Pastoral Counselors." Driskill. Joseph D. Co-published simultaneously in *American Journal of Pastoral Counseling* (The Haworth Pastoral Press, an imprint of The Haworth Press, Inc.) Vol. 8, No. 3/4, 2006, pp. 69-85; and: *The Formation of Pastoral Counselors: Challenges and Opportunities* (ed: Duane R. Bidwell, and Joretta L. Marshall) The Haworth Pastoral Press, an imprint of The Haworth Press, Inc., 2006, pp. 69-85. Single or multiple copies of this article are available for a fee from The Haworth Document Delivery Service [1-800-HAWORTH, 9:00 a.m. - 5:00 p.m. (EST). E-mail address: docdelivery@haworthpress.com].

Available online at http://ajpc.haworthpress.com
© 2006 by The Haworth Press, Inc. All rights reserved.
doi:10.1300/J062v08n03_05

mation of academic and professional societies committed to the study of spirituality (such as the Society for the Study of Christian Spirituality) and to the development and support of spiritual direction and formation programs (such as Spiritual Directors International). As these guilds developed specialized, peer-reviewed journals such as the *Christian Spirituality Bulletin* (now *Spiritus*) and *Presence: An International Journal of Spiritual Direction*, journals in the field of pastoral care and counseling began to receive and accept articles that brought the academic fields of pastoral care and spirituality into conversation with one another.

This emerging, interdisciplinary dialogue has developed in the context of postmodern and post-colonial approaches to meaning and knowing. As the postmodern world-view emerged and de-centered rationality as the primary mode of knowing, the experiential and devotional aspects of spirituality and faith received renewed attention. At the same time, the post-colonial focus on deconstructing the power and authority of social and cultural privilege–including the privileged values and practices that shaped the professional identities of pastoral counselors during the middle decades of the twentieth century–opens both pastoral care and spirituality to new modalities of understanding and practice.

In a broad sense, this de-centering has resulted from the recognition that truth and meaning are socially located. "Culture informs all that people *do* as well as all that they *are*. The culture in which we were raised instructed us on how to eat, dress, wash, play, speak, and touch, and it affected the way we are in every role we play" (Molina and Haney, 2005, p. 150). The implications of this are threatening for those who have had the power to name what is valued and important for formation, especially if they are reluctant or unwilling to share this power. In our professional lives as pastoral counselors, those who have held this power are primarily white, middle-class, heterosexuals. As we gradually acknowledged the diversity of voices within our changed context, we have made attempts to invite "others" to the table–while failing, initially, to recognize that both the rules for conversation and the table itself were shaped by the norms and paradigms of the culture of privilege. Even extending the invitation betrays that people with privilege have the authority to invite others to join the conversation. If we are to celebrate rather than merely tolerate diversity, we must create anew the mode and means for relating to one another. Those who have the power of privilege must surrender their hegemony in the interest of the not-yet-known and the unknown.

Surrendering hegemony in support of the agenda for justice and compassion begins by identifying who we are and recognizing the socially lo-

cated nature of our contributions and our limitations. Identifying ourselves allows us to acknowledge that our particular perspective may or may
not be helpful to persons from other cultures and social locations. I am an
Anglo-American, middle-aged, straight, educated, male. I teach in a diverse seminary context with women and men who are Asian-American,
African-American, Hispanic, Latino/a and Caucasian. Students and colleagues
self-identify as lesbian, gay, bisexual, transgendered and straight. Students
represent more than forty denominations and a variety of faith traditions;
some have no formal religious affiliation. I find it is important to note that I
am writing from a mainline Protestant context that differs in significant
ways from evangelical contexts. I also recognize that although a number of
diverse ethnic/cultural and faith expressions are embraced in mainline traditions, I am often unaware of the ways in which their specific communities provide unique embodiments of these traditions. Where I teach, a
consortium of seminaries has a graduate program in Christian spirituality,
and many of the nine participating schools have a pastoral theologian on
their faculties. There are a number of international students in the consortium. My classes normally embody the diversity described above. In the
midst of this diversity I seek to raise issues and draw on intellectual resources that address the needs and concerns of a variety of communities.

I turn now to a case which embodies issues raised by the role of spirituality in the formation of pastoral counselors. This case focuses first on
the Rev. Dr. Susan Wilson's response to the needs of Jamie Lin and then
raises questions about the formation needs of pastoral counselors. I
have created this case from a composite of experiences, changing the
names and identifying details to maintain confidentiality.

CASE EXAMPLE

Jamie Lin is a twenty-nine-year-old social worker employed by a
large urban county in California. She is married to John Huang, a high
school English teacher; they have a precocious three-year-old daughter.
Although they did not start dating until their first year as undergradu-
ates, they have been friends since the eighth grade. Both were active as
teens in the youth group of Eaton United Church of Christ. They strayed
from church during their college years, but returned in anticipation of
being married. Two years ago, Jamie went with several friends from
church to a Five Day Spiritual Formation Academy sponsored by the
United Methodist Church. She came away with a renewed sense of the

importance of prayer and a commitment to devote more time to spiritual growth. Her enthusiasm impressed John; although he was not interested in developing a daily prayer practice, he is highly supportive of Jamie's commitment. Lately Jamie has been sensing during prayer a deeper, more spiritual dimension to her social work career. She still enjoys working with the clients in her case load, but she feels God is calling her to some type of ministry. She is unclear about this call and has a deep inner restlessness about her vocational path. She has always thought that her call to social work embodies her religious commitments, but now she wonders if something is missing. She is befuddled but notices in her prayer this palpable movement toward "something else" or "something more."

Jamie decides to discuss her prayer life with Rev. Dr. Susan Wilson, the pastoral counselor recommended by her pastor when she and John were seeking premarital counseling. Jamie's parents were originally referred to Dr. Wilson some years ago when unresolved grief at the loss of Jamie's paternal grandfather had been stressful for her parents. Jamie was away at school at the time, but remembers her mother saying that Dr. Wilson demonstrated sensitivity to their family situation and seemed to understand the cultural assumptions that required them to care for Jamie's aunt in Taipei.

Dr. Wilson completed her seminary education at a well-known mainline Protestant seminary in the East and continued her study in a pastoral counseling internship program. Since she loved working with both families and individuals, she returned to school in her early forties and completed a D.Min. program in pastoral care. For ten years she has been employed by a pastoral counseling center. Dr. Wilson is an active church member and values her collegiality with both clergy and mental health professionals. She meets monthly for peer supervision with an interdisciplinary group of health care professionals who value her contribution to their discussions.

After meeting with Dr. Wilson for two sessions, Jamie decides to cancel her third appointment. Dr. Wilson was as warm and friendly as she had been before, but each time Jamie mentioned her prayer life, Dr. Wilson shifted the focus of the conversation. Several times Dr. Wilson raised questions about Jamie's relationship with John and his reaction to her "more intense" prayer life. When Jamie explained that John did not share a similar enthusiasm for personal prayer, Dr. Wilson asked if Jamie thought her prayer life was having a detrimental impact on the marriage. She also gently asked if issues from their Chinese cultural heritage might be influencing Jamie's interest in prayer. Jamie felt Dr.

Wilson was trying to be sensitive, but saw these topics as a distraction from her concern about God's presence in her life. When Jamie said she thought God might be working in the administrative structure of her workplace, Dr. Wilson listened and nodded but became quiet. She also asked if the vocational direction Jamie was considering might disrupt family life. As Jamie reflected on these conversations, she decided to thank Dr. Wilson and cancel their next appointment. She wondered to herself why a pastoral counselor would not be more interested in talking about God's activity in her daily life. As she thought about her denomination's motto, "God is still speaking," she wondered who might be listening and in what way.

CASE DISCUSSION

This case raises several questions that relate to spirituality and the formation of pastoral counselors. What might we infer about Dr. Wilson? She is a caring pastoral counselor who has skills working with family systems. She was able to build a relationship with Jamie's parents and with Jamie and John. While she seemed open to the importance of cultural heritage in shaping one's expectations, feelings and responses, it was less clear that she recognized differences that might exist between Jamie's Asian American identity and that of her parents' generation. Dr. Wilson was unwilling or unable to address what was happening in Jamie's prayer and how that influenced her sense of vocation. Dr. Wilson's focus on John and the marriage at the expense of Jamie's primary concern became problematic for the therapeutic relationship.

From this case I wish to identify four areas where attention to "spirituality and pastoral counseling formation" might have changed the outcome both for Jamie and Dr. Wilson. These are: (1) the role of spiritual practices in the formation of pastoral counselors; (2) using spirituality as a lens for better appreciating and understanding narratives from diverse cultural and ethnic social locations; (3) recognizing the way in which a spiritual practice can serve as a container for spiritual and emotional growth; and (4) using a spiritual direction model for raising questions with a group or individual to bring a prophetic dimension of care into the counseling session. Before moving to the issues raised by the case, I will attend to the definitions of spirituality and formation I am using here.

THE LENS OF SPIRITUALITY AND THE PROCESS OF FORMATION

Definitions of spirituality in the wider culture are numerous and varied. Spirituality is often set in opposition to religion, with "religion" referring primarily to institutional faith and "spirituality" to matters of personal faith. Another common cluster of meanings surrounding spirituality ranges from an all-encompassing embrace of anything that has to do with human beings and their spirits to a narrow focus on the inward life, often identified with a deep connection between a human spirit and a holy spirit through some form of mysticism.

The definition of spirituality I will be using in this chapter is focused on the lived experience of faith, that is, of the lived experience of one's deepest value system. Kathleen T. Talvacchia (2003) expresses it this way: "By spirituality I mean a soul force energy that connects and relates human beings to the Divine, self, and community" (p. 11). In my usage, spirituality–the lived experience of faith–is concerned with the community which shapes and celebrates this faith, the spiritual practices which sustain it, and the moral life which embodies it. This life of faith is embedded in a surrounding culture that shapes its expression and texture. Using this definition, it is possible to investigate the spirituality of an individual or family system as well as the spirituality of an organization, culture, or time period. In each case the investigator interrogates the phenomenon of interest by providing a thick description of that which animates and gives life to its existence. For the purposes of pastoral counseling, the spirituality and social location of individuals, family systems, and religious organizations are of interest.

Shaping the case example with "spirituality" as a starting point (rather than the more restrictive terms "spiritual direction" or "spiritual guidance") allows me flexibility in presenting the case. While I will address some examples that focus primarily on pastoral counseling as a one-to-one activity between a trained pastoral counselor and a client, many of my observations will address aspects of basic clergy formation especially valuable to those seeking skills in pastoral care and counseling.

The term "formation" also requires attention. *The American Heritage Dictionary of the English Language* (2000) defines "formation" as: "(1) The act or process of forming something or of taking form; (2) Something formed . . . ; (3) The manner or style in which something is formed . . . " (s.v. "formation"). The formation process suggested by these definitions is especially problematic to the extent that the recipients of such formation are viewed as passive and malleable "blank slates" on which teachers and supervisors with superior knowledge imprint preformed professional patterns.

In contrast, the recent Carnegie Foundation project on clergy education found formation in theological education focuses on "forming in students the dispositions, habits, knowledge, and skills that cohere in professional identity and practice, commitments and integrity" (Foster, Dahill, Golemon, & Tolentino, 2006, p. 100). Clergy formation in the setting where I teach seeks to honor the many ways in which people in a postmodern, post-colonial, global world engage the sacred mystery at the heart of human existence. The Carnegie authors "observed pedagogies that engage students in practicing the presence of God, holiness, and religious leadership precisely at the intersection of pastoral, priestly, or rabbinic knowledge and skill with religious commitment and professional integrity" (Foster et al., p. 100). The most common classroom pedagogical method used to "practice the presence of God" was prayer. An Auburn faculty survey in 2003 revealed that "67 percent of respondents agreed that it is 'important to open or close class sessions with some form of prayer or meditation.' Only 11 percent of participants in this study strongly disagreed with this practice . . . " (Foster et al., p. 109). These responses suggest that devotional practices are accepted by an overwhelming number of seminary faculty today as an essential aspect of pastoral formation. With professional organizations such as the American Association of Pastoral Counselors and the Association of Clinical Pastoral Education devoting more program and workshop time to spirituality, constructive conversations will continue to create ferment in the field of pastoral care and counseling at its intersection with the academic field of spirituality.

THE SPIRITUAL LIFE OF THE PASTORAL COUNSELOR

In the case example, Jamie says several times that she wants to discuss the movement she is experiencing in prayer. Dr. Wilson redirects the conversation, showing little interest in Jamie's repeated efforts. This leads one to surmise that Dr. Wilson's own prayer life has not been a significant source of direction for her personal decision-making processes. If her personal prayer life were or had ever been a dynamic expression of an experiential relationship with the divine, one would think she might consider it a worthy focus of conversation with Jamie. This example highlights the need for formation in spiritual practices.

A hallmark of pastoral counseling training–in contrast to the training of other helping professions–has been the focus on the person of the pastoral counselor. To this end, initial units of Clinical Pastoral Education focus attention on the often unexplored behavior patterns of the pastor in training. Gaining an in-depth understanding of the psychological dynamics at work in human interactions through self-understanding and self-knowledge was a cutting edge for the early leaders in the movement. The experiential dimension of pastoral formation–receiving feedback from peers and supervisors–could not be acquired as effectively through other learning modalities.

In a similar vein, the experiential dimension of spiritual growth is acquired by engaging in spiritual practices. Introducing this element into training programs is a growing edge for some, especially those shaped by a mainline Protestant ethos that focuses on psychological dynamics to the exclusion of spiritual growth. Fostering the spiritual life of the pastoral counselor is an integral aspect of the formation process. If Dr. Wilson had been encouraged to develop her spiritual life as an integral aspect of her pastoral preparation, it is doubtful that she would have remained indifferent to Jamie's needs.

Persons preparing for the ministry of pastoral counseling should be encouraged to select a spiritual practice that they find meaningful. In the setting where I teach, we introduce students to a variety of spiritual practices and encourage them to develop a "rule of life" (that is, a description of the activities that nurture their spirits and the frequency with which they plan to do them) in order to make explicit the ways in which they nurture their spirits. We start from the assumption that many students will not have a consciously chosen practice that they use at regular intervals for spiritual growth. As a group, we begin to list the many things students do to nurture their spirits. The variety of potential activities quickly grows and includes such diverse activities as gardening, sports, listening to music, visiting the ill, prayer, knitting, etc. Students are often surprised both by the types of activities that emerge from the group and by the realization they already do many things that have the potential to be spiritual practices. As they make explicit that which they have done implicitly to nurture their spirits, they also come to recognize that the intention with which an activity is engaged determines whether it is a spiritual practice. The cultural/ethnic, denominational and interfaith diversity of my context requires allowing this breadth. More traditional Christian practices, such as *lectio divina*, Luther's four-stranded garland, and prayers of examination (Driskill, 1999) are also introduced. There is not an attempt to impose any particular practice on anyone in the class.

Once practices are identified, students are asked to select and use regularly (that is, in a disciplined manner) those they find meaningful and can reasonably integrate into their daily life. Although some students associate the word "discipline" with abusive or coercive parenting, the intended understanding of "discipline" is to learn, to be a pupil or disciple of something. Musicians who practice daily to master an instrument or athletes who exercise regularly to keep their bodies in shape are disciples of their crafts. The disciplined use of spiritual practice is a way of remaining available and open for an experiential relationship with the divine.

Pastoral counselors formed by Christian traditions may find Richard Foster's (1998) scheme for classifying the direction or intent of spiritual practices helpful: inward, outward, and communal. Inward disciplines include prayer, study, contemplation, labyrinth walking, journaling, or any other activity generally done alone. Outward disciplines are those focused on action, such as visitation of the ill, peace demonstrations, caring for the poor, or working on behalf of justice in any venue. Communal disciplines include worship, small group prayer, small group bible study, or any other activity characterized by gathering as a community of faith. Obviously the categories are not mutually exclusive, but the schema helps people notice if they have a preference for one or another type of spiritual practice. Spiritual growth can be encouraged by noticing if one has a preference for one or two types of practice while ignoring others. For some people, integrating at least one practice from each category into daily life will be a meaningful way to approach spiritual growth.

In my context, weekly small group sessions are also required of students enrolled in a course on spiritual disciplines for leadership. Five to six students work with group leaders who are trained in teaching spiritual disciplines and leading small groups. While students do some emotional check-in, the focus is on learning spiritual practices and sharing experiences of practice. While these groups cannot necessarily be described as spiritual direction groups, they do give participants an opportunity to discuss their faith. Given the diversity in our setting, we allow these groups to negotiate their common life. Some develop a sense of trust that allows them to function as covenant groups while others devote more time to experiencing a variety of spiritual practices. Those who teach the class believe that these small group experiences are good preparation for students who will serve Protestant parishes where much of the common life occurs in small group settings.

The spiritual life of the pastoral counselor will also be strengthened by having a spiritual director during the formation process. "Spiritual direction serves two purposes: first, identifying how God is present in a person's life (which is always experienced in unique and particular ways), and second, discerning an appropriate response to God's presence and action" (Bidwell, 2004, p. 2). The lived experience of faith as it is expressed in the stuff of daily life provides the content for spiritual direction conversations. Considering that clergy are called to engage the mystery at the heart of existence and to assist others in interpreting their lives in the light of this mystery, it serves clergy well to have had the experience themselves. When one has experienced conversations focused on spiritual growth and healing, engaging others in such conversations has an authenticity that is otherwise lacking. As pastoral counselors are enriched by having experienced the role of counselee, so too are they made richer by having discussed their life of faith.

Much mainline seminary training is concerned with the life of the mind and the development of critical thinking. Seminary students need to have their inherited faith, often the faith of childhood teachings, challenged. This faith, a first naiveté, needs to be deconstructed and wrestled with in order for them to develop their own voice. Yet some mainline Protestant seminaries and pastoral counseling training programs have been slow to recognize that discerning God's presence in one's life, relationships, society and world requires tools for a hermeneutic of retrieval–that is, an interpretative process that listens for the authentic world-disclosing power of language. This process requires the use not only of critical skills but also devotional praxis. Spiritual formation requires tools of discernment unavailable to the unpracticed. Those who are going to hear the stories of others and join with them in the process of interpretation cannot notice what they have never been trained to see in their own encounters with the holy. The spiritual direction relationship provides a venue for processing in the presence of the holy the move through critical questioning to second naiveté, where faith is affirmed not only in its ambiguity and complexity but also as a source of meaning and life.

VALUING AND CELEBRATING DIVERSITY

In the case example, Dr. Wilson demonstrated an awareness of the importance of cultural heritage in counseling an Asian American family with a Chinese heritage. The depth of her knowledge in this area is unclear from the case. As in early attempts at "cross-cultural" counseling, she may have been working with oversimplified knowledge of the role of kinship in Chinese traditions. Her inability to distinguish generational issues between the concerns of Jamie's parents and those of Jamie and John may suggest this. More recently pastoral counselors working in intercultural spheres open themselves to a genuine encounter that de-centers the privileged assumptions of the counselor–if the counselor is white or embodies a white paradigm–for the sake of authentic communication (Driskill, 2003). This allows for the possibility of a genuine transformation by all the participants in the conversation. As pastoral counselors, we have much to learn from those we serve.

In my professional context, pastoral care providers, including pastoral counselors and spiritual directors, are taught to understand the socially located nature of the spirituality they are exploring. The "lived experience of faith" is profoundly shaped by one's cultural and ethnic context. For example, it would be difficult for a counselor who does not understand the importance of filial piety in the East Asian context to work with a Chinese couple around spiritual issues related to intergenerational expectations. Filial piety involves a level of commitment and obligation between parents and children shaped by a deep level of respect. Respect involves such things as providing care and services for elders, serving the food and drinks which elders prefer, using respectful language with elders, and providing places of honor for elders at family events. Public respect is extended to all relatives with the same last name (Pang, 2000, pp. 5-6). This understanding of filial piety carries a spiritual valence which differs from Western approaches to family life, where the relationship between parents and children is shaped more by independence and autonomy.

Spiritual issues such as the experience of the divine, the understanding of community, and common spiritual practices are all shaped by the cultural and ethnic values of the social context. Unfortunately, white students are often not aware that they are socially located. Caucasian students frequently assume that their cultural stance is the "norm" from which others differ. Their resistance to exploring the implications of this privilege reflects the structural racism that remains endemic in the United States.

The required pastoral care class taught by one of my colleagues introduces students to a model of systemic thinking essential for analyzing family dynamics, organizational structures, and inter-cultural social locations (Smith and Riedel-Pfaefflin, 2004). The diversity of both students and faculty in my educational setting fosters what Emmanuel Y. Lartey (2004) calls "internationalization." "Internationalization is the process in which an attempt is made at dialogical engagement, where American understandings interact with non-Western ones in a quest for practices that are more contextually appropriate" (p. 89). The aim "is to honor contextual particularities, the social and political dynamics in the construction of various perspectives on experience, and the priority of authentic participation for all persons in their own voices" (Ramsay, 2004, p. 35). Pastoral care providers need to be comfortable listening to and honoring the narratives of individuals and families from cultural structures whose spiritualities differ from their own. The ability to describe, understand and appreciate the spirituality of another person requires a sensitivity to the limitations of one's own perspective and an openness to the way in which "the lived experience of faith" others discloses not only meaning but also the holy.

SPIRITUAL PRACTICES: HEALING AND THE HOLY

In the case example, Jamie wanted to discuss her prayer life and explore its implications for reconsidering her vocational path. Dr. Wilson's training did not allow her to see the potential for transformation held in Jamie's prayer. Had the pastoral counselor been more aware of the ways in which spiritual practices can be a support or an ally to a counseling process, she might have encouraged Jamie to continue listening in the depths of her prayer.

Contemporary approaches to healing and health often critique the medical model prevalent in Western cultures and speak of the value of holistic approaches. A bio-psycho-social anthropology that seeks, in the interest of health, to integrate the physiological, emotional and social aspects of being is now common. For a number of years, voices in the health care community–Dr. Herbert Benson of the Mind/Body Medical Institute in Massachusetts, for example–have argued that the spiritual aspects of health must also be recognized. Institutional chaplains and pastoral counselors are the religious professionals who most often contribute to interdisciplinary health care teams. As a result, their contribution needs to include an awareness of the way in which religious concerns and spiritual practices are an important ingredient in transformation, healing and health.

Being created in the divine image involves attending to each of these aspects of lived experience–body, mind, social relationships, and spirituality. As persons share their stories of the lived experience of faith, pastoral counselors who use a bio-psycho-social-spiritual anthropology will attend not only to emotional or mental health and to social and systemic issues, but also, when appropriate, to spiritual concerns and the role the spiritual life contributes to health and healing. Pastoral counselors skilled at recognizing how religious language can mask pathology need to be equally skilled at understanding how it supports healing.

Spiritual practices, including myriad forms of prayer, contribute to growth and healing through the depth of the relationship that is established between the counselee and the divine. Spiritual disciplines themselves can promote both growth and healing by becoming the containers for material that requires healing. As spiritual practices open a person to a relationship with the divine, the relationship deepens and the love grows. The deeply loving experiential relationship between the person and God allows for honesty and integrity on the part of the person praying, and vulnerability and transparency become increasingly possible—not unlike a deeply connected human relationship. As one becomes increasingly transparent in the depth of a loving relationship, honesty and confession become a crucial aspect of being truly real. The disciplined use of a spiritual practice intentionally keeps the transference of the person praying focused on the divine. One of the questions most often asked by spiritual directors as they listen to directees discuss dilemmas and concerns is, "Have you taken this to prayer?" In the moments of genuine relationship with God, the layers of the personality that protect us not only from others but also from ourselves are transcended.

The material that emerges in prayer is sometimes frightening because it may not previously have seen the light of day. This experiential encounter with the divine presence within us will bring into consciousness aspects of the self that have not been successfully integrated. Usually this material arises in ways that can be integrated through the spiritual encounter itself. Fears may be faced, long-standing issues confronted, hopes and dreams embraced, expectations of others transformed, calls to action undertaken. From time to time, however, speaking with a trusted counselor or spiritual guide will be necessary to further process and honor this material.

Thomas Merton described this as the journey to the true self, to the self in whose image and likeness we are created. As we engage in a spiritual discipline and confront the material that emerges, whether from our unconscious or matters related to conscious decision-making, this true self expands as the hidden or unexplored material is integrated into conscious life. Through this process there is a growth in holiness, accompanied by an acceptance of our humanity. The depth of love which enfolds us and calls us to embodiment also transforms our lives.

Pastoral counselors who are working with people of prayer need to recognize how spiritual practices can be an ally in the process of healing. I am not suggesting that pastoral counselors should become spiritual directors; at this point in our history, these are two distinct min-istries that converge at important points. I do contend, however, that pastoral counselors would benefit from integrating an understanding of spirituality and spiritual formation into their understanding of growth, healing, and health.

ENLARGING PASTORAL CONVERSATIONS WITH A SPIRITUAL DIRECTION TOOL

In the case study above, Dr. Wilson continued to raise questions with Jamie that were informed more by Dr. Wilson's psychological quest for the underlying problem than by Jamie's spiritual and vocational con-cerns. Had Dr. Wilson been aware of a particular tool discussed in the spiritual direction literature, she might well have encouraged Jamie's desire to speak about her prayer life. The contemporary dialogue be-tween pastoral care and spirituality offers a helpful model for pastoral conversations when the client brings spiritual issues to the fore.

Pastoral conversations focused on spiritual concerns can be enriched by a model (see Diagram 1) that I call "Arenas of Divine Activity." It is adapted from an approach in spiritual direction training that has various forms, including the Grid (Mostyn, 1996) and the Experience Circle (Liebert, 2005). This model conceives of God's activity in four arenas of life: intrapersonal, interpersonal, structural/organization, and envi-ronmental/cosmos. The intrapersonal area is the arena of divine activity many popular books address, such as individual devotional practices, prayer, meditation, dreams, praying with beads, and journaling. The in-terpersonal arena includes the way God is present in relationships be-tween partners, parents and their children, siblings, and coworkers. The structural and organizational arenas where God is active includes not only institutions with altruistic aims, such as churches, hospitals, and social service agencies, but also organizations such as businesses and government agencies. The environmental realm includes God's activ-ities in nature and the universe.

The arenas of this model intersect to indicate the dynamic nature of God's divine activity. For example, God's activity in the environment is sustained by the actions of individuals, small groups, and organizations committed to preserving the environment. The four arenas of divine ac-tivity are specific areas where one can discern the work of God's trans-forming love. Spiritual directors use this model to help directees notice if their understanding of God's activity is largely limited to one or two

Diagram 1

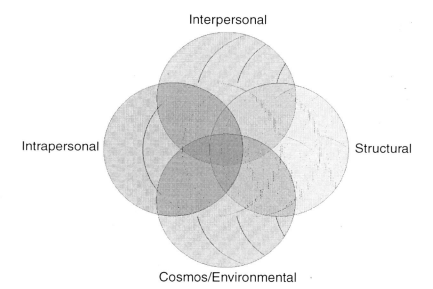

Interpersonal

Intrapersonal

Structural

Cosmos/Environmental

of these arenas. The intrapersonal and interpersonal arenas are those where many people see God's activity. Directees can be encouraged to explore how God may be at work in the structures or organizations in which they participate. They may also be encouraged to explore how God is at work in the environment. Directees are encouraged to discern where they sense that God is at work and then to begin cooperating with the divine activity.

If Dr. Wilson had been able to draw upon this model to speak with Jamie about the vocational issues she was raising, the counseling sessions might well have contributed to Jamie's vocational discernment process. This model can help pastors conceptualize divine activity in more than personal and interpersonal areas. The prophetic aspects of ministries of compassion and justice often involve the structural, organizational and environmental areas of divine activity. Pastors who understand that pastoral conversations are not limited to clinical themes can comfortably raise structural and organizational issues with those seeking pastoral care.

RECOMMENDATIONS FOR PASTORAL COUNSELING TRAINING PROGRAMS

Jamie's expectations of Dr. Wilson seem reasonable in a postmodern, post-colonial period when spirituality and spiritual concerns are increasingly valued. Religiously trained pastoral counselors who recognize the salience of a bio-psycho-social-spiritual anthropology have access both to the depths of people's lives and to health care systems where spiritual concerns are increasingly taken seriously.

Three aspects of spirituality should inform pastoral counseling formation. First, pastoral counselors should explore the thick description of narratives where the lived experience of faith shapes life's engagements. Helpful readings for this task include: Fumitaka Matsuoka, *The Color of Faith: Building Community In a Multiracial Society* (1998); and Kwok Pui-lan, *Postcolonial Imagination and Feminist Theology* (2005), especially Chapter 4, "Finding Ruth a Home: Gender, Sexuality and the Politics of Otherness."

Second, students should be encouraged to develop a spiritual practice and provided with small group time for check-in and faith sharing focused on the use of the spiritual practice. Helpful readings for this task include: Janet Parachin, *Engaged Spirituality: Ten Lives of Contemplation and Action* (1999); Dorothy C. Bass, *Receiving the Day: Christian Practices for Opening the Gift of Time* (2000); and Richard J. Foster and Kathryn A. Yanni, *Celebrating the Disciplines: A Journal Workbook to Accompany "Celebration of Discipline"* (1992).

Third, students should explore the therapeutic dimensions of spiritual practices. Helpful readings for this task include: Jean Stairs, *Listening for the Soul: Pastoral Care and Spiritual Direction* (2000), and Thomas Keating, *Open Heart, Open Mind* (1997), especially Chapter 9, "The Unloading of the Unconscious."

The contemporary cultural context offers the pastoral counselor both challenge and opportunity. Postmodern sensitivities that de-center the role of rationality in knowing offer the promise that faith can be renewed. This renewal will come not by abandoning rationality, but by integrating a critical approach to meaning with devotional practices that can both inform and sustain individuals and communities of faith. As post-colonial theorists de-center paradigms of privilege, new and exciting modalities of care may emerge. These "new" paradigms and their accompanying practices offer the possibility of transforming not only their communities of origin, but also wider communities of faith.

Practitioners of other helping professions expect pastoral counselors to know something about "the lived experience of faith" and the way in which it can promote health or mask pathology. The care and cure of souls is a sacred trust that in the foreseeable future will better serve ministries of compassion and justice because of the ongoing dialogue between pastoral counseling and spirituality.

REFERENCES

The American Heritage dictionary of the English language (4th ed.). (2000). Boston: Houghton Mifflin Co.

Bidwell, D. R. (2004). *Short-term spiritual guidance.* Minneapolis, MN: Fortress Press.

Driskill, J. D. (2003). Exploring White identity formation in pastoral care and counseling training. *American Journal of Pastoral Counseling 7*(1), 3-22.

Driskill, J. D. (1999). *Protestant spiritual exercises: Theology, history, and practice.* Harrisburg, PA: Morehouse Publishing.

Foster, C. R., Dahill, L. E., Golemon, L. A. & Tolentino, B. W.. (2006). *Educating clergy: Teaching practices and pastoral imagination.* San Francisco: Jossey-Bass.

Foster, R. (1998). *Celebration of discipline: The path to spiritual growth* (3rd ed.). San Francisco: HarperSanFrancisco.

Lartey, E. Y. (2004). Globalization, internationalization, and indigenization of pastoral care and counseling. In N. J. Ramsey, (Ed.), *Pastoral care and counseling: Redefining the paradigms* (pp. 87-108). Nashville, TN: Abingdon Press.

Liebert, E. (2005). Supervision as widening the horizons. In M. R. Bumpus & R. B. Langer (Eds.) *Supervision of spiritual directors: Engaging the holy mystery* (pp. 125-146). Harrisburg, PA: Morehouse.

McMickle, M. A. (2002). *An Encyclopedia of African American Christian Heritage.* Valley Forge, PA: Judson Press.

Molina, C. & Haney, H. (2005). Using the concept of 'co-culture' in supervision. In M. R. Bumpus & R. B. Langer (Eds.) *Supervision of spiritual directors: Engaging the holy mystery* (pp. 147-164). Harrisburg, PA: Morehouse.

Mostyn, J. H. (1996). Workshop presented to students in Program in Christian Spirituality at San Francisco Theological Seminary, San Anselmo, CA.

Pang, E. C. (2000). *Filial piety in modern time: The ideal and practice of parental care.* Paper presented at the International Conference on Searching for Meaning in the New Millennium. Vancouver, British Columbia, Canada.

Ramsay, N. J. (Ed.). (2004). *Pastoral care and counseling: Redefining the paradigms.* Nashville, TN: Abingdon Press.

Smith, A., Jr. & Riedel-Pfaefflin, U. (2004). *Siblings by choice: Race, gender, and violence.* St. Louis, MO: Chalice Press.

Talvacchia, Kathleen T. (2003). *Critical minds and discerning hearts: A spirituality of multicultural teaching.* St. Louis, MO: Chalice Press.

doi:10.1300/J062v08n03_05

Race and Ethnicity in the Formation of Pastoral Counselors

Alice M. Graham, PhD

SUMMARY. Education and training programs must attend to the unique cultural heritage of clinicians. Formation processes need to challenge internalized patterns of relational development, the ethnocentrism of psychological theory, and the impact of systems upon African-Americans and other racial and ethnic identities. Good training involves opportunities for reflection in shared-cultural, as well as multi-cultural groups. doi:10.1300/J062v08n03_06 *[Article copies available for a fee from The Haworth Document Delivery Service: 1-800-HAWORTH. E-mail address: <docdelivery@haworthpress.com> Website: <http://www.HaworthPress.com> © 2006 by The Haworth Press, Inc. All rights reserved.]*

KEYWORDS. Race and ethnicity, interrelatedness, multi-cultural, ethnocentrism, empathy, justice

All this is simply to say that all life is interrelated. We are caught in an inescapable network of mutuality; tied in a single garment of destiny. Whatever affects one directly, affects all indirectly. . . This is the way the world is made. I didn't make it that way, but this is the interrelated structure of reality. (King, 1961, p. 210)

[Haworth co-indexing entry note]: "Race and Ethnicity in the Formation of Pastoral Counselors." Graham, Alice M. Co-published simultaneously in *American Journal of Pastoral Counseling* (The Haworth Pastoral Press, an imprint of The Haworth Press, Inc.) Vol. 8, No. 3/4, 2006, pp. 87-98; and: *The Formation of Pastoral Counselors: Challenges and Opportunities* (ed: Duane R. Bidwell, and Joretta L. Marshall) The Haworth Pastoral Press, an imprint of The Haworth Press, Inc., 2006, pp. 87-98. Single or multiple copies of this article are available for a fee from The Haworth Document Delivery Service [1-800-HAWORTH, 9:00 a.m. - 5:00 p.m. (EST). E-mail address: docdelivery@haworthpress.com].

Mutuality and the interrelatedness of all life are core values in pastoral care and counseling. This realization, articulated in the quote above from Martin Luther King, Jr., captures two critical concepts that must be at the heart of formation for pastoral counseling. The first concept is the utter interdependence of all life, and the second is that human beings are intricately bound together in an inescapable network of meanings that collectively defines what it means to be human.

In a world community that is increasingly diverse, standards of training that are limited to Western cultural superiority and paternalistic systems are ineffective and immoral. Educational systems that assume the cultural superiority of one group over another, along with paternalistically toned individualism, contribute to the persistence of racism. The dominance/submission paradigm that pervades the social, religious and political arenas from which aspiring pastoral counselors emerge is problematic in the formation of pastoral counselors. It is impossible to escape the plurality of culture whether in Wal-Mart, Neiman Marcus, Macy's or in the counseling room. The values and norms of differing others impact educational objectives, business practices and the patterns of family and community life. The broadening of diversity concerns beyond black/white and male/female to black, white, Hispanic, Muslim, Asian, Iraqi, gay, lesbian, inner city urban, metro-urban, etc., intensifies the need to challenge formation standards that are rooted in traditional Western thought and practices. In order to provide a ministry of care and healing that reflects the unity and interconnectedness of all life, it is essential that in the development of pastoral counselors we grapple with the tasks of embracing the concept of mutuality and the interrelatedness of all life.

The meaning of one life is inextricably tied to the meaning of other lives. The connective pathways of meaning are concretized in the social, political, and religious constructs that shape and define the individual. It is essential for persons to struggle with the questions of "With whom do I feel a natural sense of mutuality and with whom do I escape/avoid mutuality?" and, "How come and to what end?" The formation process ought to challenge the internalized developmental pathways that create unconscious patterning in adult functioning. This is one of the central tasks of formation: to present in bold relief to the individual the "stuffings" of their particular developmental framework in its particularity rather than affirming it as normative. Though the survival of pastoral counseling is a legitimate concern for the field, that concern cannot undermine attention to the concepts of mutuality and interrelatedness. These concepts have to do with the expansion of the soul that is an expansion of the soul's eye that allows for the recognition of shared humanity in differing others.

CULTURAL IDENTITY AND FORMATION

In my own formation process, I was faced with this reality when I was assigned to do an assessment for a drug-addicted, European American nineteen-year-old suburbanite woman from a wealthy family. She had been admitted to the drug treatment center and as a part of my clinical rotation I was to do an assessment of her emotional functioning. These findings would contribute to the development of her treatment goals. My reaction to the assignment was to declare that I, as an African American woman, could not relate empathically to her, nor did I want to. Her whiteness, her wealth, and her privileged social position rendered her an unsuitable object for my attention or care. In my view, wealthy people of privilege had no meaningful rationale for drug addiction that deserved my concern much less my empathy. The world for me was divided neatly into "the have's" and "the have not's." Reflecting the prevailing thought in my community, I saw black folks as the "have not's" and white folks as the "have's." Having grown up in a low income neighborhood with a single parent mother fiercely committed to the survival of her three children, I consciously saw addiction as the final resource of the poor, the uneducated and the weak that were stripped of hope in a society that did not value their humanity. I learned in overt and indirect messages from my family and that west side community of the fifties that drug addiction was the choice of those who had given up on the value of their life. *Sympathy* for the drug addicted was reserved for the poor, uneducated and persons of color.

As I encountered this woman using the prescribed guidelines for assessment, her story of dehumanization in the midst of wealth and privilege shattered my neat categories for human experience. In the midst of having so much materially, there was much that she did not have. I was confronted with her very real human pain despite an ethnically nuanced socialized block to seeing her humanity. In subsequent supervisory sessions with an African American supervisor who had refused to change my assignment in response to my protests, I was prodded to explore what my response told me about who I was and who I could be in the world.

The supervision, in collaboration with my psychotherapeutic journey, faced me with the reality that my social, political and religious frame had both limitations and strengths. In the self-exploration that followed, it was clear that my "minority" identity distorted my view of drug addicted African Americans as well as that of the different other. There was both richness and impoverishment entangled in the soil of my developmental frame. This experience initiated, in a profound way, a more critical investigation of my assumptive world.

The process of formation urges the pastoral counselor into the life-long tasks of untangling the webbing of his/her relationship with developmental introjects in order to be in a counseling relationship with persons who are in varying stages of entanglement with their own relational history. How one has learned to view oneself in the intricacy of religious, social and political developmental networks distorts how one views the others with whom one seeks to be a facilitator of healing. This learning obviously extends to how one learns to view the continuum between pathology and health. Formation involves the exploration and discovery of the emotionally charged supports for identity that can prevent the emerging pastoral counselor from engaging the different other in a relationship based on shared humanity.

From this perspective, formation ought to move the individual beyond a culturally encapsulated worldview to a broader, expanded understanding of the human experience. Pastoral theologian and counselor Emmanuel Lartey (2003) quotes Carl Rogers (1975) in defining empathy as, "the ability to perceive the internal frame of reference of another with accuracy and with the emotional components and meanings which pertain thereto, as if one were the other person, but without losing the 'as if' condition" (Rogers, 1975, p. 140). Lartey then goes on to describe empathy in a way that underscores the challenge of empathy for persons of color:

> Empathy involves an accurate awareness of another person's feelings, the ability to 'stay with' these feelings no matter how painful or inexplicable, and being able to express or enable their expression. For this to happen, the person empathizing has to retain their own identity and inner strength. Rogers' 'as if' quality must remain the mark of empathy in order that the counselor is not swamped or engulfed by the torrents of the client's feelings. (Lartey, 2003, p. 92)

Lartey underscores the importance of maintaining a sense of one's identity and the strength that comes from having a clear sense of one's self.

One of the critical challenges for people of color is to maintain an appreciative attachment to their cultural heritage at the same time engaging that heritage critically to discern both its strengths and vulnerabilities. It is often difficult to sustain an awareness of the richness of ethnic heritage in the context of developing clinical skills in an environment whose cultural norms do not affirm and value the differing realities of people of color. Such valuing moves beyond the appreciation of the novelty of the different other toward a recognition that racial/ethnic differences are born of the varying ways that human communities in their particularity have answered three inescapable problems: (1) how to secure food and shelter; (2) how to get along with one another; and (3) how to relate themselves to the total scheme of things (Smith, 2001, p. 11). Huston Smith maintains that these are the three primary problems to be faced by any communal group.

From the perspective of pastoral counseling, then, the questions become these: What are the varying creative responses that differing communities of humanity have developed to answer these questions? What distinct capacities and understandings, for example, does the inner city African American male have to develop in order to survive? How are these different from those that a first generation immigrant/refugee male from Iraq has to have in relation to securing food and shelter, getting along in community and the relationship of God to survival? What are the emotional and intellectual capacities that must be developed in order to survive in an inner city Chicago slum and how are those different from survival as a wealthy Korean immigrant? What are the differing patterns of vulnerabilities and strengths that emerge as persons accommodate developmentally the particularities of their social, political and religious world? The common denominator in each of these contexts is survival.

Each individual has the potential for teaching others more about the range of human creativity and possibility than we can know individually through a homogenized cultural lens. In a multi-cultural learning context the tremendously imaginative resolutions discovered by differing people in response to similar human dilemmas can be affirmed while also allowing space for appropriating a fuller understanding of human possibilities. John Hinkle (1993) notes that, "multi-culturalism provides alternate definitions of self and alternate modes and contexts for pastoral counseling/psychotherapy as a frame of reference for both clearer and deeper understanding of the constructed nature of the self, and a 'non-self' lens for perceiving soul" (p. 67). To adopt uncritically European American self-definitions discounts the wisdom inherent in the legacy of the individual's particular cultural identity. Such devaluing diminishes the inner strength of the trainee and therefore diminishes the capacity of the trainee to be in positive dialogue with the legacy of cultural voices.

In the language of pastoral theology this inner strength is the soul of the individual. It is the soul of the trainee that is being nurtured toward transformation for the work of the healing ministries. As Hinkle (1993) notes, "Meta-culturalism experience is the movement toward the soul, which is an awareness of God and other beyond cultural definitions, limitations, and norms" (p. 67). In routine intentional interaction with differing others the emerging pastoral counselor can initiate the evolvement of a more authentic sense of self. Through the process of regularized contact, persons can be encouraged and supported in sharing the meaning of their lives with persons of differing ethnic backgrounds. The recognition of self in the different others precedes in the individual an awareness of divine universality. The kinship of human beings in the human predicament and the human journey can be profoundly discovered in this milieu of differentness and sameness.

The illusions, mythologies and distortions mediated through culture for the survival of the community can be engaged and re-appropriated as sources of empowerment. Homer Ashby (2003) suggests such a hope in reclaiming the concept of conjuring as exampled in the Joshua biblical story:

> The Joshua story will play this double role in the chapters that follow. It will be both a conjure and a signifier. In fact, any conjure is necessarily a signifier in that as a conjure is invoked to address a particular condition or circumstance, it critically engages that condition or circumstance in order to expose it to the transformative power of the conjure. My hope is that the Joshua conjure will work optimally as both transformer of the present reality and critical perspective for the vision of the future. (p. 13)

The experience of discovering what was not known can now serve as an emotional blueprint for further forays into the worlds of humanity. The "not known" can become an invitation rather than a barrier.

In a multi-cultural context trainees can be encouraged to entertain alternative definitions of selfhood as well as alternate modes and contexts for being that do not do violence to their heritage. Every cultural story is plagued by the limitations of knowledge and circumstance in its struggle to know truth. At the same time as the projections and assumptions entangled in the culture are explored, the cultural legacy can be plumbed for that which is life-giving. The interplay of cultural stories allows for the integration of ethnic/racial wisdom from differing realities.

TRAINING AND EDUCATION

In reviewing my formation process for pastoral counseling, certain aspects of my experience are instructive for identifying factors that would facilitate the development of educational models for persons of color for the field of pastoral theology, care, and counseling. The learning group for my first year of training was composed of three African Americans and three European Americans. An African American doctoral student who was at the dissertation stage supervised the three African Americans in their clinical work. Our clinical placements included an African Methodist Episcopal Church, a drug treatment center, and a psychiatric unit in a small Black community hospital. In retrospect, this clinical placement, combined with the racial mix of the learning group, was fortuitous. As three black students, there was comfort in the fact there were three of us, and an equal number of white students. Despite the fact that our African-American backgrounds were very different, our shared ethnicity provided a sense of "being in the same boat" in a white institution.

The program was structured so that we had to be in regular intentional dialogue with the three white cohorts whose placements were in white settings. Each of us, white and black, had the familiarity of race in our clinical placements at the same time as we confronted each other and ourselves about our assumptive worlds. As African Americans our placements gave us the opportunity to be in dialogue with our cultural legacy as we raised questions around theology, psychological theories and their applicability to the people we served. In retrospect, the gift of this placement strategy for me was that it allowed the African American students in that first year to value our ethnicity as an important contributor to our education for pastoral counseling. The fact that our supervisor was also African American for me further underscored that our ethnicity was a valuable component in our formation.

The incorporation of my cultural community in the formation process began for me the continuing dialogue between psychological theory, pastoral theology and the lived lives of human beings. At the point of my first training experience, I was an ordained elder in the AME church. Throughout my clinical training I saw clients, black and white, in the offices of the same African American Episcopal Church where I began my training. It is critical that clinical programs substantively affirm the value of the students' cultural context so that elements from that context are emotionally available in order to contribute their wisdom to the formational process. Throughout my training I was able to remain in dialogue with my cultural community as I encountered the interplay of theories, theology and practice.

Another important factor to be considered in the formation process for many persons of color is the ethnocentrism inherent in psychological theories and models of education. Cultural incompetence arises when a "one size fits all" approach to education is utilized, as opposed to the flexibility of thought and practice needed to respond to those clients whose ways of being are vastly different. Traditional psychological theories tend to emphasize the individual as an isolated biosocial unit. "These theories do not touch on the complexity of personality development in a plural society in which each is in a feedback relationship with several cultures at the same time" (Pedersen, 1981, p. 30). Persons of color who arrive at the point of training have routinely crossed boundaries of race and class, and therefore bring to their work an awareness as well as skill in negotiating systems that are not responsive to the complexity of their relational histories. Hence, it becomes important in the context of formation to explore and identify how methodology acknowledges and addresses the concerns of people of color in systems that often deny their existence.

The absence of sensitivity to the social reality of persons of color risks doing violence to the soul. For this reason, many African American psychologists and pastoral counselors raise serious questions about the effectiveness of traditional training models which rely on Western psychology. Carroll Watkins Ali (1999) sees traditional psychology as inherently racially oppressive.

> Thus, traditional psychology serves to impose the negative projections of White dominant culture on the psychology of African Americans as a racial and cultural group. In terms of personality development and identity formation, the other side of the projection is the introjection that is subject to occur as many African Americans either assimilate the views of the dominant White culture and/or internalize the distorted image of themselves. This becomes internalized oppression as African Americans accept the distortions as true and, in turn, begin to also negate their own culture and take on a kind self-loathing as they view themselves as inferior to Whites. (p. 67)

The ethnocentrism that pervades psychological theory can be instructive as well as destructive. To expose students to theories that emerge out of various cultural contexts can allow for critical engagement with the theoretical constructs against the plurality of norms and values existent in human communities. In the face of the rich abundance of the Divine imagination in creation, Lartey (2004) asserts that diversity must be assumed as the norm.

> Instead of insisting that all pastoral caregivers across the world operate on the basis of what is desirable within European or American cultures, pastoral caregivers need to assume diversity as normative true and basic. The theories and practices of pastoral care and counseling differ across cultures and these differences need to be respected. (p. 107)

To facilitate the ministry of healing in the rapidly evolving global community, it is imperative that respect for differing social identities must be woven into the fabric of training and educational models for all persons.

Implied in the foregoing is the need to be aware that all systems of government have inherent in their fabric patterns, or at least pockets, of inequities. Pastoral counselors must understand that they cannot function in their ministries of care and healing as if these patterns were non-existent or peripheral to individual functioning. As we encounter the individual, we also encounter the systems that may be contributive and/or perpetuating their pain. This concern is particularly true for persons of color who have experienced discrimination and have learned to accommodate it for purposes of survival. So, in the larger scheme of living, the maintenance of the prophetic function of ministry requires a willingness to see the perversions of systems that diminish the value of persons. For most African Americans, issues of justice have been integral to their religious experience. Given the history of slavery and the role of the black church as a refuge for nurture, comfort, and healing, formation strategies must attend to the importance of the black church as a carrier of meaning, possibility and hope. Dale Andrews (2002), in discussing pastoral care in black churches, underscores this point.

> African American religious life developed pastoral care in a campaign for meaning and value in life. Black churches concentrated great effort in nurturing the black person, teaching coping skills,

self-worth, and social justice. To this day, the Black church in-tends to empower the individual to value oneself while living a so-ciety that does not. . . . Experiences of racism and injustice shape the black perspective on how African American Christians strug-gle with their environment. (p. 24)

For people of color, the cultural symbols of nurture, care and empower-ment must be integrated into the process of becoming pastoral counsel-ors/psychotherapists as a counterbalance to the inequities that inevitably occur in institutional systems.

RECOMMENDATIONS FOR FORMATION

In summary, it is critical to incorporate the following components in educational systems for pastoral counseling.

1. Educational/training programs must develop ways for incorporat-ing the individual's racial/ethnic legacy as a learning partner in the formation of pastoral counselors. Creative strategies that sub-stantively engage the cultural context as a valued contributor to the tasks of formation increase the potential for critical self assess-ment in order to glean the cultural wisdom. This also minimizes the potential for splitting off of the denied aspects of culture in the face of the "white" dominant paradigm.
2. Students should be grouped with persons who share their racial/ ethnic history for segments of their training while also encounter-ing differing others in training modules. Intentional programmatic settings for intra- and inter-cultural dialogue are essential in order to counter the tendency to see one's own values as normative. In-terpersonal Relations Groups should provide the emotional con-tainer for a progressively authentic sharing of contrasting world views and their antecedents.
3. Programs which admit persons from varying cultural backgrounds must also have faculty and supervisors who are from varying cul-tural backgrounds. Professors and supervisors must reflect ra-cial/ethnic inclusivity beyond token participation in educational and training offerings for all students. Tokenism is racism. Even in formation programs that do not have persons from differing ethnic backgrounds students would benefit from the presence of persons that do not mirror their cultural reality. It is in the variation of voices

that a student has the opportunity to hear their own voice more clearly as well as to experientially realize that their voice is not the only voice.

4. The theories, theologies, and modes of practice that have emerged from the wide range of thought and contexts in the global community must be integrated into the curriculum. The absence of non-Western thought in the curriculum of graduate programs and training modules seriously handicaps students in providing pastoral counseling to non-white/non-Western populations. Students could then be evaluated on their ability to integrate, apply and utilize these theories, theologies, and practices in providing pastoral counseling, as well as assessed on their ability to identify and incorporate the learnings gleaned from their particular cultural legacy.

5. Educational and training programs should have collaborative learning initiatives with the global community of pastoral counselors. Every pastoral counselor should have the opportunity to explore the practice of pastoral counseling in non-Western settings through conferences and/or immersion experiences.

6. Supervisors and professors should be culturally competent in a culture other than their own. This would mean they would have substantive experience in acculturating to another a worldview that is distinctively different from their own. Without this kind of experience, it is difficult to appreciate the challenges to acculturation endured in the training process.

7. In the educational process persons would be expected to integrate the wisdom of their particular racial/ethnic background in the process of training. This would include attention to the inequities and injustices in social systems that perpetuate pathology. Students would be encouraged to explore how social contexts control one's world view.

REFERENCES

Ali, C. A.W. (1999). *Survival and liberation.* St. Louis: Chalice Press.

Andrews, D. P. (2002). *Practical theology for black churches.* Louisville: Westminster John Knox Press.

Ashby, H. (2003). *Our home is over Jordan.* St. Louis: Chalice Press.

Feagin, J. R. (1994). *Living with racism: The black middle class experience.* Boston: Beacon Press.

Hinkle, J. (1993). Whom, how and for what do we train? In J. McHolland (Ed.), *The Future of Pastoral Counseling* (pp. 63-68). Washington, DC: American Association of Pastoral Counselors.

King, M. L., Jr. (1961). The American dream. In J. Washington, (Ed.), *A testament of hope* (pp. 208-216). San Francisco: Harper.

Lartey, E. (2003). *In living color: An intercultural approach to pastoral care and counseling.* New York: Jessica Kingsley.

Lartey, E. Y. (2004). Globalization, internationalization, and indigenization of pastoral care and counseling. In N. J. Ramsey, (Ed.), *Pastoral care and counseling: Redefining the paradigms* (pp. 87-108). Nashville, TN: Abingdon Press.

Pedersen, P. (1981). The cultural inclusiveness of counseling. In P. Pedersen, (Ed.), *Counseling across cultures* (pp. 52-57). Honolulu: For the East-West Center by the University Press of Hawaii.

Smith, H. (2001). *Why religion matters.* New York: Harper.

West, C. (1993). *Race matters.* New York: Vintage Books.

doi:10.1300/J062v08n03_06

Pastoral Formation of Counselors in Intercultural Societies

Tapiwa N. Mucherera, PhD

SUMMARY. Pastoral formation and counseling in intercultural contexts takes a different form from that of the West. Intercultural or indigenous contexts refer to traditional societies, formally colonized. Pastoral formation in these contexts refers to the processes by which a pastoral person acquires an identity and authority to practice as a counselor in the context of an indigenous faith community. Some aspects important to consider in training are: the historical and traditional religio-culture of the intercultural contexts; the impact of colonialism and Christianity; and the lack of contextualized written material relevant for the education and training of pastoral counselors. The training of pastoral counselors must be pragmatic, have a global focus, and force counselors to go beyond the four walls of their offices and be advocates. doi:10.1300/J062v08n03_07 *[Article copies available for a fee from The Haworth Document Delivery Service: 1-800-HAWORTH. E-mail address: <docdelivery@haworthpress.com> Website: <http://www.HaworthPress.com> © 2006 by The Haworth Press, Inc. All rights reserved.]*

KEYWORDS. Intercultural, colonialism, globalization, identity and authority

[Haworth co-indexing entry note]: "Pastoral Formation of Counselors in Intercultural Societies." Mucherera, Tapiwa N. Co-published simultaneously in *American Journal of Pastoral Counseling* (The Haworth Pastoral Press, an imprint of The Haworth Press, Inc.) Vol. 8, No. 3/4, 2006, pp. 99-111; and: *The Formation of Pastoral Counselors: Challenges and Opportunities* (ed: Duane R. Bidwell, and Joretta L. Marshall) The Haworth Pastoral Press, an imprint of The Haworth Press, Inc., 2006, pp. 99-111. Single or multiple copies of this article are available for a fee from The Haworth Document Delivery Service [1-800-HAWORTH, 9:00 a.m. - 5:00 p.m. (EST). E-mail address: docdelivery@haworthpress.com].

In traditional societies pastoral formation of counselors takes a slightly different course from the commonly known Western route. In this chapter, I will use the term "intercultural contexts" to refer to traditional societies or indigenous peoples such as Africans, Native Americans, Aboriginals, Asians and others who experienced colonization in their own lands. Intercultural or indigenous pastoral counselors are those pastors and caregivers who function in the cultural context of their homelands. In this chapter I address pastoral formation in an African intercultural context.

Pastoral formation in an intercultural context refers to the processes by which a person acquires a pastoral identity and the authority to practice as a counselor in the context of an indigenous faith community. Such formation is based on: one's personal endowments (especially God-given spiritual gifts one brings into this world); rootedness in a faith community; the faith community's molding of the person, acknowledging and supporting the person's spiritual giftedness; and, if the opportunity is available, the person being taught or supervised by another for a period of time in order to hone one's skills and techniques as a pastoral counselor. As part of formation, it is essential that the pastoral counselor in these contexts be conversant and able to integrate the traditional religio-culture and the Christian-Western understandings of the human condition to address whatever issues parishioners bring to them for counsel.

It is not unusual in intercultural contexts, in both indigenous and mainline churches,[1] to find lay people without any formal theological and theoretical training assuming the work of pastoring or pastoral counseling. These situations are a result of the fact that there is no other alternative for the churches to cope with the membership growth and special needs of the parishioners, including the devastating problem of the HIV/AIDS pandemic and poverty. It is therefore important to note that much of the work of pastoral counseling in intercultural societies is being provided by pastors without the specialized training of "pastoral counselors" in the West.

Some pastoral counselors in Africa receive training by *experience*, or "on the job *clinical* training," leading independent or indigenous churches. They participate in *apprentice-type training* within their faith communities without receiving any formation training. Historically, when the indigenous faith community recognized one's spiritual giftedness, elders with similar gifts mentored the person. For example, if the community noticed that one had a gift such as herbal practice, wisdom in conflict resolution, faith healing, prophecy, teaching, or storytelling, the person would practice within the context of that community under the supervision of elder(s). After having served as an apprentice, gaining the confidence of the community and led in a ritual blessing performed by the community and led by the elders, they were inducted into the group of elders. There was and is full participation by the community to approve, disapprove, discontinue or encourage the process of apprenticeship through word and community action. In the mainline churches, about two-thirds of the pastors receive training at the diploma or bachelors level (BA in Theology or Religious Studies). This does not mean that there are no trained pastoral counselors (by Western standards); it means only that many of the pastoral counselors are not trained following the Western modes.

FUNDAMENTAL PARTICULARITIES OF INTERCULTURAL CONTEXTS

There are at least three aspects crucial to pastoral formation for counselors in intercultural societies that one simply cannot ignore. These particularities include the need to understand the history (the traditional religio-culture of the contexts), the impact of colonialism and Christianity, and the lack of contextualized written material relevant for the education and training of pastoral counselors.

The first particularity for pastoral formation is the need to understand an intercultural community's history and communal orientation. Common to the histories of intercultural societies is their communal orientation. Compared to most Western contexts, the sense of community is more pronounced. The common saying from the African perspective, "I am because we are, and since we are therefore I am," rings true to most indigenous/intercultural contexts. In these societies the needs of the community are a priority over those of the individual. This does not mean that individual needs are ignored; they are assessed in light of the community needs. Life is lived in the context of community and one belongs not to the nuclear but the extended family.

The definition of community is not limited to humanity but includes the spiritual world (God and ancestors), and all of creation. It would be a rare occasion to find an intercultural context where the people do not have a belief in God or a supernatural being. Traditionally, ancestors are venerated but not worshipped as mediators between God and humanity. The names and attributes of God used today in these contexts are still the same as the ones from pre-colonial days and the advent of Christianity. One of the goals of life is to live life in harmony with others, with creation and with the spirit world.

Rituals are the means by which harmony is maintained, and there are rituals for almost any occasion, such as the building of a new house, planting crops, child naming, initiation, marriage, death, and other family and communal events. Historically, problems were resolved through the family and/or community gatherings. In intercultural societies, religion and culture are intertwined. Family, community elders, and medicine persons play a big role in these rituals.

The role of traditional healers or the medicine person was and is similar to that of the psychiatrist in the West, counseling as well as prescribing medicines. Missionaries referred to traditional healers as "witch doctors." Thus, the healer, the traditional medicine person, whose cultural role was to be concerned about the welfare and health of the community, was designated the destroyer of the community. Because of the association with witchcraft and pagan practices, a "true Christian" in today's intercultural societies is not to consult a medicine person or herbal practitioner. Pastoral counselors and/or pastors in these contexts have to think through the dilemmas of parishioners who may see no problem in consulting an herbal traditional healer as opposed to going to Western trained doctors.

In pastoral formation, one has to have a general understanding of the traditions, worldviews, religion, culture, myths, symbols, and legacies of intercultural contexts. The ways of life in the intercultural contexts are influenced today by traditional worldviews, historical colonization and ideas of the postmodern world.

The second particularity of the intercultural context is the experience of colonization, including the arrival of Christianity, which still has a great impact on the formation of today's pastoral counselors. Indigenous contexts had their own pastoral counseling approaches and methods before the coming of colonization. Mpolo (1985), one of the first Western-trained African pastoral counselors writing from the Congo, argues that pastoral care, counseling, and psychiatry systems in the Western sense are new in the African context, but that similar systems have always been aspects of the indigenous African religion and medical system (p. 1). However, with the coming of colonization and Christianity, these indigenous systems were deemed heathen, pagan, backward, and unscientific and were to be discarded. Colonization and Christianity were not compatible with intercultural contexts, their ways of life, problem solving, worldview, cultural and social structures, and religion. Religio-cultural systems that were foundational to some of the traditional formation processes were therefore replaced by new Western scientific and Christian methods of pastoral training.

Missionaries and colonizers did not find anything that was worthy of redeeming from the indigenous religio-cultural and traditional practices, viewing them as "savage." The best way to "save the savages," or the indigenous people, was by re-educating them using superior Western methods, as well as the new religion, Christianity. Native American theologian George Tinker (1993) notes the impact of colonization on the indigenous peoples of North America:

> Psychologically, both at the level of individual and community, American Indians have so internalized the missionary critique of Indian culture and religious traditions and so internalized our own concession to the superiority of Euroamerican social structures that we have become complicit in our own oppression. (pp. 118-119)

The impact of colonization and Christianity can be seen in indigenous pastors who favor Western structures over traditional ones, since the traditional ways are perceived as backward. Pastoral formation has to deal with this internalized oppression and self-hate.[2]

The third particularity of intercultural contexts is the lack of written, contextualized training material to educate pastoral counselors. The educational systems were and are still modeled after those of the West. Often, pastoral counselors or pastors end up frustrated because what they learn from the books imported from the Western context does not always translate to their everyday experiences and settings. There is great need today for material for theological and theoretical training to be contextual, as noted by Third World theologians in 1977:

> We believe that African Theology must be understood in the context of the African life and culture and the creative attempt of African peoples to shape a new future that is different from the colonial past and the neo-colonial present. . . . Our task as theologians is to create a theology that arises from and is accountable to African people. (Appiah-Kubi and Torres, 1977, p. 193)

Similar sentiments were echoed by Howard Clinebell (1984), who said that pastoral care and counseling in the contemporary world "must become transcultural in its perspective, open to learning new ways of caring from and for the poor and powerless, ethnic minorities, women and those in non-Western cultures. On a shrinking planet, our circle of consciousness, conscience, and caring must become global" (p. 27).

The globalization of formation for pastoral counseling requires both traditional and Western knowledge. On the one hand, attending to gestures, eye contact, verbal tracking, and social distance are important aspects of Western methods, but these behaviors may have indigenous meanings specific to particular cultures. It is the work of those training pastoral counselors and those counseling in these contexts to understand when and how to use these skills appropriately. In addition, remembering that intercultural contexts are communally based societies is important to formation.

On the other hand, there might be some parishioners, particularly those who live in urban areas, who identify more with the Western culture. Today's intercultural societies are neither fully traditional nor Western. Because of colonization and Christianity, indigenous peoples were forced to live in between cultures and religions, thereby making them truly intercultural. As Mwikamba (1989), an African Catholic priest from Nairobi University, says:

> Many Africans are torn apart: in some sense, they are 'falling apart.' The sense of being 'double,' 'a split personality,' of being 'half,' is felt by many Africans, who are influenced by dualities: 'two cultures,' 'two morals,' 'two value-systems' and 'two worldviews': the African and the Western. (p. 92)

People in these contexts experience the push of Westernization and the pull of traditional, religio-cultural worldviews, making them "cultural refugees" in their own contexts. These marginalized people cannot fully claim and/or embrace the circumstance of the two cultures existing side by side without experiencing dissonance or conflict about which cultural framework is primary at any given time.

It is important that pastoral counselors and pastors in these societies understand that they are taking the role of the community elder and traditional medicine person (using prayer rather than herbs) in counseling with people. The pastoral counselor, who might be a stranger or known only by one person in the family, may be called upon to provide counseling to the family, especially in urban areas. Pastoral counselors in these contexts must be trained in the skill of "blending." Blending is the process of constructing new approaches to suit the parishioner, being sensitive to both traditional and Western counseling methods. It therefore follows that pastoral counselors trained and/or serving in these contexts must have a *double consciousness,*[3] consciously able to shift from one culture to the other with much ease.

PRACTICAL RELEVANCY OF TRAINING: AN ILLUSTRATION

There are many issues particular to the intercultural contexts. As stated above, some ideas, concepts, and procedures do not always translate from one context to another. To illustrate the point that well-intended norms from one culture do not always translate equally well to another, it is helpful to look at confidentiality in relationship to HIV/AIDS, organizational accountability and the need to be pragmatic. From this illustration it is possible to draw out implications for the formation of intercultural pastoral counselors.

In intercultural societies, the wellbeing of the community is a priority; it is more honorable to protect the community than to protect the interests of an individual. The HIV/AIDS pandemic has created a relational conflict in most intercultural contexts. The disease has at the present moment no known cure and those who suffer from it are stigmatized, forced to hide their illness. Traditionally, it was rare that people would shun one who was dying of a disease because it was a community's responsibility to make sure that people took care of those who were in their last days. Today, because of both a mixture of cultures and Western approaches being deemed superior while traditional knowledge is ignored, many indigenous cultures seem to be losing the battle in the fight against the HIV/AIDS pandemic. Mugwagwa (2006), a newspaper columnist from Zimbabwe, argues for the use of indigenous knowledge in the fight against HIV/AIDS:

> I have to amplify the cultural whispers to encourage Zimbabweans to appreciate the relevance of accounting for culture in curbing HIV infections and transmission. Attempts to ignore indigenous cultures, rather than transform them, during this era of HIV are gradually yet imminently leading the indigene to HIV infections, transmission and resentment of the prevention methods introduced to them. . . . Thus, ignoring cultural issues that are essentially constitutive of the indigene's humanness may act against attempts to implement effective prevention, counselling and treatment methods. . . . Against this background it is necessary to expose the role indigenous cultural practices have in HIV and Aids prevention and infections . . . Most challenges inherent in the prevention, trans-

mission, counseling and treatment of HIV are obvious given the lack of knowledge of indigenous cultures' impact on the afore-mentioned. The issue of indigenous cultures, as a knowledge base that can provide elementary alternatives in the prevention, trans-mission, counselling and treatment of HIV is hindered by the na-ture of the national constitution, media used for information dissemination and the relative disregard of indigenous cultures by funding institutions. (Part 1)

The stigma attached to the HIV/AIDS pandemic, together with the stan-dards of "confidentiality" used by Western trained medical doctors practicing in intercultural hospital contexts, have created deeper psy-chological and physical loneliness for those who are dying from HIV/AIDS. Traditionally, one could not keep quiet about something that could bring harm to the community. In other words, if a person had a disease, the community found ways to treat the person without isolating him or her. Confidentiality and the stigma that AIDS/HIV carries are causing people in intercultural contexts today to isolate themselves from the community, causing people to die alone.

The problem is exacerbated in these contexts when, for example, a husband keeps his HIV/AIDS status "confidential" and does not dis-close it to the wife and family, but continues to have unprotected sexual relations with the wife. Since the doctors cannot force their patients to reveal their status, the disease eventually kills both parents and leaves young children as orphans. This is not the only factor contributing to the many children being left behind as orphans, but it is definitely one of the contributing dynamics. How is a pastor to help a parishioner who wants to have the pastor hold the parishioner's HIV/AIDS positive status con-fidential? What counsel does the pastor offer to such a person without breaking confidentiality? What if the parishioner remains adamant not to tell, but continues to have unprotected intercourse with his wife? These are all issues that pastoral counselors from intercultural contexts must find ways to address, since "confidentiality" may spell a death sentence to the parents, leaving children as orphans.

Confidentiality, in other words, is no longer serving the community, or even the infected individuals. It has translated into "a secret weapon of mass destruction" that is exterminating the society. When people eventually discover someone is dying from the disease, the person ex-periences a lonely death because of the anger from the family and com-munity at the person for having brought such a pandemic to others. I leave this discussion without answers, but use it to raise the question of how some of Western standards of practice, such as confidentiality, do not necessarily work positively; instead they pose a danger to many women and children of intercultural contexts.

Given the devastation posed by the HIV/AIDS pandemic and issues of poverty in many intercultural contexts, pastoral counselors must be trained to be very pragmatic. It is not enough for pastoral counselors just to know proper counseling theories or have good skills in these contexts. The pastoral counselor sometimes has to take the role of the social worker. One has to have skills necessary to mobilize the community to be able to take care of and feed the hungry and orphaned children and the poor in their community. One has to be able to listen beyond the words of pain expressed, and to give hope by connecting people to resources where they can get the next meal for that day. As stated above, there are children as young as 12 years old who have become heads of household due to the HIV/AIDS crisis and who need food, shelter, clothing, school fees and books. Because the church may be their only hope, the skills of the pastoral counselors and/or pastor are needed to help provide for the children and the poor in the community. The pastoral counselor has to think as an advocate and social service provider, and to be in the business of saving both the body and the soul. As in the Letter of James, pastors are trained to realize that, "If a brother or sister is naked and lack daily food, and one of you says to them, 'Go in peace; keep warm and eat your fill,' and yet do not supply their bodily needs, what is the good of that? So faith by itself, if it has no works, is dead" (James 2:14-26, NRSV). Pastoral counselors and pastors have to be trained to think and act theologically in such a way that their faith and action go hand in hand.

Pastoral counselors and/or pastors in these intercultural contexts, especially those in areas that have been highly affected by HIV/AIDS, need to be trained to deal with grief and bereavement. Many of the pastors are burying the dead not less than one every other week. They have to deal with their own, as well as parishioners' or community, grief. Issues of theodicy are constantly brought to the fore due to the constant experiences of death. Besides the diseases such as HIV/AIDS, natural disasters such as catastrophic tsunamis, earthquakes, and hurricanes in also raise questions of theodicy. Why do we continue to experience devastating natural disasters in a world created by a good God? Does God care if we perish and where is God's love if we perish? Why is the world so unfair, with some having too much and others dying because they don't have anything? People from intercultural societies watch the Western television programs describing how some Westerners are struggling to loose weight or are dying of obesity, while some of these intercultural pastoral counselors or pastors' neighbors and parishioners are dying of hunger and starvation.

Accountability for those practicing pastoral counseling in intercultural societies is different from Western standards. There are not many intercultural societies, as mentioned above, where people practice under ethical standards established by an independent board such as one might find in the American Association of Pastoral Counselors. It is usually the case that one is held accountable by one's faith community or denomination in terms of understanding the ethics, norms and standards of practice. The laws of the government of one's country, and many times of the village courts also play a very big part as to one's practice. These are but just a few examples of how pastoral formation in these intercultural contexts needs to pay close attention to the daily experiences of the people with different societal standards.

PASTORAL FORMATION OF COUNSELORS IN INTERCULTURAL CONTEXTS AND IMPACT ON THE FIELD

It is time for those involved in shaping the pastoral formation of counselors (professors and clinicians) in the West to start being intentional about shifting methods and approaches in order to think in terms of serving the global village rather than just "my backyard." We need to shape the mindset of those in training for pastoral counseling to understand not only their own immediate community needs, but the needs of those in the global context.

As it pertains to intervention in caring for the orphans of HIV/AIDS victims, there have been numerous projects started in many of the intercultural societies which are attempting to know how best to counsel with orphaned children and to take care of them in their environment (homes) rather than placing them in institutions. As much as there are still some orphanages within these intercultural societies, intercultural pastors have become convinced that "institutionalization of children" is not the best way to give them a future. These community projects are being driven by the design of "re-villaging" (Wimberly, 2005) where people are persuaded, as they once were in traditional days, that it is the responsibility of the "village to raise the children." They have established "Children Orphan Trusts" or "Children Trust Funds" within these communities to care for the children. In contrast, the West tends to insist on the idea of "institutionalization." It would be a good learning experience for pastoral counselors being trained in the West to visit, as part of their cross-cultural immersion, some of these community home-based programs that are shying away from institutionalizing children. Children are being cared for in their own homes. They are not uprooted from their families or familiar community into a foreign environment, and they have people trained to counsel and care for them in their homes.

Pastoral counselors, caregivers, pastors or mothers are trained to provide holistic care, counseling and support as stated above, which includes physical, emotional, moral and spiritual. Formation has to do with the internalization of attitudes, knowledge, skills and dispositions related to practices of holistic care similar to "re-villaging," making sure that the pastoral counselor is concerned about the *whole wellbeing* of the counselee, rather than focusing solely on the *emotional* wellbeing of persons. My challenge to the field of pastoral counseling is to train people to go beyond the four walls of the office and 50-minute sessions to a more pragmatic approach. Because people are more than emotions and they have physical, spiritual, and relational needs, pastoral counseling formation needs to be more innovative in its approaches and must not settle merely for duplicating or mirroring psychotherapy and other secular therapies. Pastoral counseling must not lose its faith base, nor make the mistake that individual "autonomy" is the goal of life; but rather, it must teach how one's relations with the self, community, and God form the basis of our existence.

In addition, it would be beneficial to everyone if Western publishers, in particular, start to take an interest in the work of those from intercultural societies. I can personally testify that, in trying to have my work from an intercultural perspective published, I have received negative responses saying that my proposed work was very interesting, but that it was too particular (from a Third World and a minority perspective), and that the company could not publish it because it would not be able to sell enough copies *to make a profit*. It would be my recommendation that more works co-authored by Western and intercultural persons be produced. Seeking integration of approaches and creating new paradigms that are relevant to a variety of contexts is essential for the formation of intercultural pastoral counselors.

Equally important is the need for a paradigm shift that challenges the Western world to move from middle class, white male, individual approaches to pastoral counseling to ones that are shaped by a communal perspective. Training that has a global focus will encourage pastoral counselors to embrace a perspective which says that all hungry, poor, homeless Hindus, Moslems, Africans, Mexicans, and others across the ocean are my neighbors. Pastoral counseling must be more than giving people individuality and autonomy to function. It must lead people to understand how connected we are as a global community. God created all of humanity to function as a community, rather than fragmented communities.

Since many of the pastoral counselors are trained using texts that are Western based, it is my recommendation that those who train them use ethical standards and guidelines that are not contrary to intercultural societies' values, norms and morals. While an ethical standard may work well in the West, it does not necessarily follow that it will serve an intercultural context properly. Coupled with this is a recommendation for those intending to serve in intercultural societies (professors and pastoral counselors) to be trained to be sensitive to the worldview, values, traditions and culture of the people group they are serving. Many times these traditions, values, etc., which have been marginalized as backward, ancient and sub-standard, need to be reclaimed in training of the intercultural pastoral counselors. If an individual is going to serve a community that is cross-cultural, s/he needs to be exposed to the people under someone's supervision for an extended period of time before immersing oneself in working with the particular community or people group.

NOTES

1. Indigenous or Independent churches were founded by the local people who converted to Christianity but as breakaway from the Western missionary formed churches. The main reason for the breakaway was that they wanted and still integrate Western Christianity with the religio-cultural traditions of their contexts. The Mainline churches are those started by missionaries, which still may have direct connections with their sister churches in Western countries.

2. The gist of the argument on colonialism and Christianity presented in this chapter is similar to that in my book (2005), *Pastoral care from a third world perspective*. In this chapter I present material not discussed in the book such as the issues of the HIV/AIDS pandemic, confidentiality, training, organizational accountability, and pragmatism in intercultural societies.

3. See W. E. B. Dubois (1969). In this book Dubois says that Blacks (African-Americans) in order to function in the North American context have to develop a double consciousness. They have to learn and function under the white middle class culture as well as in their own Black neighborhood. Blacks need to consciously be able to move in and out of these cultures easily to survive the North American context.

REFERENCES

Appiah-Kubi, K. and Sergio, T. (1977). *African theology en route.* New York: Orbis Books, Maryknoll.

Berinyuu, A. A. (1989). *Towards theory and practice of pastoral counseling in Africa.* NY: Peter Lang.

Chikara, F., & Manley, M. R. (1991). Psychiatry in Zimbabwe. *Hospital and community psychiatry, 42,* 943-947.

Clinebell, H. (1984). *Basic types of pastoral care and counseling.* Nashville, TN: Abingdon Press.

Cokesbury (1989). The Bible (NRSV), Nashville,TN: James 2:14-26.

Dubois, W. E. B. (1969). *The souls of black folk.* New York: New American Library.

Edards, S. D. et al. (1983). Traditional Zulu theories of illness in psychiatric patients. *Journal of social psychology, 121,* 213-221.

Jongh van Arkel, J. T. de (1995). Teaching pastoral care and counseling in an African context: A problem of contextual relevancy. *Journal of pastoral care, 49,* 189-199.

Kapenzi, G.Z. (1979). *The clash of cultures: Christian missionaries and the Shona of Rhodesia.* Washington, DC: University of America Press.

Marrett, R.R.. (1914). *Threshold of religion.* NY: Macmillan Company.

Mbiti, J. (1997). *African religions and philosophy* (2nd ed). Portsmouth, NH: Heinemann Publishing.

Mpolo, M. (1985). *The risk of growth: Counseling and pastoral theology in the African context.* Nigeria: Daystar Press.

Mucherera, T. N. (2005). *Pastoral care from a third world perspective: a pastoral theology of care for the urban contemporary Shona in Zimbabwe.* New York: Peter Lang Publishers.

Mugwagwa V. (2006). HIV, AIDS and culture: Omissions, implications (part 1). *The Daily Mirror* (Jan. 04, 2006) Available: http://www.zimmirror.co.zw/daily

Mwikamba, C. M. (1989). A search for an African identity. *AFER-African ecclesial review,* 31, 92.

Tinker, G. E. (1993). *Missionary conquest: The gospel and Native American cultural genocide.* Minneapolis, MN: Augsburg Fortress.

Wimberly, A. S. (Ed) (2005). *Keep it real: Working with today's black youth.* Nashville, TN: Abingdon Press.

Wimberly E. P. (1992). *African American pastoral care.* Nashville, TN: Abingdon Press.

doi:10.1300/J062v08n03_07

Gender Identity, Sexual Orientation, and Pastoral Formation

Joretta L. Marshall, PhD

SUMMARY. The formation process for pastoral counselors needs to attend to gender identity and sexual orientation. The dynamics inherent in these concepts are present in our embodiment as pastoral counselors and our work with clients. Formation processes can assist pastoral counselors in examining our cultural, religious, and conceptual biases, as well as re-constructing understandings of gender identity and sexual orientation. doi:10.1300/J062v08n03_08 *[Article copies available for a fee from The Haworth Document Delivery Service: 1-800-HAWORTH. E-mail address: <docdelivery@haworthpress.com> Website: <http://www.HaworthPress.com> © 2006 by The Haworth Press, Inc. All rights reserved.]*

KEYWORDS. Lesbian, gay, bisexual, transgendered, gender identity, sexual orientation, heterosexism

Once a week, a group of pastoral counselors meets to discuss cases from theological, spiritual, and clinical perspectives. Today, Shelly is presenting a case that involves a 27-year-old man with whom she has met only a few times. Timothy presents with several issues, including mixed feelings about his relationships. During his teen years

---

[Haworth co-indexing entry note]: "Gender Identity, Sexual Orientation, and Pastoral Formation." Marshall, Joretta L. Co-published simultaneously in *American Journal of Pastoral Counseling* (The Haworth Pastoral Press, an imprint of The Haworth Press, Inc.) Vol. 8, No. 3/4, 2006, pp. 113-124; and: *The Formation of Pastoral Counselors: Challenges and Opportunities* (ed: Duane R. Bidwell, and Joretta L. Marshall) The Haworth Pastoral Press, an imprint of The Haworth Press, Inc., 2006, pp. 113-124. Single or multiple copies of this article are available for a fee from The Haworth Document Delivery Service [1-800-HAWORTH, 9:00 a.m. - 5:00 p.m. (EST). E-mail address: docdelivery@haworthpress.com].

Available online at http://ajpc.haworthpress.com
© 2006 by The Haworth Press, Inc. All rights reserved.
doi:10.1300/J062v08n03_08

Timothy dated women, but while in college he began to notice an attraction to men. He feels shameful about his "unnatural" relationships with men and doesn't talk about them to his family or his co-workers. His family is described as "fairly religious." Timothy recently met Alton, another man with whom he has begun to develop a relationship. Alton is ready to settle down and has invited Timothy to move in with him. This has caused a great deal of anxiety for Timothy and has put him into a crisis. When asked by Shelly whether he self-identifies as gay, bi-sexual, or straight, his response was a hesitant, "I'm not sure."

Shelly's question about his identity emerged from her own experience. A beginning therapist and single parent, she was briefly married to a man before falling in love with a woman and divorcing her husband. Although her first relationship with a woman did not last, Shelly has now been in a relationship with another woman for five years. She self-identifies to her closest friends as lesbian, but knows that were she to state this more publicly, she might lose custody of her son. Additionally, Shelly is ordained in a denomination where her standing as a minister would be jeopardized by such self-disclosure.

In the supervision group, only two people know that Shelly self-identifies as a lesbian. The group consists of:

- The supervisor, Ron, who is a Diplomate in the American Association of Pastoral Counselors (AAPC) and a mainline Protestant minister. He is married to a woman with whom he parents three teen-age and young adult children.
- Mark, a Euro-American, who is a beginning therapist with a degree from a conserving theological seminary. He graduated about three years ago, became ordained, and served a church. He is heterosexually married and has two young children.
- Evelyn, a traditionally identified heterosexual who is Roman Catholic, married, and the parent of adult children.
- Chung-Ho, an ordained clergyman from Korea who has been studying in the United States for two years. He intends to practice pastoral counseling in Korea, where his wife and two elementary-age children still live.
- Jason, a divorced Euro-American with no children and a peripheral connection to a denomination. He is a part of the supervisory group because he finds conversation about spiritual issues to be important in his work as a licensed mental health practitioner.

When Shelly presents the case her colleagues respond with the normal questions, concerns, and comments about family of origin and other matters. Finally, Jason suggests that Timothy needs to come out of the closet and be open and honest with his family. Mark hesitantly disagrees, noting that perhaps the conflicting feelings about orientation represent a deep desire not to participate in gay behavior, and Chung-Ho seems to nod in agreement with him. Evelyn suggests that perhaps the issue is not Timothy's orientation, but his fear of commitment and of settling down and getting married. She notes that the homosexual nature of the relationship doesn't really matter because, "marriage is marriage." Shelly listens to it all, without responding a great deal. She has only talked about her sexual orientation with Evelyn, whom she finds supportive.

Ron, the supervisor of the group, also does not say much initially in the conversation. He does individual supervision with Shelly and, like Evelyn, knows that Shelly self-identifies as a lesbian. Ron is also aware that there is much at stake for her personally and professionally in this conversation. Ron has said to Shelly before that he doesn't care whether she is a lesbian or not, and that his main concern is only that she be a "healthy lesbian who does good therapy." He is now a bit uncertain about how to assist the group and can't decide whether to protect Shelly or push her to deal with her own issues in the context of the group. This is not the first time that a case like this has been presented. It is, however, the first time that one of the therapists in the room–and more pointedly, the primary clinician for the case–is lesbian or gay.

Shelly and her colleagues are wrestling with the complex dynamics of gender identity and sexual orientation. These issues are not only embedded in the case, but embodied in the pastoral counselors as they sit in the room together. Their individual clinical theories, religious perspectives, theological convictions, and personal experiences appear as they begin to assess Timothy and his needs. The case highlights two issues related to the formation of pastoral counselors. First, the individuals in the supervisory group bring their own particularities, along with concomitant interpretations about gender and orientation into their conversation with one another. Naming issues of gender, gender identity, and sexual orientation is important not only for the clients with whom we work, but also because these realities are alive in the pastoral counselor's personal and professional lifelong formational processes. Second, the case draws attention to one of the less fortunate realities in clinical training and formation. We sometimes wait to reflect together on the meaning of issues until a client raises them for us. Gender identity and sexual orientation are among the important aspects to attend to intentionally in formation processes.

Formation is the lifelong circular process of shaping, examining, deconstructing, re-shaping, re-constructing, and then examining once again our theology, clinical theory, spiritual insights, personal experiences, and ecclesial connections. The process is life-long because we never fully integrate our personal and professional life stories, particularly as they relate to issues of sexuality, gender, or orientation; these dynamics live in us in ways that continually surprise us, and at times annoy us. The formation process ought to offer pastoral counselors the tools, experiences, and opportunities to become more deeply integrated and whole as pastoral theologians, counselors, and leaders in the community. Central to the formation process for all pastoral counselors ought to be the invitation to de-construct and re-construct our often unconscious and culturally formed understandings of gender identity and sexual orientation.

This article will first talk about the complexity of defining gender identity and sexual orientation. Second, unique formational concerns for pastoral counselors who self-identify as lesbian, gay, bisexual, or transgendered (LGBT) will be identified, along with a sense of how addressing these issues in a formation process for all pastoral counselors can lead to better pastoral counseling and care.

The goal in this article is to maintain two commitments. The first commitment is to offer *one* perspective and voice on the formation of pastoral identity from within the LGBT community as a pastoral theologian and clinician. Second, I am committed to the role of pastoral counselors to shape and form the broader ecclesial and cultural contexts in which we live. Toward that end, formation processes can provide proactive and prophetic pastoral counseling to persons within the LGBT communities, seeking to change the broader cultures of which we are all a part (Marshall, 1997). The reader will quickly see that I am unapologetically proactive and affirmative of lesbians, gay men, bisexual, transgendered, and queer persons (LGBT). However, I also know and respect the fact that not all pastoral counselors, religious organizations, denominations, or theological perspectives agree with me on these points (Malony, 2001).

GENDER AND ORIENTATION

A more intentional look at the dynamics of gender identity and sexual orientation requires that we attempt to define these concepts in some way, even though gender and orientation are filled with nuances and complexities that make them difficult to clearly compartmentalize. The conceptual fluidness of these terms points to the intersection of our theological, psychodynamic, social, and cultural understandings alongside changes across time and contexts. The formation process for pastoral counselors ought to provide the tools necessary to recognize the shifting nature of these concepts and, at the same time, to engage participants in critical self-examination about how these concepts hold meaning for our own lives and the lives of those with whom we work in counseling. A central formational concern for pastoral counselors is how to pay attention to the constructions of our ideas and internalized understandings of gender and orientation as they are shaped by the particularities of our context.

In most postmodern circles there is little debate that gender is a socially constructed reality (Butler, 1999; Gorsuch, 2001; Neuger, 2001; Neuger and Poling, 1997; Wilchins, 2004). The dialogue between the essentialists (those who understand that biology and genetics largely and universally determine a sense of one's gender) and social constructionists (those who understand that meaning is given to our biology and gender by the cultures and systems around us) is a fascinating one. Gender is something with which, and into which, we are born. We are born *with* biological realities that result in persons being assigned a gender at birth, even if the child is born as an intersexed child whose biology may make gender assignment less clear (Wilchins, 2004). At the same time, we know that being identified as a girl or a boy brings with it a host of assumptions, notions, and ideals *into which* we are born. The social networks of our family, community, school, church, and culture provide us with numerous personal experiences that either confirm for us our role as a particular gender, or challenge our self-understandings or the culture's assumptions. While this seems fairly simple on the surface, what we know is that life is never this neat and clean. If we are to assist clients in a critical self-understanding of these issues, one goal of formation ought to be to deepen self-awareness among pastoral counselors about how the social construction of gender influences our own experiences and perceptions.

Central to pastoral formation is the ability to analyze how we come to understand and assess both our own *gender expressions* ("the manifestation of an individual's fundamental sense of being masculine or feminine through clothing, behavior, grooming, etc." (Wilchins, 2004, p. 8)), as well as those of our clients. How do we communicate our gender to others? What makes us feel comfortable or uncomfortable about the way that we or others express gender identity? What do we think is normative for male pastoral counselors/clients or female clients/pastoral counselors?

Similarly, analyzing *gender identity* ("the inner sense most of us have of being either male of female" (Wilchins, p. 8)) raises self-awareness about the limitations of a binary definition of male and female. For the most part, pastoral counselors have become more comfortable with analyzing gender expression, allowing for greater variances. We have greater difficulty thinking beyond the binary realities of male and female in gender identity. In a postmodern world, such categories are seen as superficial, at best. An increasing attention to transgendered issues–youth who self-identify as gender-neutral, individuals who feel as if they are living in the wrong gendered body, those who self-identify as queer, or others who refuse to abide by culturally defined norms of male and female–confront our once-static understandings of the connection between biology and gender. Binary categories of gender and orientation are being challenged from multiple perspectives (Wilchins, 2004; Butler, 1999; Marshall, 2001). An astute pastoral counselor will want to re-think the basic concepts of male and female.

Formation processes for pastoral counselors can help us examine our assumptions, images and ideals about gender identity, recognizing that these affect our relationship and experience with clients. For example, how do we feel when someone uses the term, "queer," to self-identify? When a teenager seeks support in transitioning from a female to a male, do we immediately assume a diagnosis of gender disorder? Or, do we think that perhaps the young person does not know what s/he is talking about, is too young to identify with any gender identity and will outgrow this phase of life? Do we recognize the need for support and assistance in working with multiple systems (family, school, church, culture, insurance companies, counselors, and physicians) in transition?

Sexual orientation refers to one's primary emotional, physical, spiritual, and sexual intimacy attachments. For some, opposite gender attractions identify that they are heterosexual. Others have primary attachments to persons of the same gender and are usually referred to as gay men or lesbian. Still others experience primary affections with both men and women and might self-identify as bisexual (Ritter and Terndrup, 2002). Understandings and assumptions about orientation are also culturally bound. As Adrienne Rich noted long ago, we live in a culture that fosters "compulsory heterosexuality" as the norm (Rich, 1980). One should not underestimate the strength of these cultural norms to encourage women and men to be heterosexual or to act as heterosexual; nor should one overlook the courage and internal wisdom it takes to develop relationships in non-heterosexual ways.

Developing an identity around sexual orientation is a fluid process for many. While there are persons who know from early in their child-hood that there is something different about them and who later self-identify these differences as non-heterosexual orientation, it is more often the case that the development of an identity takes time and expe-rience, and the evolution occurs within contextual realities that may not always be supportive. Shelly represents a large number of women who traditionally marry men (either because of attachments they have created and/or the influence of a culture that expects the norm of het-erosexuality) only to later self-identify as bisexual or lesbian (Mar-shall, 1997; Marshall, 2001).

Cultural privileging of male-female relationships–heterosexism–is often reinforced implicitly or explicitly by religious belief systems. Churches, for example, tend to focus on marriage and families in ways that assume that everyone ought to find a partner and mate, settle down, and have children. Or we think that marriage and relationships are the same whether it is between persons of the opposite or those of the same gender/sex. In many ways the clinicians at the beginning of this article represent heterosexual perspectives that are deeply embedded, as does Timothy in reflecting the shame he experiences (Kaufman and Raphael, 1996).

The impact of sexism and heterosexism is evidenced as the collusion of gender, gender identity and orientation make it difficult for women and men, much less gay men and lesbians, to discern how the socio-reli-gious constructions negatively impact their relationships and friend-ships. Gay or bi-sexual men and lesbian or bi-sexual women may have very different ways of understanding the nature of relationships, of emotions and intimacy, of power, and of many other aspects of their lives. In the case above, an important aspect would be to analyze Shelly's understanding and experience of relationship and to examine how it might be different from Timothy's or from other men and women in the group who self-identify as heterosexual.

The formation of pastoral counselors occurs in contexts that are always full of gender constructions, gender identity, and sexual orientations. We bring our own gender, gender identities, and sexual orientations into the counseling room with everyone we meet, including our colleagues and those with whom we are in supervision. There is no escaping these reali-ties. To ignore their power in shaping our diagnoses of clients, our inter-ventions with clients, or our relationships with one another results not only in our own self-imposed limitations, but also is done at the peril of every client and community we serve.

FORMATIONAL ISSUES FOR PASTORAL COUNSELORS

It would be a mistake to say that shame, homophobia, heterosexism, and the complexities of disclosing a same-sex orientation primarily influence pastoral counselors who self-identify as lesbian, gay, bisexual, transgendered, or queer. In truth, these issues also affect heterosexually identified men and women. Because of the cultural privilege that comes with self-identification as heterosexuals, however, "straight" persons do not have to be as self-conscious about their orientation or gender. This can contribute to a lack of self-awareness, false assumptions, and misdiagnosis of clients. Pastoral counselors within the LGBTQ community can assist heterosexually identified people in reflecting consciously on the ways in which orientation and gender shape their self understandings and practices of ministry. By their very presence, LGBTQ pastoral counselors make everyone in the room mindful that gender, gender identity, and sexual orientation are alive in every encounter in the clinical realm and in our social, personal, spiritual, and ecclesial lives. While there are multiple formational issues at stake in this conversation, I will highlight only four.

First, formation processes must wrestle theologically with issues of gender identity and sexual orientation. Pastoral counselors need to reflect critically on the creation stories in Genesis, the role of biblical interpretation in our understandings of what is normative and healthy, or the power of claiming an identity in the faith narratives of which we are a part. Where is God in the midst of these conversations and how do we understand God's agency or that of human beings? Theologically, it is important to continue to work on sexuality and sexual identity in ways that are more complex than simply noting that some are born women and some are born men, or some are heterosexual and others are not. We need a theologically fluid understanding of sexuality and gender that contributes to understanding wholeness and holiness in our living. Such a perspective challenges some of our traditional theological anthropologies, doctrines, and assumptions about what it means to live as embodied creatures. In turn, this will require that we re-think our primary clinical interpretations and interventions around issues of gender and orientation.

In the formational process, listening to our own faith narratives as well as to those who are different from us culturally, socially, or sexually is imperative. Beginning with the stories of the non-heterosexual women and men in our culture rather than with our traditional paradigms opens new creative formational places for pastoral counselors. This educational and reflective theological work needs to be done in the context of diversity and community such as the supervisory group that begins this article.

Second, if pastoral counselors are to work effectively then formation processes have to be intentional about inviting trainees to internally reflect on gender and orientation and providing the personal space necessary for such reflection. Assessing and challenging our internal worlds can be painful as well as insightful. Such personal reflection requires openness, honesty and trust among colleagues. Cultural sexism in combination with heterosexism means that no one can escape the internal shaping effect of these dynamics on our psyche and souls. Whether one self-identifies within the LGBTQ or heterosexual community, gender and orientation are significant realities with which we all must deal.

The issues of our clients uniquely touch us in our own lives. In the case above, for example, one wonders how Timothy's experiences intersect with Shelly's coming out process, or coming to terms with families of origin and religious traditions, or the difficulties of creating and nurturing primary relationships in a culture that does not support them. Or, how do the responses of the clinicians reflect stereotypes we carry about men–or gay men in particular–in our culture? Shelly may have internal wrestling that is different than her colleagues as she reflects how her journey intersects with Timothy's. Pastoral counselors unconsciously carry the same kind of cultural baggage as the rest of the population. Our sophistication in matters related to psychodynamics and systems thinking does not make us immune from those realities in our unconscious lives and those who self-identify as LGTBQ do not escape the scars of a world that would rather we be someone else, even as much as we try. Indeed, one of the tragedies of heterosexism is that it prevents many LGBTQ persons from living fully, wholly, holy lives. As a community of pastoral counselors we need to probe deeply into our biases about family, marriage, and the raising of children and the way in which our constructions of gender, gender identity, and sexual orientation shape these understandings. Pastoral counseling formation programs must have an intentional curriculum that requires clinicians to identify, assess, and evaluate theologically, psychodynamically, and spiritually the effect of gender and orientation on their lives personally and professionally.

A word of caution is important here: There is a complex dynamic between those who represent minority positions in pastoral counseling centers and their colleagues. It often falls to the minority representatives (whether around gender, orientation, race, ethnicity, or culture) to educate colleagues and to raise critical issues. Formation processes ought to find ways not simply to educate the intellect, but to raise everyone's unconscious to the level that we are able to recognize our biases more quickly and be accountable to one another.

Third, formation processes need to engage seriously the multiple racial, ethnic, and cross-cultural differences that exist around gender and sexuality. It is not enough to simply note that there are differences; instead, we must find ways to creatively engage and dialogue about those differences. There is a healthy line between respecting diversity and taking a stand that challenges the *status quo* of our culture. In similar ways, it is imperative that pastoral counseling formation processes not separate issues of racism and classism from those of heterosexism and sexism. These are inter-connected realities that are detrimental not only to our clients, but to the very health of our communities and our churches.

Finally, pastoral counseling formation processes need to shape and form public theologians at two levels. First, there is a need for pastoral counselors to state publicly their support and affirmation of persons within the LGBTQ community. Centers and individuals in practice must be visibly present to the community as safe spaces for persons to engage in therapy and counseling. Taking extra measures to articulate the theological reasons for their pro-active therapy and approach and crafting a public theology to match our affirmative pastoral counseling practices occurs best in formation programs where, in the context of colleagues and peers, we risk sharing our theological differences and forging new visions. This means that some pastoral counseling centers will have to do the sometimes uncomfortable work of responding to the challenges of faith communities that may not support such affirmative stances.

Parallel to this, formation processes must teach pastoral counselors how to recognize and consciously confront cultural sexism and heterosexism, becoming educators and advocates in the public and ecclesial debates about sexuality, family, ordination, and marriage. Becoming public theologians in the culture, in our ecclesial traditions, and within our communities requires care and attention so that LGBTQ persons who have less advantage and power are listened to carefully as positions are stated and claims are made. It is imperative that pastoral counselors not unintentionally overshadow or get in the way of those whose voices they seek to advocate for. Working carefully and alongside the LGBTQ community results in forging new alliances and new public theologies of affirmation. Formation processes that nurture and foster pastoral counselors to become public theologians will ultimately serve communities and churches in positive and healing ways.

CONCLUSION

Returning to the supervisory group with which we started, it is possible to imagine how gender, gender identity, and sexual orientation might emerge in the reflections and conversations about this case. Each pastoral counselor in the room has some vested interest in gender identity and orientation simply because we all live out of those social constructions in our personal and professional lives. A good formation process provides clinicians with the opportunity to intentionally self-examine their deeper understandings about gender, gender identity, and sexual orientation. The question is not whether gender or orientation makes a difference in our own formation or the experience of our clients; rather the key is to understand and uncover how these differences both get in the way of, and enhance, our pastoral counseling work.

Formation processes must be more than intellectual education and reflection in our professional guilds. Instead, formation encourages intentional theological reflection, honest internal wrestling with how gender and orientation have been shaped and re-shaped in our own lives, and deep respect for the manifestation of these issues in particular clients and communities, taking seriously issues of context and culture. Such formation processes are bound to produce pastoral counselors who faithfully and carefully work with issues of identity, gender and orientation.

REFERENCES

Butler, J. (1999). *Gender trouble: Feminism and the subversion of identity.* New York: Routledge.

Gorsuch, N. (2001). *Introducing feminist pastoral care and counseling.* Cleveland: Pilgrim Press.

Kaufman, G. and Raphael, L. (1996). *Coming out of shame: Transforming gay and lesbian lives.* New York: Doubleday.

Malony, H. N. (Ed.). (2001). *Pastoral care and counseling in sexual diversity.* New York: The Haworth Press, Inc.

Marshall, J. L. (1997). *Counseling lesbian partners.* Louisville: Westminster John Knox Press.

Marshall, J. L. (2001). Pastoral care and the formation of sexual identity: Lesbian, gay, bisexual and transgendered. In H. N. Malony (Ed.), *Pastoral care and counseling in sexual diversity,* pp. 101-112. New York: The Haworth Press, Inc.

Neuger, C. and Poling, J. (1997). *The care of men.* Nashville: Abingdon Press.

Rich, A. (1980). Compulsory Heterosexuality and Lesbian Existence. In *Signs: Journal of Women in Culture and Society 5,* 631-660.

Ritter, K. and Terndrup, A. (2002). *Handbook of affirmative psychotherapy with lesbians and gay men.* New York: The Guilford Press.

Wilchins, R. (2004). *Queer theory, gender theory: An instant primer.* Los Angeles: Alyson Books.

doi:10.1300/J062v08n03_08

Formation in the Context
of Economic Disparity

Zina Jacque, ThD

SUMMARY. Clinicians are transformed by their reflection on and work with economically disenfranchised people. Formation in this context contributes to enhanced relationships with the Transcendent, the ability to live a more integrated life, new vocational understandings of clinical work, and new insights into the power of a spiritual community. Formation programs need to recognize the presence of God as a participant in the process, the development of the self within the context of community, the offering of sufficient time for good clinical work, the opportunity to practice, and changed perceptions of clients. doi:10.1300/ J062v08n03_09 *[Article copies available for a fee from The Haworth Document Delivery Service: 1-800-HAWORTH. E-mail address: <docdelivery@haworth press.com> Website: <http://www.HaworthPress.com> © 2006 by The Haworth Press, Inc. All rights reserved.]*

KEYWORDS. Economically disenfranchised, integrative counseling, transcendence, spirituality

In the mid-1990s, I served a church in the greater Boston area located halfway between the campuses of Harvard and the Massachusetts Insti-

---

[Haworth co-indexing entry note]: "Formation in the Context of Economic Disparity." Jacque, Zina. Co-published simultaneously in *American Journal of Pastoral Counseling* (The Haworth Pastoral Press, an imprint of The Haworth Press, Inc.) Vol. 8, No. 3/4, 2006, pp. 125-141; and: *The Formation of Pastoral Counselors: Challenges and Opportunities* (ed: Duane R. Bidwell, and Joretta L. Marshall) The Haworth Pastoral Press, an imprint of The Haworth Press, Inc., 2006, pp. 125-141. Single or multiple copies of this article are available for a fee from The Haworth Document Delivery Service [1-800-HAWORTH, 9:00 a.m. - 5:00 p.m. (EST). E-mail address: docdelivery@haworthpress.com].

tute of Technology and across the street from a public housing community. In part I was charged to oversee congregational care and, when appropriate, to make referrals for pastoral care. As a pastor in the resource-rich Boston area, I hoped I would be able to refer parishioners to facilities that utilized faith as a positive resource in the delivery of mental health care. In fact, those members who had health insurance and/or disposable income were quickly placed in appropriate pastoral counseling settings. However, those who were without the economic means to obtain therapy were left without readily available options for service.

My search for a counseling center open to economically disenfranchised people was met with limited success. The few therapy slots available were often offered during working hours, not accessible by public transportation, and located in clinical settings that did not honor the role of faith. Given the absence of appropriate referral placements, I entered into conversation with more than 100 clergy whose mosques and churches were located in economically-disenfranchised communities; clinicians; faculty members of graduate schools of theology, social work, and psychology; grant funders; and community-based leaders. These conversations led me to believe that the Boston area would benefit from the development of a counseling center designed to meet the needs of people who were religiously oriented and in economic difficulty. Moreover, the clergy with whom I spoke clearly and consistently noted that the development of such a center was necessary but faced a high risk of failure. Many suggested that a center would fail if it did not honor the clients' faith, utilize the resources of the clergy as partners, or employ clinicians who were experienced in understanding and working with the needs of the poor. Failures of this sort, my conversation partners suggested, would further disenfranchise the target population and leave them even more unwilling to enter therapy.

In the fall of 2000 I began a search for both a location for this new pastoral counseling center and licensed clinicians who would volunteer their time in exchange for a rigorous program of training focused on the integration of faith and psychology. A local Episcopal church and clinicians from many communities joined me in the creation of the Pastoral Counseling Center at Trinity Church (here after referred to as the Center). By the fall of 2001, the Center was housed at Trinity Church Boston and had successfully recruited eleven clinicians. These intrepid men and women were willing to articulate a belief in a higher power consonant with the monotheistic understanding of God/Allah and to participate in an 18-week program of training focused on the integration of theology/religion and psychology as related to working with religiously-oriented poor people. In addition, they committed to on-going monthly training and community-building meetings, to provide at minimum 10 volunteer hours per month to the Center, and to see no fewer than two clients concurrently.

Since the Center opened to clients in the spring of 2002, 28 volunteer clinicians have served more than 450 men, women, and children. African American women are the largest demographic group served. Most of the clients are assessed as poor and pay an average per-hour cost for therapy of $12.42. The vast majority of clients are referred by local pastors and/or other clients. Almost all are committed to their religious life, and as part of the intake process indicate that they desire to use faith and/or religion as a part of their therapy.

While much has been learned through this project about working with this population, my focus here is the formative opportunity opened to clinicians through their work with religiously oriented, economically disenfranchised clients. The Center's context of economic disparity offers unique challenges and opportunities for the formation of pastoral counselors.

METHODOLOGY AND BACKGROUND

Clinician reflections used in this article were collected as part of my doctoral research in 2004-2005 (Jacque, 2005). Each clinician associated with the Center was invited to participate in the research. Twenty-one of the 28 agreed to be interviewed in a face-to-face, 90-minute session; their comments form the data set for my doctoral dissertation and this article.

By the time of the interviews, all 21 of the participating clinicians had completed the Center's 18-week training program and had been affiliated with the Center between one and four years. Each clinician was either actively engaged in seeing clients of the Center or had previously seen clients. Subsequent to the original interviews, all of the clinicians noted that their current economic standing was middle-class or higher. The demographic characteristics of the clinicians are listed in Table 1.

While the clinicians describe themselves as middle-class or above, the vast majority of the Center's clients pay a fee in the bottom quartile of the Center's need-based sliding fee scale ($1.00-$85.00 per therapy hour). Though not a precise measurement of the income level of the clients, the average fee suggests a significant level of economic disparity between the Center's clients and clinicians.

TABLE 1. Aggregated Data for All Participants in the Study

Gender		Race		Age		Denomination	
Female	17	Black	4	Under 30	2	African Methodist Episcopal	2
Male	4	Hispanic	3	31-40	4	Baptist	2
		White	14	41-50	6	Catholic	2
				51-60	2	Congregational	1
				Over 60	7	Episcopal	12
						7th Day Adventist	1
						Unitarian	1

Though many questions emerge from the concrete setting and partic-ular circumstances of the Center, as noted above, the question that occu-pies this article is *in what ways did the delivery of psychotherapy to religiously committed, economically disenfranchised people open up avenues of formation for the clinicians?* Though the original study did not ask this specific question, responses drawn from the interviews sug-gest the clinicians felt their participation with the clients and in the work of the Center created unique opportunities for personal and professional formation. In fact, a significant finding of the research study was that the clinicians reported their work with the Center impacted their lives. This article will consider what the clinician responses might reveal about the effect on the clinicians of working with religiously oriented poor clients.

THE EFFECT OF SERVING RELIGIOUSLY ORIENTED, ECONOMICALLY DISENFRANCHISED PEOPLE

The clinicians who formed the initial cohort of volunteers were li-censed therapists experienced in many areas. However, only four had any extended experience in counseling poor people and only two had any formal or supervised theological training. None of the 11 thought of themselves as pastoral counselors; they only became comfortable working in a center with this title as they came to understand the con-cept of pastoral counseling as "a psychotherapeutic approach which attempts to integrate theological/spiritual and psychological/behavioral concepts in an intentional, unified manner" (Giblin and Stark-Dykema, 1992, p. 362).

The staff and the clinicians chose the term *integrative counseling* to describe psychotherapy that intentionally draws on the domains of theology, faith, and psychology. Thus, the term *integrative counseling* is used in this article in lieu of the term "pastoral counseling."

As clinicians began to see clients, they recalled the caution of the clergy with whom I had spoken during the planning phase of the Center. Remembering the insistence of clergy that clinicians associated with the Center honor the faith of the clients, support them in feeling empowered, utilize the resources of the church as a partner, and recognize the available assets of clients (e.g., their faith), the Center developed its program of training focused on, among other things, the role of faith and of the church in the lives of religiously oriented poor people (cf., Ali, 1999; Aponte, 1999; Satcher, 1999).

As part of the training, clinicians presented case studies of their clients. Three religiously trained psychologists, whom we called "listeners," then responded to the cases from both psychological and theological perspectives. The listeners' responses generated discussion around an array of topics, including the location and role of God/the holy/the sacred in the case as proffered by the client and understood by the clinician, the positive and/or negative affect of religion/faith for the client, the location of evil and/or sin (understood as "missing the mark"), the presence or absence of religious/spiritual themes as heard by the clinicians, and the effect on the clinician of listening for and sitting with religious/spiritual data.

Several themes emerged as clinicians and listeners engaged in the case studies. Among the more expected topics were the following: the mediating effect of faith/religion/spirituality as it relates to disappointing life circumstances (cf., Pargament and Brandt, 1998, p. 125); the relationship between the client's faith and her/his willingness/ability to persevere in the face of challenging circumstances (see Larson and Larson, 1991, p. 5); and the relationship between a client's faith and the presence of an improved quality of life (see Shafranske, 2000, p. 525).

However, other themes emerged from the training sessions that were of a less predictable nature. For example, clinicians noted that clients seemed to develop a therapeutic alliance more quickly than expected. Clinicians attributed this to their willingness to utilize the clients' spirituality, religion, and faith as a part of a strength-based approach (Bidwell, 2001). Moreover, clinicians noted that clients seemed willing to remain in therapy longer than was typical for the few poor clients with whom they had worked in the past. Clinicians observed that the longer stay in therapy might be attributed to the clients' sense that their faith tradition would not be diminished, that they did not have to edit out the language of faith or religion, that they felt welcome in the physical edifice of a church, and that they sensed they were working *with* the clinician as opposed to the clinician working *on* them. This sense of cooperation was often mentioned in conjunction with language describing the clinician and the client as being made equally in God's image, equally held in esteem by the creator, and equally on a journey toward all that they had been created to be.

An astute reader of this article will observe that all of the comments thus far have focused on the *clients'* response to an engagement with integrative therapy. However, as clinicians sat with the stories of religiously oriented poor clients, they reported an effect on their professional lives based on working with this specific clientele. One clinician observed that the depth of the clients' faith life provided an opportunity for the clinician to utilize more spiritually focused interventions (e.g., prayer, confession, scripture, and the lighting of candles; see Faiver and O'Brien, 2004). Other clinicians observed that the clients' willingness to engage in integrative counseling brought about the opportunity for the clinician to bring into the room a unified self (i.e., both professional and spiritual/religious self). The use of the term "unified self," or terms like it, occurred in 13 of the 21 interviews. When asked to describe what was meant by this family of terms, clinicians noted that their experience in prior clinical settings had limited their ability to utilize religious/spiritual resources in therapy and thereby had caused them to segment off that portion of their experience and skill. One clinician, a faculty member engaged in teaching about the nexus between faith and therapy, noted that he had more energy for clinical work when he did not have to bracket off, disguise, or make light of resources drawn from his spiritual and theological experience. John Karl (1998) notes that the development of the unified self is an important move for those who wish to work in the field of integration. In an article written for the *American Journal of Pastoral Counseling*, he notes, "Work is detached from spirituality. They reside in distinct mental compartments, like separate blocks of material for an unfinished quilt" (1998, p. 2). The work of the Center provided an opportunity for clinicians to bring both their spirituality and their work, the pieces of the quilt, together into a more unified whole.

However, clinicians also reported that working with the clients of the Center had an effect on their personal lives. One clinician observed that the client's desire to share the activity of spontaneous prayer with the clinician enlarged the clinician's capacity to pray in this way. The clinician noted that her use of spontaneous prayer was not limited to the clinical setting but had an affect on her private practice of spirituality. A second clinician commented that her clients had an expressed capacity to draw on biblical stories of poor and marginalized people. The clinician observed that one specific client had a practiced and particular ability to use biblical stories as an "exquisite mirror for reflection on her circumstances and a window on hope for her future." This clinician, who also viewed herself as in some ways marginalized, drew from the client new ways of accessing biblical works for her own study and growth. Finally, one of the most senior clinicians indicated that the clients of the Center spoke with such power about their faith lives and communities that the clinician felt drawn to study her own faith history.

In each of these instances, and in many others, clinicians noted that the non-material resources of the clients' faith extended the client's ability to focus on the positive and to move toward solutions. The clinicians' observations of and interactions with clients encouraged the clinicians to explore ways to deepen their spiritual lives; first as a tool to use with clients and in integrative therapy, and second for their own personal benefit. This particular move toward an enhanced spiritual life is highlighted in the work of James Hightower (2000), who suggests that clinicians well trained in counseling theory who wish to engage in integrative counseling must have something (spiritual) to integrate with their counseling theory. In particular, he urges clinicians to develop a deeper spiritual practice and to bring that practice into relationship with their theory. The clinicians associated with the Center found that the lessons they learned from the clients of the Center prompted them to do just that, to deepen their own spiritual lives, and therefore to have more to bring to the work of integration (see also Driskill, this volume).

LITERATURE IGNORES CLINICIAN FORMATION

As it became clearer that the clinicians were being opened to deeper levels of spiritual and religious development as a by-product of working with religiously oriented, economically disenfranchised clients, I turned to the research on integrative mental health care to gain a better understanding of how the Center might continue to enhance an experience of formation for the clinicians. However, a review of the literature turned up scant data regarding how clinicians are or should be affected and formed as a result of working with religiously oriented, poor clients.

A review of recent and widely acknowledged works in the field of integration (e.g., Griffith and Griffith, 2002; Richards and Bergin, 2002; Gorsuch, 2002; Sperry, 2001; Swinton, 2003; West, 2001; Miller and Thorensen, 2001; Mahrer, 1996; Miller, 2000; Richards, Rector, and Tjeltveit, 2000; Wulff, 1997; Becvar, 1997; Bergin, Payne, and Richards, 1996; Lovinger, 1996; Shafranske and Maloney, 1996; Shafranske, 1996; Tan, 1996) indicates that much attention is paid to clinicians as a primary factor in the *delivery* of integrative mental health care. However, the topics covered in these publications tend to focus on what a clinician ought to know, do, and be in the integrative process and not on the effect this work has on the clinician.

Though it seemed astonishing that the literature did not note *how* a clinician might be transformed by work in integrative mental health care settings, I found it even more sobering to think that the discussion seemed sufficiently unimportant as to be completely missing from the literature. Could it be that the ways in which clinicians are affected by integrative work with any particular community might add to an understanding of the transformative power of the work with clients and for clinicians? And might not this data be important to the field? Richard H. Cox (1997) points to this possibility:

> [T]he messenger is the message. . . . The transcendent psychotherapist is personally in the process of transcending, always unfinished, but continuing to be [a] finished product. This message is clear to all who come in contact with that therapist. . . . Herein lies another important message. Psychotherapists do not develop techniques for patients. They develop styles of life, communication, and energy that are vibrant and living. . . . The transcending personhood of the therapist is the key. (pp. 518-19)

Cox's addition of the "ing" suffix to the term *transcend* suggests action or an on-going process. It is an understanding of this action, this on-going process of being formed, that seems to be absent in the literature. William West (2001), agreeing with Cox (1997), continues the discussion of the effect of practicing mental health care in general as the process relates to the personal development of the clinician. He notes that models of therapist training and development "tend to de-emphasize or even ignore the role of personal change, focusing primarily on the therapist's development as a practitioner" (p. 86). But West emphasizes that "the therapist is not a fixed, unchanging person who simply acquires therapeutic skills and then becomes increasingly effective in the practice of therapy. The process of personal change continues well beyond" (pp. 86-87).

An analysis of the subject matter addressed in three respected texts in the field of integration shows that the impact of participating in integrative mental health care on the formation of the clinician is an under-researched topic. Books by Edward P. Shafranske (1996), William R. Miller (2000), and P. Scott Richards and Allen E. Bergin (2002) devote their approximately 1,300 pages, allotted by percentage in descending order, to the following areas: techniques/specific issues that arise with clients, 59.4% (722 pages); history and context of the field, 23% (299 pages); appendices/references, 8.3% (108 pages); future research/training issues, 5.46% (71 pages); and other (e.g., introductions, etc.), 3.84% (49 pages).

Another concern raised by the lacunae in the literature is that the needs of *previously* trained therapists are not on the horizon of integration scholars. Miller (2000) signals this important and disturbing notion when he ends his acclaimed edited volume with an emphasis on training those clinicians who are to *come*: "What matters most is to prepare future psychotherapists to work in a competent, professional and ethical manner with clients who vary greatly in spirituality" (p. 261). Additional research into the experiences and needs of the *current* cohort of clinicians engaged in integrative mental health care might prove beneficial to an expanded understanding of the growth potential for the field and protocols for training.

However, despite the absence of information in the literature, the experience of the clinicians associated with the Center at Trinity Church suggests that there is an effect on the lives of the clinicians. The following section of this article identifies what the clinicians reported as the most salient effects rendered on their personal lives as a result of working with the religiously committed, economically disenfranchised clients of the Center.

HOW THE LIVES OF THE CLINICIANS WERE AFFECTED

Responses from the 21 clinicians suggest that their work with the Center affected their personal formation in the following five ways: the development of an enhanced relationship with the Transcendent, the ability to be a more confident religious person, the transformation of clinical work into a clinical vocation, the fostering of an ability to live a better life, and a new understanding of the power of a spiritual community. Brief descriptions of each of these effects are noted below.

The Development of an Enhanced Relationship with the Transcendent. Based on their exposure to the clients' faith, 17 of the 21 clinicians noted they had an increased desire to attend church, study sacred Scripture, develop a prayer life, and/or seek spiritual direction. As noted above, one clinician gained a new understanding of how to use biblical texts to support marginalized people, including herself. Another clinician, a life-long Christian, articulated that in her previous (i.e., prior to the Center) faith life she did not practice an active personal relationship with the second person of the Trinity. Yet, through her work with her clients, she saw evidence of the power of this relationship and the possibility for a deeper personal relationship. Thus, prompted by her work with clients, she began to explore and question her own beliefs and relationships. In particular this clinician observed that even though her clients were without extensive resources, several remained able to face the difficult circumstances because of the presence of hope as articulated in the gospel story.

The Ability to Be a More Confident Religious Person. Eight of the clinicians interviewed emphasized that their time with the Center encouraged them to be more confident in their general expressions of faith. Some clinicians noted that their work with the Center had allowed them to investigate childhood memories of church and faith and to address questions, concerns, and issues they had left unattended for years. Others suggested that the Center's program of training had given them access to safe spaces in which they could reflect on and dialogue about faith/religion/spirituality. Still others averred that the ways in which they practiced talking about faith with fellow clinicians and clients provided them with experience such that they were able to speak about their work at the Center and their faith development in other settings, including with colleagues who were not engaged in integrative mental health care. One clinician in particular observed, "I know more about me and I am now more confident in my ability to speak about what I believe and in the way I walk through this work and life. . . . This . . . began . . . at the Center."

Fostering of an Ability to Live a More Integrated Life. As noted above, many of the clinicians indicated a unifying of the professional and the spiritual/religious self through the work of the Center. One psychologist who had considered leaving the field noted that through his work with the Center he did not have to leave his spiritual side tucked away at home. Specifically he said, "In coming to work (at the Center) I do not have to jump over the chasm that has always separated my professional self and my church self. Here I can bring in all of me." Another clinician, one of the most senior in years, responded, "Finally, after over 30 years of practicing, my insides and my outsides match and it feels good." Additionally, one of the youngest clinicians noted that his clients' refusal to separate things into sacred and secular categories encouraged him to see the inextricable connections between the sacred and secular aspects of his client's life and his own.

The Transformation of Clinical Work to Clinical Vocation. In relationship to their work with the Center, clinicians used the terms *vocation, call* or *calling, mission,* and *ministry* in 15 out of 21 interviews. Clinicians seemed to recognize both the training and the delivery of mental health care at the Center as the locus of an activity that took on divine proportions. The sense that the work in which they participated was somehow made special or holy pervaded the comments of the clinicians. Eleven of the 21 spoke about their participation with the Center as something offered to God as sacred gift, offertory, or tithe. One clinician described her work by saying, "This is holy work. It is our best gift. . . . I think it is sort of being a channel of the Holy Spirit as we minister to people. And, now I know this is my call in life." Contemplating whether her work at the Center was a mission or a job, another clinician said, "My work (at the Center) . . . comes out of a sense of sacredness and wholeness; and by that I mean wholeness/holiness. . . . Each and every person that I am allowed to interact with, to work with, to team up with . . . has changed me in profound ways and called, no calls, me . . . to see this work as a higher thing than" just therapy.

Creation of a New Understanding of the Power of a Spiritual Community. Twenty of the 21 clinicians spoke about the power of the community created at the Center. Many talked about it in multiple ways, but overwhelmingly the clinicians observed that the concrete actuality of the community of the Center enabled the work of integration and of their own transformation. This community, according to the clinicians, was created and sustained during the time spent together during the training sessions. In essence, clinicians found they were able to serve clients and to learn about integrative work and themselves because of the presence, support, learning laboratory nature, and grace of the community that was formed. One clinician noted, "The Center is a place where people are held accountable to one another, in an incubator-like setting, in a defined and consistent space, which makes it safe." Additionally, clinicians commented that the Center had a subversive nature because it turned the delivery of mental health care upside down and embraced the religious/spiritual/faithful as ways to make meaning and to engage, test, and find what might be meritorious for all who were involved.

However, the most poignantly stated purpose served by the community of the Center was conveyed in phrases that suggested the Center took on sacred proportions. Clinicians note that the Center became a worship space, a consecrated setting, and a place where "God had skin on." In particular, one clinician commented, those who gather at the Center do so as a *sacred band of souls*. This same clinician offered,

> It was very important . . . to have the camaraderie among the clinicians. . . . Souls [were] present, welcoming in the presence of the Holy Spirit or Jesus Christ or whatever higher power . . . different people invoked and we had church. So it certainly marked me and was very important because it gave the Center a soul and it wasn't just a place to do business. It was a soul turned toward God, waiting for God, feasting on God, and moving toward God. We are *a* soul and so the therapy was more whole and so were we.

SALIENT ASPECTS OF A PROGRAM OF FORMATION

A review of the information gleaned from the interviews with the clinicians suggests that their personal and professional formation was effected by the clientele and the culture of the Center. The clients, most of who were religiously oriented and poor, sought services from the Center because they knew their faith, one of their methods of making meaning out of life, would be utilized as a helpful tool. The culture of the Center promoted the growth toward wholeness and healing of client *and* clinician. Therefore, the clinicians found themselves in a setting that honored their growth as much as it honored their clinical work.

A review of the information gleaned from the interviews with the clinicians suggests that their transformation took place as a by-product of the culture of the Center and their work with the clients. While this article cannot do justice to the impact of the relationship of the clients and the clinicians, it can report on one of the central aspects of the Center, its program of training, and what the clinicians noted as most salient about the training. These aspects are noted below.

The Presence of God as Participant. Most of the clinicians interviewed for the research study were trained during a time when religion and spirituality were held as anathema to psychotherapy (Sperry, 2001,

p. 6; Hill et al., 2000, p. 58; Gorsuch, 1998, p. 205; Larrimore et al., 2002, p. 69; McMinn and McRay, 1997, p. 102). When queried about their graduate training, each of the clinicians indicated that religion and spirituality were thought to be, at best, another component of a client's culture or, at worst, an area to be worked around. As such, the ability to bring purposefully the presence of God into therapy as a positive resource constituted a new and welcomed phenomenon for the clinicians associated with the Center. Several clinicians commented on the gift of being able to sit with clients whose life circumstances had created in them a deep faith and to work with that faith as a primary resource in moving forward. Additionally, clinicians noted that it was refreshing and a source of renewal to be able to ask colleagues for prayer and to participate in activities that brought God into the counseling encounter not only for the client but for them. One clinician pointed to the Center's logo of two upraised, prayerfully positioned hands. She averred that she felt the hands sometimes held her, sometimes held the client, but most often held them both. In addition, seven clinicians spoke about their ability to conduct therapy or sit in a physical space that had been anointed and commissioned for sacred work by the clinicians themselves.

Development of the Self in the Presence of Community. Also important to the formation of clinicians associated with the Center was the presence and role of community. Most important about this community was its consistently safe, gracious, reverent, and nurturing characteristics. Clinicians commented over and over that in the presence of the other clinicians prayer for one another was standard, times of fellowship anticipated and always present, intense conversations were not fatal, disagreements would not cause irreparable damage, honest challenges would be seen as open doors, and discussion that did not end by end of day would be held as a promise of future conversation. In the company of clinicians who were conservative and liberal, black and white, Jewish and Catholic, Unitarian and Protestant, gay and straight, and all other possible permutations, all understood and respected the gift of community and relied on it to help nurture and hold accountable all of the individuals that comprised its whole. One clinician noted that, no matter how tired he was when he came to the training sessions, he left feeling energized and alive because he had been in the midst of a community of people who, like him, were made more whole by the dialogue and the silence, the action and the stillness of time spent together.

Presence of Sufficient Time. During the interviews one clinician compared his time with his clients and with the other clinicians to cooking with a crock pot instead of a microwave. Put in other words, he recognized that the sufficiency of time allowed clinicians the opportunity to build relationships slowly and securely. As relates to the training and the clinicians' formation, the promise that each cohort of clinicians had 18 full weeks together to work on and to work out issues, followed by on-going monthly meetings with the entire cohort, allowed the clinicians to slowly and deliberately develop their relationships with one another and to their volunteer work. One clinician noted that the profound nature of the work that seemed underway *between* the clinicians could be due, in part, to the training. She suggested it offered the clinicians the opportunity to step out of the violence of society's encouragement to "do more, faster," and to step into the Center's intentional practice of slowing down, spending time relating to one another and trusting the sufficiency of time.

Opportunity to Practice. The clinicians who volunteered at the Center were drawn from an educated and senior cadre of therapists. As such, from the beginning, it was unclear how they would feel about becoming novices as they worked to learn more about integrative counseling. Clinicians were encouraged to think of the training program as a laboratory space where they were meant to learn techniques, practice skills, acquire language, and participate in rituals that would be a part of their work with clients. The notion that they were free to *practice* under the prayer-full eyes of other colleagues and the guiding hands of the listeners freed many of the clinicians to try new concepts, fall, try again, and continue to progress without fear of stigma or reprisal. The freedom to practice over many weeks became a significant part of the formation of the clinicians.

*Ability to See Clinical Work as **More Than***. Scholars understand the concept of the word "vocation" to mean a call to engage with God in the realities of (the world) (Kaye, 1996, p. 5), or as the place "where (one's) deep gladness and the world's deep hunger meet" (Jones and Paulsen, 2002, p. 218) or finally, "as that thing that keeps making more of you" (Jones and Paulsen, 2002, p. 212). As noted, 17 of the 21 participants described their work with the Center in terms of tithe, offering, vocation, gift, call or calling, mission, or ministry. Each of these words signals something more than mere work. The clinicians associated with the Center began to see their work as taking on divine proportions. In doing so they found new energy for the work, a new impetus to learn about things of faith, and a new pattern after which to model their own lives.

CLOSING

It would be easy to see the development of the Center as a function of the hard work of the clinicians, the culture of the Center, and the commitment of Trinity Church Boston. But these essential parties cannot claim all of the glory. Without the contribution of the clients–without the authentic, in-your-face, particularity of their faith and a determination to use it as source and resource in counseling–the Center might have been just another mental health care clinic. However, it has been so much more. The Center that exists at Trinity Church Boston is a space where affluent clinicians and economically disenfranchised clients bring the best of themselves together, working cooperatively to find the best way for both client and clinician to move toward wholeness and healing.

Wayne Oates (1982) suggests that the " . . . central objective of all *pastoral* care and personal counseling is that 'Christ be formed' in the personality of those individuals who seek help" (p. 77). Though it was not the mission of the Center to transform the lives of the clinicians, the unique contribution of mission, clients and clinicians accomplished this feat of transformation just the same.

In the end, the clinicians have, through their engagement with the Center and its clients, been made aware of a new way of conducting therapy *and* they have been changed. As one clinician noted, "I came here to learn how to do something I always wanted to do, to bring my inside spiritual self and my outside professional self together. I did not think (the Center) would change me, just integrate those halves. But it did (change me), and now I am whole."

REFERENCES

Ali, C. W. (1999). *Survival and liberation.* St. Louis: Chalice Press.

Aponte, H. J. (1999). The stresses of poverty and the comfort of spirituality. In F. Walsh (Ed.), *Spiritual resources in family therapy* (pp. 76-89). New York: Guilford Press.

Becvar, D. (1997). *Soul healing: A spiritual orientation in counseling and therapy.* New York: Basic Books.

Bergin, A. E., Payne, I. R., & Richards, P. S. (1996). Values in psychotherapy. In E. P. Shafranski (Ed.), *Religion and the clinical practice of psychology* (pp. 297-326). Washington, DC: American Psychological Association.

Bidwell, D. R. (2001). A competency-based initial assessment form for pastoral counseling. *American Journal of Pastoral Counseling* 4 (2), 3-15.

Cox, R. H. (1997). Transcendence and imminence in psychotherapy. *American Journal of Psychotherapy* 51, 511-21.

Favier, C. O., & O'Brien, E. M. (2004). Spirituality and counseling. *American Journal of Pastoral Care* 7, 25-49.

Giblin, P., & Dykema, S. J. (1992). Master's level pastoral counseling training. *The Journal of Pastoral Care*, 46, 361-371.

Gorsuch, R. L. (2002). *Integrating psychology and spirituality*. Westport, CT: Praeger.

Gorsuch, R. L. (1998). Psychology of religion. *Annual Review of Psychology* 39, 201-21.

Griffith, J. L., & Griffith, M. E. (1999). *Sacred encounters*. New York: Guilford Press.

Hall, M. L., & Hall, T. W. (1997). Integration in the therapy room. *Journal of Psychology and Theology* 25, 86-101.

Hightower, J.E. (2000). Enriching theological integration: One pastoral counselor's story. *American Journal of Pastoral Counseling* 3 (2), 15-21.

Hill, P. C. et al. (2000). Conceptualizing religion and spirituality: Points of commonality points of departure. *Journal for the Theory of Social Behavior* 30, 51-77.

Jacque, Z. (2005). A Practical Theological Exploration of Psychology and Theology as Collaborative Partners: The Pastoral Counseling Center Trinity Church, Boston, Massachusetts. Unpublished doctoral dissertation. Boston: Boston University School of Theology.

Jones, L. G., & Paulsell, S. (2002). *The scope of our art: The vocation of the laity.* Grand Rapids: Eerdmans.

Karl, J. C. (1998). Discovering spiritual patterns: Including spirituality in staff development and the delivery of psychotherapy services. *American Journal of Pastoral Counseling* 1 (4), 1-40.

Kaye, B. (1996). The forgotten calling? Theology and the vocation of the laity. *St. Mark's Review* 167, 3-2.

Larrimore, W. L., Parker, M. & Crother, M. (2002). Should clinicians incorporate spirituality into their practices? What does the evidence say? *Annals of Behavioral Medicine* 24, 63-73.

Larson, D. B. & Larson, S. S. (1991). Religious Commitment and Health. *Second Opinion* 17 (1), 26-41.

Lovinger, R. J. (1996). Considering the religious dimension in assessment and treatment. In E. P. Shafranski (Ed.), *Religion and the clinical practice of psychology* (327-364). Washington, DC: American Psychological Association.

Mahrer, A. R. (1996). Existential-humanistic psychotherapy and the religious. In E. P. Shafranske (Ed.), *Religion and the Clinical Practice of Psychology* (433-460). Washington, DC: American Psychological Association.

McMinn, M. R., & McRay, B. W. (1997). Spiritual disciplines and the practice of integration: Possibilities and challenges for Christian psychologists. *Journal of Psychology and Theology* 25, 102-10.

Miller, W. R. (2000). *Integrating spirituality into treatment.* Washington, DC: American Psychological Association.

Miller, W. R., & Thorensen, C. E. (2001). Spirituality and health. In W. R. Miller (Ed.), *Integrating spirituality into treatment* (pp. 1-18). Washington, DC: American Psychological Association.

Oates, W. E. (1982). *The Christian Pastor* (3rd. ed. rev.). Philadelphia: Westminster Press.

Pargament, K. I., & Brant, C. R. (1998). Religious coping. In H. G. Koenig (Ed.), *Handbook of religion and mental health* (pp. 112-129). San Diego: Academic Press.

Richards, P. S., & Bergin, A. E. (2002). *A spiritual strategy for counseling and psychotherapy*. Washington, DC: American Psychological Association.

Richards, P. S., Rector, J. M. & Tjeltveit, A. C. (2000). Values, spirituality, and psychotherapy. In W. R. Miller (Ed.), *Integrating spirituality into treatment* (pp. 133-60). Washington, DC: American Psychological Association.

Ritter, R. H. (1998). If pastoral counseling is religious, then how do personal beliefs influence the process? *American Journal of Pastoral Counseling* 1 (3), 47- 65.

Sathler-Rosa, R. (2002). Pastoral action in the midst of a context of economic transformation and cultural apathy. *American Journal of Pastoral Counseling* 5 (3/4), 225-237.

Satcher, D. (1999). *The US Department of Health and Human Services: A supplement to mental health: A report to the Surgeon General on mental healthcare: Culture, race and ethnicity*. Washington, DC: US Department of Health and Human Services.

Shafranske, E. P. (1996). Religious beliefs, affiliations, and practices of clinical psychologists. In E. P. Shafranski (Ed.), *Religion and the clinical practice of psychology* (pp. 149-164). Washington, DC: American Psychological Association.

Shafranske, E. P. (2000). Religious involvement and professional practices of psychiatrists and other mental health professionals. *Psychiatric Annals* 30, 523-32.

Shafranske, E. P., & Maloney, H. N. (1996). Religions and the clinical practice of psychology: A case for inclusion. In E. P. Shafranske (Ed.), *Religion and the clinical practice of psychology* (pp. 561-86). Washington, DC: American Psychological Association.

Sperry, L. (2001). *Spirituality in clinical practice: Incorporating the spiritual dimension in psychotherapy and counseling*. Philadelphia: Brunner-Rutledge.

Swinton, J. (2003). *Spirituality and mental health care*. London: Kingsley Publisher.

Tan, S. Y. (1996). Religion in clinical practice: Implicit and explicit integration. In E. P. Shafranske (Ed.), *Religion and the clinical practice of psychology* (pp. 149-162). Washington, DC: American Psychological Association.

West, W. (2001). *Psychotherapy and spirituality: Crossing the line between therapy and religion*. London: Sage Publications.

Wulff, D. (1997). *Psychology of religion: Classic and contemporary*. New York: Doubleday.

doi:10.1300/J062v08n03_09

SECTION II:
MODELS AND PRACTICES

Formation Through Parallel Charting:
Clinician Narratives and Group Supervision

Duane R. Bidwell, PhD

SUMMARY. The narrative nature of identity and theological reflection suggests that pastoral counselors can benefit from intentionally engaging clinician narratives about counselees and about training experiences. The parallel charting process from narrative medicine provides a method for engaging clinician narratives in group supervision. It contributes to the formation of pastoral counselors by increasing self awareness, broadening theological reflection, clarifying pastoral identity, and shaping values, commitments, and dispositions helpful to the practice of pastoral counseling. doi:10.1300/J062v08n03_10 *[Article copies available for a fee from The Haworth Document Delivery Service: 1-800-HAWORTH. E-mail address: <docdelivery@haworthpress.com> Website: <http://www.HaworthPress.com> © 2006 by The Haworth Press, Inc. All rights reserved.]*

KEYWORDS. Narrative, supervision, theological reflection, clinical formation, identity formation, parallel charting

[Haworth co-indexing entry note]: "Formation Through Parallel Charting: Clinician Narratives and Group Supervision." Bidwell, Duane R. Co-published simultaneously in *American Journal of Pastoral Counseling* (The Haworth Pastoral Press, an imprint of The Haworth Press, Inc.) Vol. 8, No. 3/4, 2006, pp. 143-154; and: *The Formation of Pastoral Counselors: Challenges and Opportunities* (ed: Duane R. Bidwell, and Joretta L. Marshall) The Haworth Pastoral Press, an imprint of The Haworth Press, Inc., 2006, pp. 143-154. Single or multiple copies of this article are available for a fee from The Haworth Document Delivery Service [1-800-HAWORTH, 9:00 a.m. - 5:00 p.m. (EST). E-mail address: docdelivery@haworthpress.com].

Active, intentional formation of pastoral counselors occurs largely through the reflective processes of group and individual supervision. In these settings, clinicians and supervisors work with the raw materials of empathy, self-knowledge, and spiritual awareness to shape and give form to a coherent identity for clinical ministry. To a greater or lesser extent, this identity incorporates the traditions, values and commitments established by the community of pastoral counselors; it is informed as well by theological and therapeutic knowledge and training. But something even more significant plays at the heart of formation: the personhood of the pastoral counselor. Our ability to construct meaning with counselees, to affect change in their lives, is predicated on who we are. And who we are, the mosaic of shifting identities that we call the "self," emerges from our stories.

By now, the narrative nature of identity is well established. "Whether or not we view ourselves as story-tellers, and whether we proceed consciously or unconsciously," writes diaspora studies scholar Rima Berns McGown (2003), "narrative is how we order our world and make sense of its events" (p. 163). The stories we tell shape our personhood, and evolutions in personhood require that we tell new stories about ourselves (McAdams, 1993 and 2001; Richert, 2002 and 2003). For pastoral counselors, much re-authoring of personal stories begins in the process of clinical supervision, where we articulate, deconstruct, and retell stories about the relationships between counselees, clinicians, and supervisors (Bob, 1999; Speedy, 2000; Behan, 2003). The clinician narratives that emerge in and through supervision—that is, the stories that clinicians tell about their relationships with counselees, their experiences in training, their efforts to live out theological commitments in their practice of therapy, and the ways in which their personal stories and histories intersect with the counselee's stories and with the therapeutic process—express the values, skills, beliefs, and practical wisdom (Carlson and Erickson, 2001) of the person in formation. Clinician narratives are the life and breath of formation for pastoral counseling.

Unfortunately, supervision rarely emphasizes or strengthens an ability to notice and reflect on the personal, clinical, and theological stories that pastoral counselors tell to themselves during the therapeutic process. Instead, supervisors seek to hone an ability to hear and reflect on counselee stories with accuracy and skill. Yet, as family therapist Roger Lowe (2000) observes, in the background of every clinical case, is the ongoing project of the therapist story, the evolving narrative of the practitioner's "life as therapist." . . . This story focuses on the significant experiences, continuities, turning points, emerging themes, discontinuities, and challenges that mediate the practitioner's sense of identity and progress as a therapist.

While these elements of the clinician narrative rarely belong in the formal clinical record, they nonetheless shape the therapeutic relationship and the clinical process. Say, for example, you are working with a woman whose fiancée suddenly ends their engagement. Every time you meet with her, you are reminded of the unexpected death, decades ago, of the partner you believed would enter into a life-long covenant with you. In the psychodynamic therapeutic traditions, a situation like this is usually identified as an instance of counter-transference. Yet it is also a narrative event; your story about the death of a partner becomes intertwined with the counselee's story about a broken engagement, creating a new and richer narrative that incorporates–gives body to–both experiences. The meaning of this new narrative is performed, intentionally or subconsciously, in the context of the therapeutic relationship, the clinical process, and the supervisory hour. Your supervisors and peers may become an important audience for this evolving story.

Thus, what is needed in formation is a supervisory process that makes explicit these implicit stories "so that new, shared meaning (can) be explored" (Aggett, 2004, p. 44). Attending to clinician narratives, and their theological implications, can be an effective way of cultivating the arts of ministry and theological reflection in pastoral counselors who do not have theological training (see Townsend, 2003). Further, participation in a structured process for attending to these narratives develops skills for self-supervision that will be vital when the clinician completes formal training (Lowe, 2000).

THE PARALLEL CHARTING METHOD

In my educational and clinical context, the process of *parallel charting*, pioneered by practitioners of narrative medicine at Columbia University (see http://www.narrativemedicine.org), has provided a helpful process by which students can learn to attend to clinician narratives. Because the process emphasizes context, relationship, and narrative, it is particularly suited for communal-contextual approaches to pastoral theology and for training programs that engage in social constructionist approaches to psychotherapy and supervision. The parallel charting process recognizes and affirms the "multi-voiced, communal experience" (Behan, 2003) of clinical work and training and the personal dimensions of formation as a pastoral counselor (see also Bob, 1999; Speedy, 2000; Carlson and Erickson, 2001; Berg and Schnare, 2005).

But parallel charting is more than a process for learning. It is also a constitutive practice that gives voice and form to values, commitments, and dispositions that clinicians may choose to make central to their ministries and identities as pastoral counselors. To paraphrase Rita Charon, the Columbia University physician who pioneered this approach to formation,

> All good pastoral counselors know a great deal about their counselees that does not belong in the case notes, and yet such knowledge becomes available to the counselor only when it is put into words. . . . Writing in ordinary language about counselees and their care allows pastoral counselors to pause, to reflect on the meaning and consequences of their interactions with counselees, and to acknowledge their own complex responses to experiences of distress. Such reflective pauses are required for examining the meaning of one's actions; to let one's thoughts achieve the status of language by writing them down is the critical step in making the reflections available for growth. (see Charon, 2000, p. 288)

Charon created the parallel charting process in 1993 as a way to incorporate the existential concerns of patients and doctors into medical training. "We were very effectively teaching students about biological disease processes," Charon (in press) writes, "and we were systematically training them to do lumbar punctures and to present cases at attending rounds, but we were not being conscientious in helping them to develop their interior lives as doctors." Her goal was to discover a method that enabled students "to recognize more fully what their patients endure and to examine explicitly their own journeys through medicine."

She began asking students to write in ordinary language about an encounter with a particular patient, recording "clinical and personal considerations that are critical to their care of the patient but that do not belong in the hospital chart" (Charon, 2000, p. 289). These documents are limited to a single page, and students write with the knowledge that they will read their documents aloud to teachers and classmates in weekly case conferences. Through writing, and by listening to others discuss what they have written, students recognize how their memories, dispositions, and associations are present in clinical encounters and see more clearly how these elements influence their clinical approaches.

THE PARALLEL CHARTING CONFERENCE

In the professional context of pastoral counseling, a parallel charting conference is similar to a clinical case presentation. Before the group conference, trainees write in non-clinical language about their encounters with particular counselees. They focus primarily on their own responses to a counselee rather than on theoretical or clinically salient elements of the case. Solitary writing about their experiences encourages students to develop perceptual skills and to strengthen their ability to provide rich descriptions in every-day language (Charon, in press). The writing, limited to one page, contains no names or details that would identify the counselee. (Indeed, because these documents are discoverable and subject to subpoena, it is essential to omit private health information completely.) Students are entirely free to decide what they will write and what form it will take. The literary forms chosen by trainees vary; I have received parallel charting documents that are poems, psalms, journal entries, obituaries, philosophical and scriptural reflections, breakup letters, prayers, songs, and want ads. Invariably, the content reflects an encounter in which the trainee's (and sometimes the counselee's) "sensibilities are jarred" (Townsend, 2002), initiating personal and theological reflection.

During the conference, students read their documents to a group of peers, including a faculty supervisor. Participants do not receive copies of the documents; as Charon (in press) notes, the oral process improves listening skills and teaches students to attend to narrative details while allowing them to "practice and strengthen the skills of observation, perception, and interpretation" (Charon, 2000, p. 287). Some students find that learning to listen to what their peers have written can be the most helpful aspect of parallel charting. One student, reflecting on her first experience of a parallel charting session, said:

> I always thought I was a good listener. But this taught me that I listen for information and not for stories. I'm missing a lot by focus-

ing just on the facts and information I need to include in my case note.

When a reader has finished speaking, the rest of the group begins an interpretive process that attends to the form, genre, tense, voice, plot and other literary elements of the writing (including its symbolism and use of metaphor). Through this process, listeners skilled at attending to stories will notice "who the teller is, what points of view are enacted, what points of view are excluded, what images govern the story, how the temporal sequence configures events into plot, and what gives the story its closure" (Charon, 2000, p. 287). Charon (in press) recommends that facilitators use three questions to shape this discussion: What do you see? What do you hear? What do you want to learn more about?

During the group discussion, the writer simply listens. When the group has finished, the facilitator invites the writer to enter the conversation. The writer may respond to the things that the group wanted to learn more about; share what was most significant or helpful about the group discussion; reflect on how the parallel charting process is influencing the way a case is approached or conceptualized; or decline to respond. I find that students almost invariably want to engage the group by exploring what particular comments suggest about their clinical practice and conception of a case, especially the ways in which embedded theologies and subconscious stories about and attitudes toward counselees (which are often made explicit during the group discussion) influence their clinical approaches. Always, writers decide for themselves how to make use of the group's conversation in their own formation processes. In this way, the process is similar to what Behan (2003) calls the "co-authoring" approach to narrative supervision: "Each person contributes to the story being told and the person at the center–in this case the supervisee–has the last word on what to keep and what to leave out" (p. 35).

As the writer is reflecting with the group, I often use particularly "formative" questions, informed by the theory and practice of narrative therapy, to evoke richer descriptions of the ways in which the writing reflects or influences the author's pastoral identity, theological commitments, and evolving story about being a pastoral counselor. For example, I might ask:

> After hearing us discuss your writing, how has your sense of pastoral identity shifted or coalesced?

What does this piece of writing suggest about you as someone who seeks to integrate spirituality and psychotherapy?

How congruent is the story you are telling in this piece of writing with your preferred ways of "being with" counselees?

What aspects of your own stories (from childhood, from school, from being a trainee) are shaping your story about this case?

What did you learn about your embedded theology or spirituality as a result of listening to the group's reflection on your writing?

How congruent is the theology reflected in this piece of writing with your pastoral identity or your "publicly claimed" theological stance? In what ways, specifically, is it congruent? Incongruent?

During this parallel charting conference, what has become clearer (or muddier) about your professional commitments, values, and preferred ways of embodying the ministry of pastoral counseling?

"A MARRIAGE THAT IS PLEASING TO GOD": *PARALLEL CHARTING IN PRACTICE*

One clinician, who belongs to a conservative religious tradition, found herself revising her personal, pastoral and theological stories about Christian marriage after counseling two women who struggled for wholeness in their marriages. In writing about her experience with these counselees, the clinician began with a quote from one of the women: "I want to be a godly wife. I want us to have a marriage that is pleasing to God." In response, the clinician wrote:

"A marriage that is pleasing to God"–what does that look like? Scripture gives us some idea . . . (*the clinician quotes four bible verses*). But these scriptures don't seem to cover it all. There is more to a good marriage–a godly marriage–than faithfulness and submission and even passion. As counselors, we add good communication, common goals, respect, and effective conflict management. But there's got to be more than that. . . . Marriage is a *covenant* relationship in which two people share a covenant relationship with God. There is *mutuality*–give and take. There is *fel-*

lowship and *friendship* and *intimacy*. There is *love for the other* above self and *love for neighbors* of the marriage. There is new *love of self* that comes from knowing self through the experiences of another. Love of self–does this make it easier for her to love another? Does this make her easier to love? She is asserting her thoughts and ideas like never before–she is loving herself enough to put her self out there to be loved. And he is responding to that. He's putting himself out there, too. So maybe a godly marriage involves some *authenticity* and *vulnerability*. And she is setting boundaries–taking responsibility for what he has ignored. She's caring for herself and refusing to meet his spoken issues until he takes some responsibility, too. And he is responding to that. So maybe a godly marriage involves *responsibility* as well as some mutual *accountability*.

A member of the training group responded by saying that the piece of writing "seemed almost like a Pauline epistle," in that it offered a pastoral interpretation that could broaden a particular community's understanding of the Christian tradition. When the writer joined the conversation, the group engaged what it meant for the clinician to offer pastoral interpretation within a religious tradition that does not ordain women; whether the embedded theology of the writing was congruent with the clinician's "public" pastoral identity; and how an emerging, richer story about marriage might influence the ways in which the clinician approached counseling with couples and families.

After this conversation, the writer-clinician noted that parallel charting requires a quality of reflection she otherwise would not take the time to engage in.

> It's challenging me to think about questions that I have inside, to take a stab at an answer–even if it's not the end-all, to at least engage it. . . . There's an experience that I'm having with a counselee that I feel like is stretching my theology a little bit, so I'm going to write about it and see where it is that it takes me. And it formulated a theology based on that experience, which I probably wouldn't have done otherwise.

NARRATIVE AND THEOLOGICAL REFLECTION

This sort of narrative reflection on personal experience has been a staple of theological reflection and spiritual formation at least since the time of Augustine. Drawing from Augustine's understanding, evangelical scholar Alan Jacobs (2003) states that such reflection allows us

> to review our past actions and discern a variety of important themes: we can see when we were moving towards God and (conversely) when we were moving away from Him [sic]; when we discerned the good rightly and sought it properly and (conversely) when we misidentified the good and sought experiences or possessions that were bad for us; when God was calling us towards Himself [sic], whether we heard His [sic] voice or not; and so on. (p. 28)

This process, Jacobs says, eventually enables a person to give "some account of the coherence (not perfection) and development (not fulfillment) one discerns in one's own life" (p. 29).

But this requires an imaginative reciprocity between theology and storytelling, as noted by cultural critic Catherine Wallace (1999). "The life of faith," she says, "is lived in storytelling and not in doctrine. And yet we need both" (p. 41). She believes that theological doctrine is a concise way of summarizing, in formal language, particular human encounters with God. Behind every doctrine, she argues, dances a story– "a human experience, an event or series of events, and . . . a community in which and for whom both the experience and the story became exemplary of God and of their connection to God" (p. 45). Our stories embody the inheritance of our faith; through them, "we discover what our lives mean, what our values are, what differences our virtues make, and how we are connected to the past and to the community in vital ways" (p. 54).

In my experience, the clinician narratives brought to light through parallel charting can function in precisely this way. By writing about their experiences with counselees, clinicians discover what their life as a therapist means to them personally, spiritually, and theologically; reading aloud what they have written, and listening to peers respond, clarifies their therapeutic and pastoral values, their understandings of the effect of their care on counselees, and their sense of connection to their faith tradition and the faith communities that nourish it. These outcomes can make parallel charting a powerful ancillary to more formal theological reflection and an important contribution to the formation of pastoral counselors.

CONCLUSION

Formation for pastoral counseling, as stated in the introduction to this volume, shapes and integrates the personal, professional, and pastoral dimensions of a clinician's identity. The parallel charting process touches all three dimensions, increasing self-awareness, contributing to spiritual and theological integration, clarifying pastoral values and commitments, increasing clinical choices, and encouraging flexibility. The process itself illustrates the ways in which community can contribute to the social and narrative aspects of identity formation.

Different clinicians, of course, experience the parallel charting process differently. But trainees generally say that parallel charting broadens their theological reflection, allowing them to hear the multiple voices that belong to the clinician and to explore how those voices affect therapy and case conceptualization. (They are sometimes startled and dismayed to discover that their loudest interior voices about a particular case are those of hopelessness, powerlessness, and despair.) By externalizing these multiple voices in writing, clinicians can more clearly discern the stories they are telling about counselees that have the greatest therapeutic utility and then work to amplify the effects of these stories on their pastoral identities and the process of therapy. Clarity most often emerges, students say, as they read their writing aloud and "listen in" on the training group's subsequent conversation. Finally, trainees say that parallel charting creates a permanent record of their own evolution as pastoral counselors and the ways in which "counselees are teaching and changing us." The result, they suggest, is greater respect for counselees, clearer theological conceptualization of cases, and a quality of self-awareness that permits more intentional and frequent use-of-self to therapeutic advantage.

From my perspective, parallel charting helps pastoral counselors develop the narrative competencies (Montello, 1997; Charon, 2000) necessary for clinical practice and for the ongoing, life-long formation of professional identity. In addition to clinical distance, empathy, and pattern recognition (Montello, 1997, pp. 190-193), these narrative competencies include:

- an ability to hear a counselee's story as a holistic entity comprised of genre, plot, characterization, tense, voice, symbolism and other literary elements;
- an ability to distinguish the clinician's stories about the counselee from the counselee's own stories;

- an ability to skillfully and creatively identify possible intersections between sacred stories and the stories told by those who participate in the therapeutic process; and
- skill at holding these multiple storylines in tension during the process of intentional theological reflection.

REFERENCES

Aggett, P. (2004). Learning narratives in group supervision: Enhancing collaborative learning. *Journal of Systemic Therapies 23(3)*, 36-50.

Behan, C. P. (2003). Some ground to stand on: Narrative supervision. *Journal of Systemic Therapies 22(4)*, 29-42.

Berg, S., & Schnare, T. (2005). Re-storying the training experience: The application of reflecting team and narrative practices. In S. J. Cooper & J. Duvall (Eds.), *Catching the winds of change: A conference to inspire healing conversations and hopeful stories with individuals, families and communities* (pp. 47-54). Conference Proceedings. Toronto: The Brief Therapy Network.

Bob, S. R. (1999). Narrative approaches to supervision and case formulation. *Psychotherapy 36(2)*, 146-153.

Carlson, T. D., & Erickson, M. J. (2001). Honoring and privileging personal experience and knowledge: Ideas for a narrative therapy approach to the training and supervision of new therapists. *Contemporary Family Therapy 23(2)*, 199-220.

Charon, R. (in press). *Narrative medicine: Honoring the stories of illness.* New York: Oxford University Press.

Charon, R. (2000). Reading, writing, and doctoring: Literature and medicine. *The American Journal of the Medical Sciences 319(5)*, 285-291.

Jacobs, A. (2003). What narrative theology forgot. *First Things: A Monthly Journal of Religion and Public Life 135*, 25-31.

Lowe, R. (2000). Supervising self-supervision: Constructive inquiry and embedded narratives in case consultation. *Journal of Marital and Family Therapy 26(4)*, 511-521.

McAdams, D. P. (1993). *The stories we live by: Personal myths and the making of the self.* New York: The Guilford Press.

McAdams, D. P. (2001). The psychology of life stories. *Review of General Psychology 5(2)*, 100-122.

McGown, R. B. (2003). Writing across difference: Standing on authentic ground. *Journal of Muslim Minority Affairs 23(1)*, 163-171.

Montello, M. (1997). Narrative competence. In H. L. Nelson (Ed.), *Stories and their limits: Narrative approaches to bioethics* (pp. 185-197). New York: Routledge.

Richert, A. J. (2002). The self in narrative therapy: Thoughts from a humanist/existentialist perspective. *Journal of Psychotherapy Integration 12(1)*, 77-104.

Richert, A. J. (2003). Living stories, telling stories, changing stories: Experiential use of the relationship in narrative therapy. *Journal of Psychotherapy Integration 13(2)*, 188-210.

Speedy, J. (2000). Consulting with gargoyles: Applying narrative ideas and practices in counselling supervision. *European Journal of Psychotherapy, Counselling and Health 3(3)*, 419-431.

Townsend, L. (2002). Theological reflection, pastoral counseling, and supervision. *The Journal of Pastoral Theology 12(1)*, 63-74.

Townsend, L. (2003). Ferment and imagination in training in clinical ministry. In N. J. Ramsay (Ed.), *Pastoral care and counseling: Redefining the paradigms* (pp. 109-132). Nashville: Abingdon.

Wallace, C. (1999). Storytelling, doctrine, and spiritual formation. *Anglican Theological Review 99(81)*, 39-59.

doi:10.1300/J062v08n03_10

A Model for the Spiritual Formation
of a Pastoral Counseling Center

P. Mark Watts, DMin
David B. Reynolds, DMin

SUMMARY. Formation occurs not only to individual pastoral counselors, but to pastoral counseling centers as well. The organic development of the model presented here builds upon stages in the historic context of the center. The marks of a mature pastoral counseling center include an articulated identity, integration, the ability to develop new structures, tolerance of differences, and the willingness to build community and maintain both self and group. Benedictine spiritual formation grounds this pastoral counseling model. doi:10.1300/J062v08n03_11 *[Article copies available for a fee from The Haworth Document Delivery Service: 1-800-HAWORTH. E-mail address: <docdelivery@haworthpress.com> Website: <http://www.HaworthPress.com> © 2006 by The Haworth Press, Inc. All rights reserved.]*

KEYWORDS. Benedictine spirituality, pastoral counseling center, identity, integration, koinonia, organizational development

(Monastic community) has been from the beginning, a grace of communion in shared quest and a participated light. It is then a

[Haworth co-indexing entry note]: "A Model for the Spiritual Formation of a Pastoral Counseling Center." Watts, P. Mark and David B. Reynolds. Co-published simultaneously in *American Journal of Pastoral Counseling* (The Haworth Pastoral Press, an imprint of The Haworth Press, Inc.) Vol. 8, No. 3/4, 2006, pp. 155-166; and: *The Formation of Pastoral Counselors: Challenges and Opportunities* (ed: Duane R. Bidwell, and Joretta L. Marshall) The Haworth Pastoral Press, an imprint of The Haworth Press, Inc., 2006, pp. 155-166. Single or multiple copies of this article are available for a fee from The Haworth Document Delivery Service [1-800-HAWORTH, 9:00 a.m. - 5:00 p.m. (EST). E-mail address: docdelivery@haworthpress.com].

charism of special love and of mutual aid in the attainment of a difficult end, in the living of a hazardous and austere life. (Thomas Merton, 1998, p. 18)

A pastoral counseling center is an organic entity. After spending almost 30 years working in and observing pastoral counseling centers, the reality of the organic nature of a pastoral counseling center allows us to reflect on formation in a systematic way. We have observed the stages of development of the center in which we work and have some observations that have helped us to be intentional about the process of formation. These observations have also given us a perspective that we believe has been nurturing to the work we do and to the community in which we do this work.

Although this model of formation has come from our particular place, influenced by the persons who have joined our community, we believe that this model's implications may be instructive for other pastoral counseling centers. We begin with a brief history of our community and the way it has developed. Next, we present the structure of our formation process and the forces that we believe have shaped it, including Benedictine spirituality and community life. Finally, we discuss some of the resources that have helped us build on the work of other communities.

A HISTORY OF OUR COMMUNITY

Pastoral Counseling Services in Manchester, New Hampshire, was founded in 1979 by two United Church of Christ clergy to provide needed services in Manchester and southern New Hampshire. Originally, ordained clergy who were licensed as pastoral counselors by the state of New Hampshire provided services. All of the staff members were ordained UCC clergy. Very quickly the staff was modified to include other Christian clergy and a Jewish rabbi. There was also a training program for ordained clergy. When non-ordained persons applied to be part of the training program, the board and staff conducted a study and determined that only ordained clergy could participate. Thus, the religious core was easy to maintain and the training was built on the common experience of theological education. All persons in training held a Master of Divinity degree or its equivalent.

This model worked for 15 years but could not be sustained because the pool of candidates for the training program began to shrink and the demand for service continued to grow, exceeding the number of pastoral counselors able to provide counseling. The question of staff composition was again debated, and after vigorous study the staff was opened to non-ordained, clinically trained persons licensed by the state of New Hampshire as mental health providers. The transition was gradual, but significant. Concurrently, the pool of training candidates became unsustainable, and the training program was discontinued. This happened over time and was a painful shock to the staff because for many of the clinical staff, training was the center's *raison d'etre*. The training and theological reflection, done as part of the program, was no longer there. The staff's identity as supervisors and teachers was no longer the primary role. Counseling and psychotherapy became the principle enterprise of the center. As a result, theological reflection and the pastoral work of the center became more ambiguous and diffuse. How do you speak of theological needs with a staff of psychologists, social workers, pastoral counselors, and mental health counselors? What are the common core values? How is community defined? It was out of these transitions that the ideas we are presenting were developed.

THE CENTER'S DEVELOPMENTAL STAGES

We began to see the stages of development that our center was going through and identified ways to be more intentional about understanding and articulating what we were doing. In observing the way communities develop, we were especially informed by the model that Scott Peck, MD, presents in his book, *The Different Drum* (1987).

Briefly, he offers a four-stage model of community development based on group theory and practice. The stages of the community are: (1) *Pseudocommunity* based on the belief that "all are one" and that there is no difference in the community or that differences between people do not matter; (2) *Chaos*, in which differences become more important and the focus of the group is uncertain. People retreat into their identities beyond the group; (3) *Emptiness*, when differences are acknowledged and seem to overwhelm the group identity; and (4) *True community*, when persons can celebrate what they have in common, acknowledge differences, and hold that tension without falling into loss of self or group (p. 86).

Another way of identifying these stages is using object-relations theory to label the stages: (1) Symbiosis, (2) Differentiation, (3) Rapprochement, and (4) Object Constancy. These stages in any group happen over and over. But allowing for both self and group boundaries creates a more stable and engaging structure in the community.

In time, the staff members of Pastoral Counseling Services began to talk about what we were doing as an organization and reflecting on the changes that had occurred. The conversation about change was initiated in community meetings that included most of the staff. The authors developed our ideas into a workshop and presented them to our colleagues at the center and in a workshop at a national AAPC conference. We have also applied them to other centers where we have done consultation. We continue to be in formation and are working to keep our center life growing.

MARKS OF A MATURE PASTORAL COUNSELING CENTER

At Pastoral Care Services, we began our conversations about theological reflection by asking the question that so many centers (in our experience) ask: "How do we bring together theologically trained and 'secular' counselors to do theological reflection? What common language can we use in reflecting theologically both about clients and our own experiences as clinicians?"

We gradually realized that we were asking the wrong questions. Instead, we began to approach the question of theological integration from the perspective of how formation occurs in the community of a pastoral counseling center. First, we identified shared core values that we affirm and use to organize our life together. These include respect, hospitality, communal healing, and intentional community, as discussed below. After we identified core values, we identified the forces that create tension in any community, but especially in our community. Based on our experience and the experiences of other communities, we have identified five hallmarks of a mature and well-functioning pastoral counseling community.

The first mark of a mature pastoral counseling community is that it has an *articulated identity* focused around a mission or shared goal that is affirmed and voiced by all members of the community. This may take the form of a "mission statement," but is deeper in that it is affirmed by the actions and intentions of the members of the community on a daily basis.

The second mark is *integration*. The identity can be seen and recognized throughout the different areas of the center, i.e., the board, the staff, the administration, and by the ways in which that identity informs the behaviors and interactions of community members. An integrated identity becomes part of how work is done and how community is formed.

A third mark is that the community has *the ability to develop new structures in a responsive, non-rigid way.* The mature community is aware of the feedback necessary to respond to needs for structure and autonomy. Persons in the community experience the community as responsive to them as individuals and are in turn responsive to the community as a whole.

This leads to the fourth mark of a mature community: it *strives for "real community" tolerant of differences* and does not settle for a "pseudocommunity" focused on homogeneity to the exclusion of differences. Persons are able to define themselves to the community and bind to the community by affirming the shared identity. An example of this is tolerance of religious differences and the ability to allow members to express their faith in ways genuine to them and to share these expressions freely.

The fifth hallmark of a mature pastoral counseling center is the recognition that it *takes work to be in a community.* Members are willing to participate in the work of community by showing up and contributing to its ongoing life. This includes being honest about both the needs of the self and the purpose of the community. It means at times living with ambiguity while change and growth happens.

Thus, a mature pastoral counseling community, in our definition, has a clear and integrated identity, is responsive to the members and tolerant of individual identity within the shared identity, and is willing to do the "work" of community building and maintaining both self and group.

TENSIONS AS STRENGTHS

We look to the New Testament theological concept of "koinonia" as our model for community. The translation from the Greek is that of holding in common or to share. From this meaning develops a powerful image of a healing community. Another image of koinonia is an environment for spiritual growth. This theological model of the early church is close to the community we hold as an ideal for the healing community of PCS.

We know that in the early church there were tensions present in the community. Much of the post-gospel New Testament is concerned with conflicts between members of the churches. People vied for position and influence, and the individual was in tension with the community. We believe that this tension is important in order to hold community together and must be acknowledged to maintain a healthy community.

All relationships include tensions that create polarities within the relationship. There is tension in marriages between the need for together time and the need for individual time. There is tension in relationships between parents and teens because of the need for the teen to develop autonomy and the parents to maintain their role of nurture and protection. By identifying the tensions in a community, we can better respond to the structure of the community and to the needs of individual members. The tensions that shape community life are normal and healthy, and it is at the nexus of such tensions that real community is formed and forged on a regular basis. Tensions create strength; if one side of the polarity overwhelms the other side, an important source of energy is lost. We believe four continuums of tension are inherent to a pastoral counseling center: (1) hierarchy vs. consensus, (2) autonomy vs. community, (3) task vs. affirmation, and (4) structure vs. change.

At Pastoral Counseling Services, the community is arranged in a hierarchical fashion with lines of authority and responsibility. But we also value consensus and work to allow persons in the community to have input in decisions. We work at processing decisions as a group, but the lines of responsibility allow for decisions that are responsive to the environment. All of our counselors are licensed by the state to practice at an independent level. That means that they are able to make choices about treatment and function autonomously. They are also encouraged and given many opportunities to connect with colleagues about their clinical work. We need to get certain tasks done to keep our center open and function as a business. However, all persons need affirmation about their work and help with "blind spots." We allow opportunities for community where we can receive feedback and test the reality of the work we are doing. Finally, our structure is important to allow us to do our work, but that structure also needs to change to meet the changing needs and demands of our environment.

CORE VALUES AT PCS

The four core values around which community is built at Pastoral Counseling Services are: (1) All persons are created by God for respect and wholeness, (2) We are called to offer hospitality to all who come to our community, (3) Healing is best done in a community that provides support to its members, allows faith affirmation, and does not require faith suppression, and (4) Community is a task that takes work.

The first of the four core values is rooted in scripture's assertion that all persons are created by God for respect and wholeness. From the creation story in the Hebrew Scriptures, we learn that God "creates humankind in God's image" (Genesis 1.27, NRSV). The Christian scriptures illustrate this point by saying that the goal of humanity is "abundant life" (John 10:10 NRSV). Every client, regardless of ethnicity, spirituality, gender, sexual orientation, etc., is accepted as a child of God. Usually, some type of brokenness brings a person to the office of a pastoral counselor; but we believe that there is a hidden wholeness in each person. When all members of a pastoral counseling center operate from this principle, clients will feel the respect that is necessary for healing.

Second, hospitality is extended both to staff and clients as an expression of the biblical duty to regard the alien as "the citizen among you" (Leviticus 19. 33, 34, NRSV). We who are Christian also see this value as recognizing the "Christ" within the other. We see all are on a journey and all in need of hospitality. We attempt to create a community that has an expanded "tent" which welcomes all. We meet on the common ground of our shared community time and shared mission. By listening, sharing, feeding and caring for each other, we set the tone for extending this to those who come seeking counsel from us.

The third core value is that healing is best done in community. For the demanding work of providing pastoral psychotherapy, community is absolutely necessary; pastoral psychotherapists need settings where they can receive support, input, and correction. When hearing stories of abuse, neglect, and pain, caregivers need a place to detoxify, which is to neutralize the suffering that they have heard. The balance of the individual and community provides a healthy tension for living out this value.

Community, however, is a task that takes work, and we attend to this by providing intentional times for gathering to focus both on the work we do and on our own needs. We have two staff times per week, and we also have a retreat each quarter to allow for case presentations, sharing of community concerns, and nurturing of all of us. At the beginning of our Thursday staff gathering, we take turns being "chaplain" and leading in some form of worship, which is not highly stylized. Our community has suffered great loss, great joy, and all the human experiences in between. It is in the sharing that we are able to be with others in a deep way.

A BENEDICTINE MODEL OF SPIRITUAL FORMATION

One model of formation for pastoral counseling centers is the religious order founded by and based on the writings of St. Benedict, the sixth-century founder of Western monasticism. Benedict sought to develop a spiritual community that allowed for the growth and nurture of the individual as well as the community. His classic work *The Rule of St. Benedict* (Fry, 1982; hereafter referred to as "RB") outlines the basic tenets of his thought. Contemporary interpretations of that rule provide the basis for this discussion.

Some members of the Pastoral Counseling Services staff have attended retreats at Benedictine monasteries; others have read books based on Benedictine thought. In planning the structure of our life together, the staff has drawn from this rich tradition. When we began having quarterly retreats, for example, we drew from the Benedictine tradition. The retreat model grew out of the tension of growth of the institution and the needs of the individual.

The Benedictine approach to formation emphasizes three particular monastic dynamics that shape spiritual life, which we call stability, change, and balance.

Stability

Stability is the commitment to a place, practice, and community. In Benedictine life, a person makes a commitment to a geographical location for life to contribute to and receive from the community. In pastoral counseling centers, people commit to a particular setting for a period of time. In that setting, in ways similar to the religious members of the Benedictine order, members contribute to and receive from community. At Pastoral Counseling Services, therapists find a stable place for clinical, business, devotional, and collegial practices, as well as a place for receiving the support of the business administration department for billing, typing, phone messages, and reminders of insurance authorizations for treatment.

While the last sentence may sound strange in the context of a monastic model, Benedict was very practical, believing that one should "regard all utensils and goods of the monastery as sacred vessels of the altar" (RB 31.10; Fry, 1982, p. 55). The clinical staff at Pastoral Counseling Services does more than receive from the community; however, staff members also contribute to the community by leading case studies, devotionals, and theological reflections; attending retreats; and contracting to give a portion of their income to support the operations of the institution.

Benedict's emphasis on stability echoes the rhythm of the structure of the pastoral counseling center. It is the daily, weekly, and monthly structure that gives shape to the life of the community. Structure is flexible and can be changed; yet it provides the foundation for life together. For example, during a staff retreat, the idea arose that a different time for our community meeting would be better. The idea came from the staff and made sense to all who were present. After checking with those who were not present at that particular retreat, the meeting time was changed and it works much better.

Change

Paradoxically, Benedictine thought calls for continuous change. The concept of repentance (or *conversatio morum*) suggests that life invites transformation at all stages. In the Benedictine communities that we have known, the order exists for the maximum benefit and growth of the individual and the community. Earlier, we spoke of the tension of autonomy vs. community. Both points of this polarity are nurtured by being open to changes that allow optimum functioning. As discussed earlier, the transition from a staff of ordained clergy to one that includes laypeople signified a necessary though difficult transition in the life of Pastoral Counseling Services.

Institutions tend to resist change. Structures, modes of functioning, personal habits, and tradition tend to cause sluggishness when internal or external forces require transition in order to maintain optimal function. Chapter four of *The Rule of St. Benedict* suggests traits that keep the community and individuals open to change, including discipline, love, consideration, listening, and hope. Thus, by utilizing these traits, each member of a pastoral counseling community commits to growth and transition.

After the decision to include laypeople on the staff, we wondered how to nurture the spiritual and theological dimensions of our center. After attending a workshop on theological reflection, several staff proposed that one staff meeting per month be devoted to a "theological case presentation." Through consensus, the group agreed, and every second Thursday, a staff member presents a clinical case from a theological point of view. The presenter reflects on the case from a spiritual or theological understanding. At first some of the non-theologically trained staff were uncomfortable presenting, but with time everyone realized that the diversity of training enriched theological reflection.

Balance

An emphasis on balance is where the wisdom of Benedict and the tensions mentioned earlier dovetail. The examples of changing the time of meeting or adding theological case presentation illustrate stability (keeping community time and case presentation) and change (time and mode). Stability is a reality. Core values deeply ground the life of a counseling center. Key tasks that keep the center running smoothly are ongoing. At the same time, listening to staff needs and the cultural context requires continual evaluation.

Benedictine communities seek a balance between prayer and work. The sustainability of the Benedictine order since the sixth century is directly related to the ability to adapt to cultural, geographical, and ethnic differences across the world and across the centuries. Adapting is demanding but necessary for staying alive and viable. Balancing core values and responding to the need for change nurtures longevity for any institution and allows healthy adaptation.

In the mid-1990s, Pastoral Counseling Services was faced with the challenge of "managed care," with insurance companies seeking to control costs through greater involvement in treatment decisions. Psychotherapists raised many legitimate questions about the changes happening in mental health care. Health insurance was changing, challenging the stability of the practice of pastoral counseling. Through the leadership of its executive director, Pastoral Counseling Services decided to join as many insurance panels as possible and to make some changes in psychotherapy practices. A number of colleagues in other settings made the legitimate decision not to make those changes. But Pastoral Counseling Services decided that the changes were necessary in order to provide services to our constituency.

In making these changes, we believe we maintained our core values. Hence, Pastoral Counseling Services was able to maintain stability while learning new approaches to psychotherapy. The short-term, issue-oriented approach advocated by managed care companies contrasted with the long-term, psychodynamic approach that many of us learned in our clinical training. We discovered that the new modalities actually worked better with certain populations. Hence, maintaining balance required change in learning a new theory, and at the same time, maintaining our core values.

CONCLUSION

Intentional community, as Merton said, is " . . . a *charism* of special love and of mutual aid in the attainment of a difficult end, in the living of a hazardous and austere life." This article highlights the history, functioning, reflection, and models that have shaped the formation of community and individuals at Pastoral Counseling Services in Manchester, New Hampshire.

The day-to-day "living into" our values and commitments has informed our theory. We believe that spiritual formation is an ongoing process for individuals and communities. Staff members go through life transitions; new staff members join the organization; culture and business practices change; staff members leave. The rhythm of life affects and is affected by the process of community development. The core values have often been seen clearly in hindsight rather than being set out from the beginning.

One sign of practicing these principles is the long-term stability of our staff. Various clinical and business staff members have been at Pastoral Counseling Services for 10, 15, 18, 20, and even 26 years. At the same time, our center continues to grow and new staff members are joining us. Presently the center has 27 staff members, with a clinical staff composed of 10 ordained and 13 non-ordained clinicians. In the past year, two new clinicians have become part of our community. We incorporate new staff members in our community through orientation, introductions, case presentations, and quarterly retreats. We also listen to their stories and expressions of life, work, and faith. Finding balance in the Benedictine sense is never easy or clear-cut. Living our four core values in the context of the four healthy tensions has allowed and encouraged redefinition of our identity and mission.

One of our favorite theologians, Sallie McFague (2000), suggests that people of faith image the world as God's household. We suggest that pastoral counseling centers and other mental health agencies image their organization as "God's household." A pastoral counseling center does not belong to the leadership, board of directors, or supporters. It belongs to God and to each person of God's creation who is organically a part of it. It is a charism of special love and of mutual aid in the attainment of the challenging end of healing lives, relationships, and families.

REFERENCES

Fry, T. trans. (1982). *The rule of St. Benedict.* Collegeville, MN: The Liturgical Press.

McFague, S. (2000). *Life abundant: Rethinking theology and economy for a planet in peril.* Minneapolis: Fortress Press.

Merton, T. (1998). *Contemplation in a world of action.* South Bend, IN, Notre Dame Press.

Peck, S. (1987). *The different drum: Community-making and peace.* New York: Simon and Schuster.

doi:10.1300/J062v08n03_11

A Model of Formation
in the Multi-Cultural Urban Context
for the Pastoral Care Specialist

Rebeca M. Radillo, DMin

SUMMARY. The model for the formation of Pastoral Care Specialists in this article is inclusive of a broader and integrative formation process in an urban, multicultural, religious, and racial diverse context. The model is intentional in developing a keen awareness of and sensitivity to the realities of urban life and the critical role it plays in the formation and the emergence of the Pastoral Care Specialist's identity. doi:10.1300/J062v08n03_12 *[Article copies available for a fee from The Haworth Document Delivery Service: 1-800-HAWORTH. E-mail address: <docdelivery@haworthpress.com> Website: <http://www.HaworthPress.com> © 2006 by The Haworth Press, Inc. All rights reserved.]*

KEYWORDS. Urban, multicultural, pastoral care specialist, theological education, Spanish-speaking

This article focuses on the importance of contextualizing the training of Pastoral Care Specialists without compromising the educational standards for excellence and the achievement of proficiency in the practice of pastoral care ministry. The curriculum, pedagogy and methodol-

[Haworth co-indexing entry note]: "A Model of Formation in the Multi-Cultural Urban Context for the Pastoral Care Specialist." Radillo, Rebeca M. Co-published simultaneously in *American Journal of Pastoral Counseling* (The Haworth Pastoral Press, an imprint of The Haworth Press, Inc.) Vol. 8, No. 3/4, 2006, pp. 167-176; and: *The Formation of Pastoral Counselors: Challenges and Opportunities* (ed: Duane R. Bidwell, and Joretta L. Marshall) The Haworth Pastoral Press, an imprint of The Haworth Press, Inc., 2006, pp. 167-176. Single or multiple copies of this article are available for a fee from The Haworth Document Delivery Service [1-800-HAWORTH, 9:00 a.m. - 5:00 p.m. (EST). E-mail address: docdelivery@haworthpress.com].

ogy reflect the distinctiveness of the Pastoral Care Specialist track and promote the integration of critical reflection and praxis, while at the same time making possible the required skill development.

The Pastoral Care Specialist (PCS) is a non-certified category of membership in the American Association of Pastoral Counselors (AAPC). This category "is designed for pastors, students and lay pastoral care givers. . . . Pastoral Care Specialists are not qualified for long-term counseling or pastoral psychotherapy. PCS is not a clinical category of membership, but can fulfill the pastoral care practicum requirements for the Certified Pastoral Counselors" (AAPC, 2006, p. 9). The educational and formative objectives of a training program, are to, "strengthen personal pastoral identity, spirituality, and pastoral care practice. It integrates the resources of one's faith tradition with current theoretical understanding and practical skills" (p. 9).

The focal point of the process of formation is the whole person in his or her particular milieu. It is faulty to assume that the process of formation is uniform; such thinking results in processes that are exclusive and individualistic, ignoring or diminishing the importance of contextual realities. To disregard the social, psychological, biological and spiritual forces that from birth have been at work in the lives of persons leads to a partial or fragmented self-understanding. The lifelong process of formation, therefore, must be sensitive to and intentionally inclusive of context and particularity. These aspects have particular implications in the development and integrity of any Pastoral Care Specialist program, its content, and the manner in which it is approached and its participants understood.

The model presented in this article has been designed for a Pastoral Care Specialist Program for Parish Settings at the New York Theological Seminary and is an integral part of the overall seminary curriculum. The second institution where this model is in operation is at the Institute Latino de Cuidado Pastoral, Inc. (ILCP), which is a non-degree granting institution with the training being conducted in Spanish. Participants are inclusive of lay and clergy persons representing mainline and non-denominational faith communities. Because of the differences between the two institutions some areas have been adjusted in order to meet the needs and expectations of each institution and its participants.

The model emerged out of the increasing need to respond effectively to the needs of urban congregations. Pastors and lay caregivers are encountering a multiplicity of difficult situations in their churches. This is due to social and economic crises, which affect the emotional and spiritual lives of parishioners and the larger community where ministry takes place. It is safe to say that over ninety-five percent (95%) of all participants are urbanites who interface with a heterogeneous highly mobile society, which is continually on emotional overload. A large majority of them have encountered economic scarcity and experienced first hand the failures of social institutions. Urbanites experience a vast web of relationships and yet they face the danger of becoming alienated.

In the Greater New York area, the effects of the September 11th tragedy continue to linger, and it is obvious that Post Traumatic Stress Disorder (PTSD) is indeed directly or indirectly affecting the life of every person in this geographical area. Furthermore, the multiethnic and racial nature of the urban context provides, on the one hand, an invaluable opportunity to experience the richness of a global village; while on the other hand, it gives rise to inter or intra-ethnic conflicts, increasing the struggle for limited resources. Marginalization of people due to immigration status, race, lifestyle, poverty, illness, and lack of access to resources is on the increase in the urban context.

The church, as a social and cultural broker institution, must prepare its leadership to understand and address these realities. Sociology, theology and anthropology alert us to the importance of paying special attention to issues of social and cultural construction of reality (Robbins, 1997). A socio-theological perspective suggests that, "every religion, no matter what we may understand by 'religion,' is a situated reality in a specific human context, a concrete and determined geographical space, historical moment and social milieu" (Maduro, 1982, p. 41).

The Pastoral Care Specialist Program in the urban context is inclusive, creative and flexible, making certain that its participants meet the necessary professional standards that foster a pastoral competence for practitioners in this field. Simultaneously, it offers culturally appropriate training for its participants who, for the most part, serve the needs of persons and families identified as underserved in the urban context. A reality that must always be taken into consideration is that a significant percentage of these pastoral caregivers belong to the "underserved" population themselves.

To establish a training program that has relevancy and credibility to its context, meets the needs of the care-seekers, and is conducive to the recruitment of effective practitioners, one must adopt a core curriculum that correspond to all of the above. The core curriculum for urban pastoral caregivers in this model uses a bio-psycho-social-spiritual framework. This conceptual framework is particularly valuable for multi-ethnic racial and religious groups.

Initially, the bio-psycho-social conceptual structure was introduced by George Engel (1977) and the spiritual dimension was added later. This framework is conducive to examining what contributes to the identity development of the person and her/his formation. This model assists practitioners in deepening spirituality and developing respect of the "other." The bio-psycho-social-spiritual model (Figure 1) brings to the forefront the complexity of the self in society, noting how identity is never permanent or static since the internal and external realities are always in flux and unpredictable. All of these elements have a direct impact on one's theological stance and the practice of ministry.

THE SETTING AND THE PROGRAM

This model for the training of Pastoral Care Specialists is in place at the New York Theological Seminary (NYTS) and the Instituto Latino de Cuidado Pastoral, Inc. (ILCP), which was founded five years ago. I will begin with the program at the seminary, noting later some of the contextual differences of the Instituto Latino de Cuidado Pastoral, Inc.

New York Theological Seminary is committed to the intentional formation process of its seminarians and to theological and biblical education for urban ministry. The students at New York Theological Seminary as well as the faculty reflect the diversity of the city: African Americans, Hispanics, Asians, West Indians, Caucasians and Africans, among others, and is multi-denominational. The involvement of students from many cultures in the classes and in the total life of the seminary presents a wonderful challenge and a magnificent opportunity to contribute to the students' formation.

The Pastoral Care Specialist Program for Parish Settings offers preparation for the ministry of care, which is an essential function of any faith community. Theological education is rigorous and demanding. It requires discipline and commitment to pursue intellectual proficiency. Contextual education translates and integrates intellectual knowledge with the development of the necessary skills to carry out the practice of ministry. The students are aware of the complexity of the needs their parishioners are constantly facing and acknowledge that requests for assistance are beyond their realm of expertise. To respond to this reality, the seminary realizes that it is imperative for pastors to obtain a comprehensive understanding of pastoral care in the parish as well as appropriate skill development, education, support and consultation. In addition to theological and biblical disciplines, it is critical that seminarians ac-

FIGURE 1

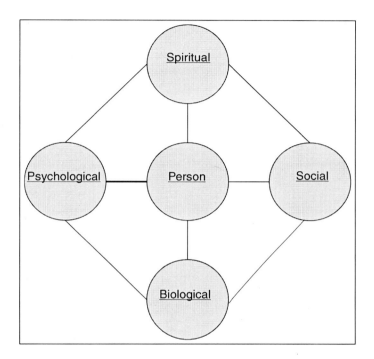

quire a profound understanding of the complexity of the internal and external dynamics that affect human behavior and emotional, physical and spiritual health.

There are at least four areas where the incorporation of the Pastoral Care Specialist Program benefits its participants and augments their theological education. First, by incorporating this training program as part of the core curriculum, New York Theological Seminary is taking an initiative to strengthen the educational experience of the students. Seminarians can pursue this specialized training while still enrolled in their biblical, theological and ministerial courses. This model fosters a deeper degree of integration due to the interplay of required courses and praxis, especially during their supervised ministry. It is important to note that this program incorporates the same standards for the Pastoral Care Specialist courses as those required for the membership category by the American Association of Pastoral Counselors.

Second, the training program addresses the reality of the increasing cost of seminary education and the time constraints for students who must work full-time in order to meet personal and family responsibilities and pay for their education. The seminary has, by incorporating this program into the overall core curriculum, made it possible for students to incorporate this training as a part of their elective courses, thus saving them from having to go through the training at a later time with the added cost of time and money.

Third, this training provides an insightful and profound education that better prepares seminarians to understand the complexities of human development and behavior, and offers practical, responsible and ethical guidelines for comprehensive parish ministry. In other words, seminarians become more conscientious of what it means to be an agent of healing and transformation in a holistic fashion.

Lastly, this program encourages seminarians to identify and to further explore areas for personal growth and formation in the ongoing process of developing their pastoral identity and competence. Even students who are not interested in participating in the full program do take the advantage of this training program by taking courses that are made available because of the inception of the Pastoral Care Specialist Program.

As stated early on in this article, the Pastoral Care Specialist Program parallels other models in terms of the established body of knowledge set up by the American Association of Pastoral Counselors. The distinctive focus at NYTS is on the intentionality of focusing every course on the urban context, demonstrating the multi-dimensionality of pastoral care as a liberating and empowering ministry in the parish. One of the required courses offered is Pastoral Formation in a Multicultural Context. The readings for this course include anthropology, sociology and theology. The course is augmented by introducing other self-awareness instruments such as genograms, the bio-psycho-social-spiritual model, and culturalgrams. The course has proven to be very helpful in that trainees are able to appreciate the importance of the development of an authentic self and to understand that such an accomplishment only comes into being through the careful process of self-discovery and an understanding of all that has shaped one's life. In a formal educational experience credibility comes from the intentional inclusion of the individual's history, core values, faith tradition and spirituality in the training program. This also applies to the subject of skill development and the group consultation process. This class widens the lenses through which others are understood and appreciated. The tools from this class also assist participants to better understand the impact of immigration on families and individuals, since immigrants are an integral and growing population in congregations.

Every course in this program also recognizes the importance of "integrating bodies of knowledge" (Lowe & Mascher, 2001) with multicultural understanding and the urban context. For instance, when a course on death and dying is taught, the instructor is certain to include the ways in which different cultures understand these issues. This integrative practice maintains the integrity of the specific discipline while acknowledges the different perspectives and experiences of the student.

There are some differences between the program at NYTS and the program offered by the Instituto Latino de Cuidado Pastoral, Inc. The ILCP includes participants with limited formal education who are serving churches as ministers and lay leaders in urban neighborhoods. There is a certain elitism that precludes the inclusion of intelligent and gifted people in formal education. Programs and individuals that can expand their capacity to serve appropriately underserved communities need to be supported by a suitable educational training. Many of these individuals come from fast growing non-denominational and storefront congregations. These persons are congregational leaders giving pastoral care to their parishioners; therefore, it is critical for them to learn how best respond in an informed and responsible manner to their needs.

The program offered by the Instituto Latino de Cuidado Pastoral, Inc. recognizes students from mainline denominations who are trained as congregational leaders and local pastors and for whom the process of formation is as critical as that received by seminarians. All training is conducted in Spanish and special attention is given to issues and dynamics that are particular to their culture.

Elizabeth Conde-Frazier (2004) reminds us, "that historically the church has had a variety of formal and informal means of equipping persons for their priesthood. Informally, we have learned through discipleship models of mentoring where the relationship, observation, and reflection have been methods of teaching and learning" (p. 40). All participants trained by the Instituto are on the life-long journey of formation as well. They have been very much engaged in the process of developing an authentic self-awareness and of the necessity to develop a deep theological, psychological and sociological understanding of self and others. They are engaged in learning the necessary skills to respond to their parishioners and to enhance their ministry.

Because the Instituto is a non-granting degree program, participants receive a certificate indicating the completion of the two years of training. I must mention that the majority of the student body either has very limited formal education, with many achieving only high school graduation or Graduate Equivalency Diploma (GED). Some have received theological and biblical education in bible institutes only accredited by their religious body. The Institute has trained over one hundred urban students in a multicultural context who are now serving their congregations and other community ministries.

The program at the Instituto offers a similar list of courses as those offered to the seminarians. The difference between the two programs is evidenced in the methodological and pedagogical approaches to training that meet the educational level for the particular students and their contexts. It is obvious that the educational expectations of a master's level program are different from those of the ILCP. The courses at the Instituto are geared to meet the specific needs of the participants in their religious setting. I dare to speculate that for many or most of the students involved in the training program at the Instituto, this is the first time that they have engaged in an intentional pursuit of self-discovery and self-awareness. They have been able to grasp the concept as a life-long learning process.

A concrete example of this is the fact that many of them are now pursuing formal education, as well as expanding their biblical and theological education. Others have entered community colleges in order to at least pursue two years of formal education. In the meanwhile, I rejoice that formation and training are not limited but inclusive. While the level of formal education is dissimilar, I submit that the level of commitment is not. If "formation is the disciplined and intentional reflection and corresponding action that shapes individuals and communities toward a particular way of being" (Marshall, 2005) the difference is not in the "formalness" of the education.

CONCLUSION

Formation in the multi-cultural urban context for pastoral care specialist is indeed an undeniable opportunity to offer a creative and innovative programmatic challenge both at the New York Theological Seminary and at the Instituto Latino de Cuidado Pastoral, Inc. Because of the contextualization and the interdisciplinary nature of this program, formation is a constant. Cognitive and experiential awareness of the "other," and the theological richness of the diverse context, serve as a fertile ground for the formative process and the student's education to take place.

My experience has been that students are eager to integrate their newly acquired knowledge with their practice of ministry in their parishes and/or community settings. What contributes to this creative and highly valued program is the contextualization of the Pastoral Care Specialist curriculum, which is inclusive and respectful of the student's cultures, ethnicity, and the particularities of urban life. This program has also challenged participants in their theological viewpoint and motivated them to deepen their self-understanding and their perspective of others.

This contextualization of the curriculum in conjunction with the introduction of the bio-psycho-social-spiritual conceptual model provides a visual and straightforward approach to the understanding of the four major contributors to their personal development. All of the above provides a firm foundation upon which the process of formation is firmly grounded.

One obvious value of the training is the palpable personal growth of the students in the program, as well as the recognition of their need to participate in a process that will enhance their knowledge, skills and personal development. As they experience and engage in the interplay between the cognitive and practical implications of this training for ministry, one can observe their unfolding as authentic pastors/leaders and as *agents of transformation* in a very difficult and complex context.

REFERENCES

American Association of Pastoral Counselors. (2006). *Membership standards and certification committee operational manual*. Washington, DC: AAPC.

Conde-Frazier, E. (2004). Religious education in an immigrant community. *Perspectivas, Ocassional Papers*. Altanta: Hispanic Theological Initiative.

Engel, G. L. (1977). The need for a new medical model: A challenge for biomedicine. *Science, 196*, 129-136.

Falicov, C. (1998). *Latino families in therapy: A guide to multicultural practice*. New York: The Guilford Press.

Lowe, S. & Mascher, J. (2001). The role of sexual orientation in multicultural counseling: Integrating bodies of knowledge. In J. G. Ponterotto, J. M. Casas, L. A. Suzuki & C.M. Alexander (Eds.), *Handbook of multicultural counseling*. Thousand Oaks, CA: Sage Publications.

Maduro, O. (1982). *Religion and social conflicts*. Maryknoll, NY: Orbis Books.

Marshall, J. (2005). *Some thoughts on formation and the American Association of Pastoral Counselors.* Paper presented at the American Association of Pastoral Counselors, Fort Worth, TX.

Radillo, R. M (2003). Pastoral counseling with Latina/o Americans. In R. J. Wicks, R. Parsons, and D. Capps (Eds.), *Clinical handbook of pastoral counseling* (pp. 101-119). New York: Paulist Press.

Robbins, R. H. (1997). *Cultural anthropology: A problem-based approach.* Itasca, Illinois: F.E. Peacock Publishers, Inc.

doi:10.1300/J062v08n03_12

Formation for Care of Souls:
The Claremont Way

Kathleen J. Greider, PhD
William M. Clements, PhD
K. Samuel Lee, PhD

SUMMARY. Claremont School of Theology understands formation as part of its academic and clinical training programs. As one of the historical programs in pastoral counseling, it integrates research and practice, multidisciplinary study, concern for the marginalized, pluralism, program flexibility, and mentoring. Concerns about the future of pastoral counseling are reflected in the ongoing development of the program. doi:10.1300/J062v08n03_13 *[Article copies available for a fee from The Haworth Document Delivery Service: 1-800-HAWORTH. E-mail address: <docdelivery@haworthpress.com> Website: <http://www.HaworthPress.com> © 2006 by The Haworth Press, Inc. All rights reserved.]*

KEYWORDS. Graduate theological education, research, clinical practice, pastoral care and counseling, multidisciplinary education, diversity, mentoring

The Claremont tradition in pastoral care and counseling education began before the Claremont School of Theology (CST) existed. It started at the

[Haworth co-indexing entry note]: "Formation for Care of Souls: The Claremont Way." Greider, Kathleen J., William M. Clements, and K. Samuel Lee. Co-published simultaneously in *American Journal of Pastoral Counseling* (The Haworth Pastoral Press, an imprint of The Haworth Press, Inc.) Vol. 8, No. 3/4, 2006, pp. 177-195; and: *The Formation of Pastoral Counselors: Challenges and Opportunities* (ed: Duane R. Bidwell, and Joretta L. Marshall) The Haworth Pastoral Press, an imprint of The Haworth Press, Inc., 2006, pp. 177-195. Single or multiple copies of this article are available for a fee from The Haworth Document Delivery Service [1-800-HAWORTH, 9:00 a.m. - 5:00 p.m. (EST). E-mail address: docdelivery@haworthpress.com].

Available online at http://ajpc.haworthpress.com
© 2006 by The Haworth Press, Inc. All rights reserved.
doi:10.1300/J062v08n03_13

University of Southern California (USC), where David Eitzen taught in both the department of religion and the professional school. Eitzen was a pioneer of graduate education in the field (Mills, 1990), and from about 1940 USC offered a Ph.D. in Church in the Community (pastoral counseling and other arts of ministry). But in 1957, after USC decided to discontinue professional education in ministry, members of the religion faculty ceded their building, endowment, and most of their library, and moved 40 miles east to the town of Claremont. The first classes at the Southern California School of Theology at Claremont (which became Claremont School of Theology in the mid-1990s) were taught in trailers and Quonset huts. From this hardscrabble beginning, graduate education in pastoral care and counseling grew and has flourished in Claremont.[1]

This essay describes enduring features of and emerging directions in Claremont's approach to formation for pastoral counselors. While some aspects of our story are idiosyncratic, the history we convey is also communal, the story of all those who embrace the rewards, continuities, changes, and dilemmas involved in formation for pastoral counseling.

Those of us authoring this essay have relatively short experience of the program: Clements graduated with a Ph.D. in 1972 and joined the faculty in 1990; Greider began her service in 1991, and Lee in 2004. We are cultivating a program founded and shaped by dedicated and distinguished educators who served here long before us, including Eitzen, Howard J. Clinebell, Jr., Frank W. Kimper, Patricia Martin Doyle, and Paul Schurman. Because we have few records of the program's first five decades, we cultivated our conceptualization of the program's history through Clements' experience as Ph.D. student/graduate and through countless conversations with persons associated with the program in its earlier years. We also studied school catalogues dating from 1956 to 2006. Other Claremont veterans might disagree with our characterizations of the program, and we welcome corrections and additional perspectives.

FROM THE BEGINNING

Throughout the history of the CST program, there have been five persistent characteristics: education that synthesizes research and practice[2]; multidisciplinary study; orientation toward the margins and the marginalized; pluralism within the student body; and programmatic flexibility, with mentoring.

Education that Synthesizes Research and Practice

The hallmark of the Claremont model of formation is the integration of research and practice within the academic program. We do not simply require clinical learning, we provide it. It is impossible to overstate the importance of this commitment and project, especially because it has become somewhat rare for academic programs in pastoral care and counseling, especially Ph.D. programs, to provide both scholarly and clinical formation. Students in many doctoral programs get clinical training from sources outside their degree programs and, thus, usually from teachers other than their professors and through study not intentionally linked to their academic coursework.

The CST program has clung doggedly to another philosophy and its benefit to formation: We believe that clinical training offered within the structure of the academic program holds the greatest promise for synthesizing scholarship and caregiving, and brings immeasurable benefit to both practices. Since 1964, when CST began its sponsorship of what is now known as The Clinebell Institute, formation at Claremont has been shaped by the school's integral involvement with a pastoral counseling center. Over the years, the faculty have been directly involved in seeing clients and supervising students. From 1988 until 2005, several persons served as staff as the Institute, most notably Dr. Marie Johnson who provided clinical teaching and supervision both as clinical and executive director. Upon her retirement, Dr. Samuel Lee became executive director of the Institute and the care and counseling faculty have resumed most of the clinical teaching and supervision. Many CST students have received clinical education at the Institute, and CST professors of pastoral care and counseling have been directly involved in the life of the Institute, especially by providing clinical teaching and supervision.

CST faculty and administrators have provided academic support for this kind of teaching and learning. It has been a priority to hire and retain pastoral care and counseling professors who are proficient not only as teachers and scholars but also as clinicians. Clinical teaching has always been encouraged and rewarded, as has the faculty's practice of continuing in various types of part-time clinical practice as part of their research and professional development. This commitment is noteworthy, since faculties in theological education and religious studies are not as familiar as faculties in other professional schools–medicine or engineering, for example–with the value of relating classroom and practicum, or the danger of divorcing them. Moreover, for students, the institution-wide commitment creates a pervading ethos in which excellence in pastoral care and counseling is built on this synthetic way of being: clinicians keep up with the literature, scholars practice what they teach.

Clinical teaching occurs most intensively in a laboratory course offered every year since the founding of the program. It is required for all students specializing in pastoral care and counseling. In addition to clinical work, the course requires 3-hour weekly seminars in which students learn best counseling practices, study various clinical approaches, offer case reports and engage in case conferences, and learn from consultants from other fields (most typically theological and mental health disciplines). In addition, they receive weekly supervision individually and in small groups.

Finally, our synthesis of research and practice is strong because clinical teaching and supervision are being done by the same faculty members who are teaching the academic seminars. This allows a fluid, two-way exchange of between clinical and theoretical perspectives. Faculty guide students to utilize the theories studied in seminar as they work with clients, but also to utilize clients' responses as one means to evaluate and modify the theory. The synthesis of research and practice is extremely complicated and is always only partially attained. Still, the fact remains that CST students experience their professors as professionals who are all at once clinicians, scholars, and teachers. They work side-by-side with us, seeing how we engage the struggle to synthesize, and what synthesis looks like when embodied.

Other aspects of the program further the synthesis of research and practice. Most students specializing in pastoral care and counseling are required to take Clinical Pastoral Education as a prerequisite to enrolling in the clinical course, and students are expected (and required, if necessary) to engage in some formal form of growth in self-reflexivity (psychotherapy and/or spiritual direction, for example). Also, course assignments often call for integration, and culminating exams in the doctoral programs require demonstration of synthetic learning.

Finally, the program's emphasis on synthesis of research and practice tends to have a snowball effect. We draw students passionate about "integration" in their studies who then, by the work they do and the questions they raise, help faculty and student colleagues progress further toward synthesis. The program tends to draw faculty and students committed to teaching and learning holistically, linking pastoral care and counseling education with intellectual, pastoral, and personal growth. Closing the distance between classroom and practice is a shared goal, as is the interrelating of intellectual abilities with interpersonal skills and self-reflexivity. Claremont faculty and graduates tend to be scholarly clinicians and clinically-oriented scholars. Many Claremont graduates have become leaders in the field–as teachers, as clinicians, and in roles that require both.[3] It is counterintuitive that a relatively small program with chronically minimal financial resources would be part of such a significant contribution. However, we suspect that the program's dedication to a holistic education, synthesizing theory and practice, is a vital factor in the program's placement record–our graduates tend to be well-rounded professionals and persons.

Multidisciplinary Study

Formation in pastoral counseling requires synthesis of multiple fields of study. Thus, multidisciplinary study has been an enduring characteristic of Claremont's approach to formation in pastoral counseling. Claremont's program has emphasized multidisciplinary study of two kinds: *inter*disciplinary and *intra*disciplinary.

We emphasize interdisciplinary study for obvious reasons. Practical theology and pastoral care and counseling are by definition interdisciplinary enterprises, engaging not only theological and religious studies but also, especially, the social sciences. Pastoral counseling is widely understood to be a discipline that integrates spiritual, theological, or religious insights and approaches with those of psychology. Thus, interdisciplinary study is a relatively common element of formation in pastoral counseling.

But because pastoral counseling formation at CST happens in an academic context where theological studies and religious studies are ongoing, we can also require intradisciplinary study–further academic work in theological and religious studies, even for our students who hold degrees in those disciplines. We find it essential that pastoral care and counseling students be conversant with the literature of the so-called classical disciplines–Biblical studies, history, theology, ethics–in order that their capacity to articulate and engage caregiving from a spiritual, theological, and religious perspective will continue to mature. In the Ph.D. program, 8 of 48 units of coursework are interdisciplinary, and as many as 20 are intradisciplinary. In addition, CST faculty from diverse fields have served as consultants in the clinical course, participating in weekly case conferences.

Orientation Toward the Margins and the Marginalized

The Claremont model of formation has tended to be oriented toward the margins and the marginalized. Perhaps this tendency was birthed when David Eitzen and his religion faculty colleagues were marginalized by USC's decision to discontinue education for ministry but, undaunted, set out to make their own way–successfully, it turned out. Certainly, it is necessitated by the school's location on the Pacific Rim and within Los Angeles County, which immerses us on a daily basis in one of the most diverse gatherings of immigrants in the world. Undoubtedly, it has been fueled by our location in the western U.S. and in California–a context that has historically harbored and fashioned misfits, renegades, and trendsetters. No doubt we can also trace this characteristic in part to one of our number–Professor Howard Clinebell–who was infamous for embracing eccentric ideas that later emerged more widely and popularly.

But even without these factors, orientation toward the margins and the marginalized can be understood as a manifestation of spiritual and religious values appropriate to our calling as pastoral caregivers. It is a theological imperative, and therein rests the importance of this characteristic in Claremont's model of formation. It is a priority for us that we equip caregivers to welcome strangers and embody the biblical value of showing a preference for the disenfranchised. As the next section will describe, many of us at Claremont know the experience of being the stranger–it easily follows that we try to live out the Christian tradition's teaching that every soul matters, no matter how lost, and deserves to be sought out. Religions of all kinds teach their adherents to offer humble service to any person in need, especially to persons despised by the mainstream.

These values have manifested in different ways in the Claremont mode of formation. Students are encouraged to pursue novel ideas, if there is any chance that those ideas might benefit careseekers. Encouragement is provided in part through professors willing to teach ideas that are ahead of their time. William Clements, who studied with Clinebell and Kimper, put it this way: "Claremont students had confidence that what we were studying would 'power up' in 10-15 years." Attending to the often-marginalized population of the aging, Clements himself was a pioneer in the field of religious gerontology.[4] CST has always struggled financially and provided only modest circumstances for study–this atmosphere leads easily to teaching students how to provide counseling at the lowest possible cost and with the widest possible outreach. Whatever its origins, pastoral care and counseling formation at Claremont has tended to make space for newcomers to the field–not only new ideas but, as we discuss in the next section, new constituencies of students, new communities of careseekers, and new forms of practice.

Pluralism Within the Student Body

CST's pastoral care and counseling program has always been characterized by student diversity (including race, ethnicity, culture, theology, class and economic background, sexual identity, and age) and faculty efforts to be responsive to that diversity. Diverse students seek us out not only because they can receive clinical training, but also because of the diversity of the student body and the priority that our formation model gives to culture and particularity. We learn from one another how pastoral care and counseling contributes to justice and healing around the world.

A diverse learning community of this sort requires and provides more diversity in instruction. Especially in regard to cultural particularity, we treat our students as teachers and learn from them.[5] However, our limited capacity to meet the diverse needs of students has made it plain that we need a more diverse faculty. Therefore, we try to educate the leaders our field needs: we have been intentional through our admission policies about creating and nurturing a pluralistic body of students and graduates whose particularity and special expertise are exactly what we, future students, and many careseekers need.

Racial-ethnic, gender, and national diversities have combined with economics to significantly affect the educational atmosphere of the program. CST's struggle to establish itself financially has made it unable to provide scholarship aid to students or remuneration to faculty on par with similar schools. For example, until about ten years ago, financial aid for students in the Ph.D. program was largely nonexistent. This mattered less when students tended to be white, male and middle-class: most had to work part-time but most also had middle-class resources and access on which to rely–savings, family finances, and easy borrowing. As the student population became notably internationalized and more economically diverse, students tended to have greater financial need and fewer resources. They undertook their studies at a greater sacrifice and economic disadvantage.

Financial constraints affecting the school and the students have resulted in several characteristics of the CST program–both negative and positive. On the one hand, too many students must earn income outside the academic program, and this often has resulted in students taking longer to complete their program than is optimal. The CST faculty have traditionally worked at wages significantly below the national average and have not been able to turn to the school for program development support. On the other hand, this means we are all making sacrifices to be here, because of the kind of community and education Claremont offers. Students don't come to Claremont because we offer the best financial package. They are here because they choose Claremont–often over a better offer elsewhere–as the best place for their education. In a way, the same is true for faculty–we are enticed to come here and stay not for financial reasons but because of the diverse community and creative atmosphere. Thus, faculty and students together tend to have strong ties to the program, chiefly out of love for the opportunity to learn amid diversity.

Programmatic Flexibility, with Mentoring

A fifth long-term characteristic of the Claremont model emerges so obviously in relation to the previous four characteristics that it needs only brief mention. If students are to attend to the many aspects of formation that we have discussed–learning that consistently seeks synthesis of research and practice, is multidisciplinary, responsive to the margins and marginalized, and tailored to their diverse contexts–then our programs have had to offer flexibility within an overall structure of study. This flexibility enables students to make the best use of faculty resources at all the educational institutions at Claremont in order to move toward their particular goals. The freedom to choose means that Claremont students can turn to any professor where faculty expertise is aligned with the student's need. When used well, the responsibility to design their own programs speeds students' progress toward being mature scholar-clinicians. Support of students through programmatic flexibility is one way Claremont acknowledges the limits of its faculty's contextual expertise and seeks to empower students to develop creative programs of study that extend our field into new ideas and divergent contexts.

Mentoring, thus, is a hallmark of the program, especially the doctoral programs. The flexibility of the programs requires the student to take initiative at many junctures to seek consultation with faculty. But if they do so, faculty strive to be accessible and responsive–indeed, we commit ourselves to generous accessibility and responsiveness as some offset to CST's modest financial resources! We mentor students regarding formal program requirements, of course. However, we also mentor students through the inevitable vocational and spiritual questions prompted by graduate study. We offer regular informal teaching for professional development–for example, personal introductions to the guilds and colleagues in other schools, mock interviews and practice sessions for paper presentations, and guidance for publication of papers. We also participate with students to develop among us a professionally social community.

NOW, AND TOWARD THE FUTURE

In this section we discuss two significant developments in our model of formation that embody some variation relative to the program's earliest emphases: (1) broadening practices in pastoral care and counseling through adding placements, leadership, and approaches; and (2) re-focusing on soul-care. The more recent history of the program that follows suggests how, in the last 15 years, these two new emphases emerged in relation to one another.

In the 1980s, a series of factors began to shift the identity of the program in significant ways. Clements recalls that when he arrived at the program in 1969, almost all the students planned to be full-time clinicians and graduated to full-time employment in the pastoral counseling centers springing up throughout the U.S. or in other clinical settings. But since the mid-1970s, especially because many theological schools began to add faculty positions in pastoral care and counseling, the Claremont program had slowly become a major supplier of faculty for schools in and beyond theological education.[6] By the 1980s, many students came to the Ph.D. program wanting formation for academic careers. In addition to preparing future faculty members to be clinicians and clinical teachers, the program now needed to attend to formation in a range of new areas: for example, pedagogy, publication, and participation in academic guilds and institutions.

Then, in the late 1980s, the state of California restricted eligibility for taking mental health licensing examinations. Graduates from CST had been eligible to take the licensing exam in marriage and family therapy (MFT). That option was revoked, unless the program became a state-accredited program in MFT. Not wanting to lose its identity as a program in pastoral counseling, CST decided against becoming an MFT program. Of course, this decision was made easier by the fact that licensure was more or less irrelevant to a growing percentage of students: given the internationalization of the pastoral care and counseling student body, and the increasing focus on preparation for teaching, the program had new priorities. Besides, with the bureaucracy of managed care beginning to emerge and benefit levels sinking, licensing was no panacea for the eligible clinicians.

An additional factor was at play: some important limitations of pastoral counseling–at least as it had developed in the late 20th century–were becoming increasingly obvious and problematic. On the one hand, amid growing awareness of cultural differences, the limitations of the westernized psychotherapeutic model that had dominated pastoral counseling were becoming clearer. While of enormous value in the cultural context in which it originated, in other contexts it was excessively individualized, unable to distinguish differing cultural standards for wellness, and likely to be shame-inducing. On the other hand, amid growing interest in spirituality, it was becoming increasingly obvious that pastoral counseling had largely lost touch with its roots in soul-care. The differences between pastoral psychotherapy and other forms of mental health care were negligible, or at least difficult to articulate.

Thus, when Clements and Greider joined the CST faculty in the early 1990s, the program was at a significant turning point. Our first effort to respond to these issues and changes was to diversify placements in pastoral counseling centers. For the first time in the history of the program, students were placed at two additional centers, mostly in the hope that they would see a more diverse clientele, especially in regard to race/ethnicity. Though it was beneficial that students were exposed to additional supervisors and colleagues in those additional settings, the diversity of clientele was not significant, nor was there much diversity in therapeutic approach–long-term pastoral psychotherapy was the norm (which probably contributed to the minimal diversity in clientele).

Our second efforts were directed at providing training options that diversified the clinical practices themselves, especially leaning more toward pastoral care. In the mid-1990s, we added two "tracks" to the clinical training possibilities. In addition to the pastoral psychotherapy track, we have a track for CPE supervisors-in-training: some elements of the certification process required by ACPE meet requirements for our Ph.D. Another track we call "clinical pastoral care": students can propose a variety of clinical training options in line with traditions of soul-care, such as combining multiple units of CPE, or completing a program in spiritual direction. This effort was moderately more successful: we attracted students interested in chaplaincy and chaplaincy supervision and thus our community of practitioners was diversified. Symbolically, after this change was in place, we changed the nomenclature used to refer to our field: after 50 years of being the CST program in pastoral counseling, we designated ourselves the CST program in pastoral *care and* counseling.

The arrival of Lee in 2004 has advanced our effectiveness enormously. His presence does not merely increase our staffing, as crucial as that is, given that we lost a position in the 1980s and have, on average, 25 students in the Ph.D. program alone. More important, his presence finally increases the racial-ethnic diversity of the pastoral care and counseling faculty. This is a long-overdue and necessary development, given the racial-ethnic and national diversity of our student body and our significant number of Korean students. His knowledge and skill have led to immediate programmatic improvements.

First, while we continue to provide pastoral psychotherapy training through the Clinebell Institute, Lee has implemented new placements where clinical practice is broadened in terms of setting, supervisor, and approach. His initial efforts assisted us to provide more appropriate formation for our Korean and Korean American students. He initiated pastoral counseling placements in Korean congregations, where some of the care and counseling happens in the Korean language. This new setting, and Lee's capacity to provide culturally-informed, Korean-language supervision and other leadership, has meant our Korean students have been able to experiment with approaches appropriate to the Korean context. They are "counseling ministers" who provide educative and small-group approaches as well as more classic psychotherapeutic approaches. Few Korean congregants would come to a pastoral counseling center, especially one without Korean leadership; now, they can access the help of a specialist in pastoral care and counseling in the familiar location of their church and in their native language (whether that is Korean or English). The benefits to Korean students are immeasurable: these counseling ministers now have waiting lists, some of their caregiving happens as needed in the Korean language, and Lee provides supervision rich in Korean cultural and linguistic nuance.

Second, Lee is designing other new settings and utilizing fresh approaches to pastoral counseling. Congregational placements are now being sought in congregations beyond the Korean context. This year an African American student who is pastor of a church on Skid Row is exploring ways to make pastoral counseling appropriate for and accessible to its homeless and low-income constituency. Also this year, Lee has implemented pastoral care and counseling placements in community service agencies where spiritual care is welcomed. Some students are providing spiritual care at a residential home for boys. Other students provided spiritual care, family, counseling, and other leadership at a family service agency operated by a congregation through use of government funds.

In all their placement settings, Lee is encouraging students to explore approaches that are preventative, oriented as much toward health as illness, and psycho-educational in style—and all of these qualities lead to counseling with broader cultural appropriateness. Especially he has been building collaborative relationships with other agencies involved in the burgeoning movement of marriage education (e.g., the Smart Marriages Conference fueled by the U.S. government's Compassion Capital Fund). The efficacy of clinically and individually-based marriage counseling has been questioned by many clinicians in recent years. In the marriage education movement, professionals teach laypersons to serve as facilitators of the marriage education, which serves as an important reminder that care and counseling do not have to be monopolized by licensed clinicians. Marriage education in the context of local congregations helps our training program to become more relevant for the local congregations' caring ministry.

Whatever their placements, students meet together in the clinical course and learn from the diverse settings, supervisors, approaches, and clientele in which care of souls is being learned and offered. Thus, Clements' and Greider's 15-year dream is becoming reality: as a service center, The Clinebell Institute provides pastoral psychotherapy, but as a training center, it is a hub for formation in a variety of settings, with the oversight of diverse supervisors, and for diverse practices of pastoral care, counseling, and psychotherapy.

A thread throughout all these developments is that we have been returning attention to our roots in pastoral care. As the diversity of our applicants and students has increased, and as the clamor for spiritual growth and nurture grows, our formation is centered more on rooting ourselves in study and practices related to soul-care. Students from underrepresented communities are more likely to be related to congregations and invested in utilizing spiritual, theological, and religious resources explicitly for their caregiving. But students of all cultures are more and more likely to be seeking clinical training that is less psychologized and caregiving that is more holistic. Our diverse students—seminarians, congregational pastors, chaplains, CPE supervisors, spiritual directors, other religious leaders, "secular" therapists, Christians and persons of other affiliations–tend to want clinical training not in psychotherapy but in spiritual care. Our teaching is getting re-centered in religious, theological, and spiritual resources that assist careseekers (and caregivers) to move beyond emotional growth to spiritual maturity, from health to abundant life.[7] In a program that had historically concentrated on the literature and methods of pastoral counseling and psychotherapy, the literature of pastoral theology and care is becoming co-equal.

Our students work in the most religiously diverse region of the world. Pastoral care and counseling faculty at Claremont can no longer assume that all our students are Christian, much less than that their careseekers will be Christian. Because CST itself is slowly becoming interreligious and not only ecumenical, and our students live and work in environments that are multireligious and not parochial, we are in the process of learning to conceptualize, teach, and practice spiritual care as much as pastoral care. We understand that this new terminology is in some ways problematic. However, we do not have the luxury of turning away from those problems but rather must work them out in day-to-day research and practice. Our changing constituency is challenging the parochial aspects of our pastoral care and yearning for religiously multifaceted spiritual growth, guided by soulful healers educated not only in theological studies but also in religious studies. Many CST students are preparing to offer soul-care outside Christian contexts: the therapists who come to study human spiritual growth so as to better understand their clientele, the Hindu and Buddhist students preparing to care for the souls of their communities, and the Christian student with a vocation for chaplaincy in public institutions–they all compel our nonpartisan response. Responsible faculty practice requires us to reach for new language, concept, and practice that form broad rubrics within which all our students can find themselves and the human souls in their care.

We also understand that those of us who have been formed in the Christian tradition do not simply shuck off the particulars of our traditions by changing our rhetoric from religion to spirituality. For this reason, we are enormously encouraged that the School of Religion at Claremont Graduate University is evolving beyond its focus on Christianity to hire faculty and develop programs in additional religious traditions–most recently, faculty have been hired and masters programs have been developed in Islamic Studies and Jewish Studies. Increasingly, we are encouraging our students to use their cognate requirements to study a religion other than their own and to study spiritual care as well as pastoral care. Always, we make our classrooms laboratories in which faculty and students teach one another from the perspective of their diverse spiritual, theological, and religious locations. In all these ways, we are at work building theory and practice for the interreligious soul care that, for us, is the logical and mandatory outcome of commitment to religious diversity. For us, these are the necessary implications of the communal-contextual paradigm that we claim as a primary standard and vision for our work.

While it is outside the scope of this essay to discuss the particulars, our colleagues in religious education have faced parallel challenges and been changing in similar ways. Thus, it is telling to note a development that is both substantive and symbolic: in 2005, we changed the nomenclature of the Ph.D. program we offer jointly. The change from "Ph.D. in Theology and Personality" to "Ph.D. in Practical Theology" is the culmination of a reformation of the program that has been in progress as the current generation of faculty has exerted its influence. One of our colleagues in religious education, Carol Lakey Hess (1998), offers a description of practical theology that suggests its appropriateness as a language and conceptualization for our work:

> Practical theology involves the process of shaping and enacting a religious vision for life practice. Those engaged in practical theology draw upon theological tradition, cultural wisdom (including the various sciences), religious practices, and the realities of life to shape their vision. . . . Practical theology is not, however, only an academic discipline; it is also a phenomenon rooted in communities of faith. (p. 51)

Lakey Hess's conceptualization suggests the themes that have been discussed in this essay as critical in pastoral care and counseling formation at Claremont. We are educating caregivers to guide persons toward emotional health but also toward a religious vision, however their community understands it. We are educating scholars to draw on theology in tandem with other resources, especially cultural wisdom. We are educating future teachers and caregivers to engage the realities of life as much from the perspectives of the communities with which we are in service as from the perspectives of the individuals by which they are comprised.

CLAREMONT FORMATION SUMMARIZED: CURRENT REALITIES, QUESTIONS FOR THE FUTURE

In a position paper prepared to provoke discussion about formation within the American Association of Pastoral Counselors, pastoral theologian Joretta Marshall (2005) offers a description of formation in pastoral counseling. Some of the questions raised by her description serve well to shape a succinct summary of Claremont's intentions in forming spiritual caregivers and pastoral counselors: Who is being (or "should" be) formed? To what end are we being formed? By what paths are we being formed? What common elements make our practices distinctively "pastoral counseling?" To her questions we add a fifth, which is our starting place: Why should we be formed?

Why should we be formed? At Claremont, we devote ourselves to formation because so many communities and the persons in them–Christians and many others–feel insufficiently related to sacred reality's many dimensions. Both within and beyond religion's bounds, they are seeking spiritual leaders and caregivers for assistance. What assistance do they seek? They seek, and we seek to form, spiritual leaders and caregivers who, in their particular way of being, synthesize and embody the human wisdom, especially holy traditions, necessary to heal illness but also to increase soulfulness, a just peace, and joy in living (Greider, 2005). It is to these ultimate ends that we are being formed–toward the capacity to assist those seeking to cultivate, both communally and personally, greater relatedness, justice, integrity, and profundity, whatever their spiritual location and/or religious location. Who is being formed? Because the human hunger for the sacred is found around the world, we seek to form a learning community that is internationalized, professionally diverse, and otherwise pluralistic. We need such a community, since knowledge adequate for cultural multiplicity is beyond the scope of any one teacher or school. In our community, teachers and students as collaborative inquirers learn from one another how to work in multicultural and intercultural modes with the diverse communities and careseekers who are seeking to form and reform themselves spiritually.

By what paths are we being formed? We embrace a communal-contextual paradigm not only in caregiving but in formation, in which pastoral psychotherapy is but one path among others toward formation as a pastoral counselor. These multiple pathways–such as preventative and educational counseling in faith-based contexts, facilitation of caregiving by congregations, clinical spiritual care, counseling in religious contexts other than westernized Christianity–necessarily indigenize and diversify the practices of pastoral counseling.[8] They also raise disconcerting questions about identity, standards, and accountability, and the answers to those questions are for the foreseeable future elusive. For now, the question of common elements centers us amid the turmoil in the field, because it yields values that guide us through this time of transition. The question is far beyond the scope of this essay, so our succinct summary is only suggestive: what makes counsel distinctively pastoral? For Claremont, care is pastoral–or spiritual–insofar as:

- It affirms the mutuality of the search for soul by both caregivers and careseekers.
- It centers on questions of power, meaning, values, and ethics.
- It honors ambiguity and values questions as much as answers.
- It strives to incarnate the sacred/holy/ultimate/G-D.
- It enhances relatedness to the sacred in all spheres of existence.
- It is holistic–responsive to interrelatedness and particularity.
- It embraces the margins and the marginalized.
- It cares for the sake of creating a just peace.
- It values human limitation as well as human growth.
- It is representative of and rooted in the spiritual search of a community.
- It builds on historical traditions of care of souls.
- It takes initiative in offering help.
- It provides universal, non-profit service.

CONCLUSION

After noting the early pioneers in graduate education, Liston Mills noted a difference between the established graduate programs in his field. Some programs, he observed, focus on the "professional service [of pastoral care and counseling] in relation to the church . . . and so emphasize clinical competence within a theological orientation as the goal of their work." Programs of a second kind "do not neglect the professional task," but, he noted, their "primary agenda . . . is to establish the field of pastoral theology in the world of scholarship and research." Emphasizing that he did not wish to draw the distinction too sharply, Mills (1990) located Claremont in the first group–the programs that "emphasize clinical competence within a theological orientation" (p. 866). When Mills wrote the entry in the late 1980s, his characterization was reasonably accurate.

But it is interesting to note that Claremont is no longer able to make the choices Mills' categories suggest were possible less than 15 years ago. Pastoral clinical service loses its moorings and otherwise grows ineffective if it does not interact with pastoral theology and the traditional disciplines of theological education–but also, as Mills, notes, a whole *world* of scholarship. Being a practical theological discipline, pastoral theology's integrity rests on it being a "phenomenon rooted in communities" as much as an establishment within academe. Both clinical pastoral care and academic pastoral theology are being beckoned beyond our relation to the church–by people whose spiritual lives have been damaged by the Christian, grown in and beyond other religious traditions, gone cold, or never been ignited. The emphases and trends described in this essay are Claremont's way of navigating pastoral care and counseling's honorable past, turbulent present, and emergent future.

NOTES

1. The general reference to "Claremont" is intentional and meaningful. The city of Claremont is home to 8 institutions of higher education, and pastoral care and counseling students can make use of faculty and library resources at all these schools: not only Claremont School of Theology (www.cst.edu) but also Claremont Graduate University (www.cgu.edu), Keck Graduate Institute (www.kgi.edu), and five undergraduate schools–Claremont McKenna, Harvey Mudd, Pitzer, Pomona, and Scripps–often collectively referred to as "the Claremont Colleges" (www.claremont.edu).

2. The impossibility of separating theory and practice is betrayed by the difficulty of finding language adequate for distinguishing between the two. In this essay we will use "research," "academics," "theory," and "scholarship" somewhat interchangeably to refer to the most abstract aspects of our work. We will use "practice," "clinical," "professional," and "caregiving" somewhat interchangeably for the most concrete aspects of our work.

3. A small sampling of this multifaceted influence is found in the contributors list for the *Handbook for Basic Types of Pastoral Care and Counseling* (Stone and Clements, 1991), edited and written by Claremont faculty and graduates, in honor of Clinebell's retirement. The graduates published in that book include: Robert H. Albers; Hunter Beaumont; Carolyn J. Stahl Bohler; William M. Clements; Harold T. Kriesel; Merle R. Jordan; Bridget Clare McKeever; Masamba Ma Mpolo; Christie Cozad Neuger; James Newton Poling; Charles L. Rassieur; Howard W. Stone; R. Scott Sullender; David K. Switzer; and Robert W. Wohlfort.

4. Clements was the founding editor of the *Journal of Religious Gerontology*, the editor of *Religion, Aging, and Health: A Global Perspective* (1989) which was compiled by the World Health Organization, and the editor of *Ministry with the Aging: Foundations, Challenges and Designs* (1981), which has been in print for 25 years and is the winner of several awards.

5. K. Samuel Lee (2002) calls this relationship "collaborative inquirers." Lee worked with the Multicultural Competencies Task Force of the Association of Clinical Pastoral Education (ACPE) from 2001 to 2005 to develop multicultural competencies for CPE training, standards, and policies, the recommendation of which was adopted in 2004 by its governing board. Samuel Lee received the ACPE's 5th International Net-

work Award for his contributions. Howard Clinebell was the first recipient of the same award.

6. A sampling of schools served by Claremont graduates: Bangor Theological Seminary; Berea College; Boston University School of Theology; Brite Divinity School; Church Divinity School of the Pacific; Colgate-Rochester Crozer Divinity School; Emory University School of Medicine; Fuller Theological Seminary; Garrett Evangelical Theological Seminary; Hanshin University (Korea); Hubert Kairuki Memorial University (Tanzania); Lexington Theological Seminary; Loma Linda University; Luther Seminary; Lutheran Theological Seminary at Gettysburg; Memphis Theological Seminary; Methodist Theological School in Ohio; Methodist Theological Seminary (Korea); Perkins School of Theology; Southern Illinois Medical School; Stillman College; Theological College of North Nigeria; United Theological Seminary (Dayton); United Theological Seminary of the Twin Cities; Universidad Methodista de Sao Paulo (Brazil); Carver School of Medicine, University of Iowa; University of Arizona College of Medicine; University of Kinshasa (Zaire); University of Winnipeg (Canada); Virginia Theological Seminary; Waterloo Lutheran Seminary (Canada); Wesley Theological Seminary; and Yale Divinity School.

7. The pediatrician and psychoanalyst Donald Winnicott (1971) observed to clinicians that "you may cure your patient and not know what it is that makes him or her go on living. It is of first importance for us to acknowledge openly that absence of psychoneurotic illness may be health, but it is not life" (p. 100). Spiritual care, including pastoral care, seems to us to be directed toward accompanying people beyond cure to the abundance of meaning that makes life not only livable, but worth living. In the Christian tradition, "abundant life" is a metaphor for a rich and soulful life. Cf. John 10:10.

8. Emmanuel Y. Lartey (2004) differentiates between exporting Western theory and practice (globalization), intercultural dialogue about the relevance of Western theory and practice in non-Western contexts (internationalization), and the reconsideration and use in ministry of theory and practice indigenous to non-Western contexts (indigenization).

REFERENCES

Clements, W. (1981). *Ministry with the Aging: Foundations, Challenges and Designs.* San Francisco: Harper and Row.

Clements, W. (1989). *Religion, Aging, and Health: A Global Perspective.* New York: The Haworth Press, Inc.

Greider, K. J. (2005). Nonviolent Conflicts and Cultural Differences: Essentials for Practicing Peace. In Ellen Marshall, (Ed.), *Choosing Peace Through Daily Practice.* Cleveland, Ohio: Pilgrim Press.

Lakey Hess, C. (1998). Becoming Midwives to Justice: A Feminist Approach to Practical Theology. In D. M. Ackermann and R. Bons-Storm, (Eds.), *Liberating Faith Practices: Feminist Practical Theologies in Context.* Leuven: Peeters.

Lartey, E. Y. (2004). Globalization, Internationalization, and Indigenization of Pastoral Care and Counseling. In N. J. Ramsay, (Ed.), *Pastoral Care and Counseling: Redefining the Paradigms* (pp. 87-108). Nashville: Abingdon Press.

Lee, K. S. (2002) The Teacher-Student in Multicultural Theological Education: Pedagogy of Collaborative Inquiry. *Journal of Supervision and Training in Ministry,* vol. 22.

Marshall, J. L. "Some Thoughts on Formation, Theological and Social Concerns, Certification, Training and Supervision, Recruitment, Retention, Revitalization, and the American Association of Pastoral Counselors." unpublished paper, April 2005.

Mills, L. (1990). Pastoral Theology, Graduate Education. In R. Hunter (Gen. Ed.), *Dictionary of Pastoral Care and Counseling*. Nashville: Abingdon Press, 1990.

Stone, H. W. and Clements, W. M. (Eds.). (1991). *Handbook for Basic Types of Pastoral Care and Counseling*. Nashville: Abingdon Press.

Winnicott, D. W. (1971). *Playing and Reality*. London: Tavistock Publications.

doi:10.1300/J062v08n03_13

A Model of Formation:
The Virginia Institute of Pastoral Care

Hunter R. Hill, DMin
Bonnasue, PhD
Dennett C. Slemp, STM
W. Victor Maloy, DMin

SUMMARY. This article presents the model of formation at the Virginia Institute of Pastoral Care (VIPCare). It begins with an historical recounting of how we have arrived at the present moment, moves to a description of VIPCare's present practices, and closes with a brief speculative look into the future. As a metaphorical narrative for this historical consideration, we offer a prime religious metaphor for journey and formation: the Exodus narrative. Within it, we find themes similar to the ones encountered by VIPCare over the past 39 years of its existence: initial security, emerging threat, wandering, wilderness times of lengthy confusion, followed by growing clarity, the sustaining providence of God, and finally the mixed reports of a Promised Land lying before us. doi:10.1300/J062v08n03_14 *[Article copies available for a fee from The Haworth Document Delivery Service: 1-800-HAWORTH. E-mail address: <docdelivery@haworthpress.com> Website: <http://www.HaworthPress.com> © 2006 by The Haworth Press, Inc. All rights reserved.]*

[Haworth co-indexing entry note]: "A Model of Formation: The Virginia Institute of Pastoral Care." Hill, Hunter R. et al. Co-published simultaneously in *American Journal of Pastoral Counseling* (The Haworth Pastoral Press, an imprint of The Haworth Press, Inc.) Vol. 8, No. 3/4, 2006, pp. 197-207; and: *The Formation of Pastoral Counselors: Challenges and Opportunities* (ed: Duane R. Bidwell, and Joretta L. Marshall) The Haworth Pastoral Press, an imprint of The Haworth Press, Inc., 2006, pp. 197-207. Single or multiple copies of this article are available for a fee from The Haworth Document Delivery Service [1-800-HAWORTH, 9:00 a.m. - 5:00 p.m. (EST). E-mail address: docdelivery@haworthpress.com].

KEYWORDS. Training center and program, pastoral counseling history, Exodus narrative, integration, being and being with

Assuming that a pastoral counselor engages in a life-long process of formation, it can be posited that "history" is not nearly as much about *what* happened as about *who* happened. This is not to suggest, of course, that *what* happened is unimportant or to be minimized; it is rather to indicate that identity as shaped by events has the potential to move a pastoral counselor ever closer to a divine-human encounter and/or an encounter between two fellow pilgrims. For the pastoral counselor, then, history may be said to lean toward the relational.

THE PAST AS PROLOGUE

"Good Enough" Egypt

Near the end of the Joseph narrative in the Genesis account (see chapters 46-50), Jacob and his descendants found that while Egypt was not ideal by any means, it served as a place where good happened to them. They received from Pharaoh " . . . the best of the land of Egypt" and were told to "enjoy the fat of the land." They were advised by Joseph to say to Pharaoh that they were shepherds. Since shepherds were needed to attend to Pharaoh's livestock and were at the same time "abhorrent to the Egyptians," their settlement in Goshen, far from the courts of troublesome power, would be assured. To sum up, Egypt was seen as a "good-enough" place to be.

The early days of formation at VIPCare were similarly far from ideal. The program was male dominated, housed in space neither attractive nor especially conducive for learning, with cast-off furniture and carpet held together in places by duct tape. Consistent with the times in a Southern tobacco-growing culture, tobacco aromas wafted through the morning air, and meetings took place in smoke-filled rooms with non-smokers expected to make the best of it. However, what the VIPCare program did have–apparently since near its beginning in 1967–was what has been called "an immersion model" of training. In large measure this immersion model arose from the culture of Clinical Pastoral Education. Most of the earliest VIPCare staff members were CPE supervisors. They brought with them a deliberate, intentional focus on the relational as well as on the practices of engagement and encounter as cornerstones of the training process for students. The connection with CPE was recognized institutionally as VIPCare moved toward becoming an accredited ACPE training center.

Specific elements in the immersion model developed simultaneously at many pastoral counseling centers during the 1960s and 1970s. VIPCare's program, with its strong emphasis on clinical training, included heavily supervised client work (usually tape-recorded) with counter-transference receiving a major focus, intense residency training programs, peer group meetings with a full time staff member providing facilitation, participation in staff meetings, reading assignments, and participation in interdisciplinary case conferences/staffings. The expectation was that trainees and staff would move toward certification as Member, Fellow or Diplomate in the American Association of Pastoral Counselors (AAPC). Participation in AAPC's regional and national meetings was strongly encouraged. Students positively experienced this formation process by using words such as: "intense," "transforming," "sometimes painful," "the stuff of engagement," "incarnational," and "both gracefully supportive and deeply challenging."

Two additional realities impacted VIPCare's training and formation program in her earlier years. The towering presence and charism of William B. Oglesby, Jr., cannot be overestimated. Bill's "main job" was as Professor of Pastoral Counseling at Union Theological Seminary in Virginia. Yet from VIPCare's birth, Bill saw to it that he faithfully attended staff meetings as well as engaged in supervision of staff and students whenever possible. Although he never counseled a VIPCare client, Bill was on the part-time staff, served as an unofficial consultant to the Institute and was a member of the Board of Directors and an early president of the Board. He assisted VIPCare in developing and strengthening its ties with Union Seminary as well as with AAPC. In his role, Bill helped create and maintain a culture of thinking theologically, pedagogically, and psychologically, drawing on his wealth of story, humor, and a profoundly humane understanding of the biblical text. Moreover, through Bill, VIPCare staff and students were introduced to other significant persons in the pastoral counseling movement, such as Carroll Wise and Seward Hiltner. Until his death in 1994, Bill was, simply put, leaven to VIPCare's educational and institutional dough.

Beginning in the mid-seventies, a second reality serving to deepen VIPCare's theological and institutional roots was VIPCare's relationship with Garrett Evangelical Theological Seminary located on the campus of Northwestern University in Evanston, Illinois. During the seventies, several graduates of Garrett's Ph.D. program in Pastoral Counseling became members of the VIPCare staff for varying lengths of time. Beginning in the fall of 1981, Garrett developed a D.Min. in Pastoral Counseling, and VIPCare became one of the training centers for that program. With the retirement of Jim Ashbrook from the Garrett faculty, one of VIPCare's staff members began to teach Ashbrook's signature course, the History and Theory of Pastoral Care and Counseling, thus maintaining VIPCare's and Garrett's partnership of theological reflection, clinical focus, and appreciation of the historical roots of pastoral counseling.

In sum, the tapestry that was the "formation process" at VIPCare in its earlier years included strong threads woven together into a rich design. There were institutional threads from ACPE, AAPC, and theological institutions (i.e., Union and Garrett seminaries). There were the threads of educational philosophy, including the emphasis on experiential learning and the relational practices of supervision, encounter and engagement. There were threads produced by a culture of theological and Biblical reflection on clinical, policy-related, and even administrative matters. There were threads of mentoring and learning by being in the presence of and being impacted by the personhood of early pioneers in the pastoral counseling movement. "Things" seemed good enough, indeed.

Pharaohs Who Knew Not Joseph

At the beginning of the book of Exodus it is noted that although Joseph, his siblings and all his generation died off, the Israelites thrived nonetheless and "grew exceedingly strong" all in a place identified as merely "good enough." Similarly, despite a less than idyllic existence during the late 1970s and the decade of the 1980s, VIPCare's training/formation of pastoral counselors went along in a fashion demonstrating some strength. Training programs in pastoral counseling were offered most years, with 2-3 persons in full-time residency classes. The immersion model attracted persons and provided a place for the new generations of pastoral counselors to mature alongside the older generation. But, just as troubles began for the Israelites when there arose a new pharaoh "who knew not Joseph," new realities arose on the horizon for VIPCare which pointed towards changes that would lead to years of transition and the necessity to rethink training and formation.

The first reality occurred as medical coverage emerged for medically necessary treatment, and insurance companies began to cover counseling for various mental health diagnoses. This resulted in the need for

VIPCare pastoral counselors to become qualified providers under insurance plans. A second change soon followed on the heels of the first and quickly became entangled with it as providers of service who were reimbursable by third-party payers needed to become licensed. These two new realities–making provision for clients to use insurance and VIPCare staff becoming licensed by the Commonwealth of Virginia–arose pharaoh-like to provide complexities not anticipated.

Initially VIPCare leadership and staff held serious reservations about moving towards becoming qualified providers. Because of the state's role in licensure there was a concern about potential violation of the separation of church and state. Similarly, there was a concern that a move towards licensure would involve a subtle eroding of pastoral identity and was perhaps to be likened to selling one's birthright for a bowl of lentils. Through discussion and consultation with colleagues who had been licensed with no apparent deleterious effects on pastoral identity, VIPCare realized that the decision we faced was in large measure a theological one involving stewardship of clients' resources. With a theologically based understanding of stewardship and the awareness that the licensing process in Virginia appeared to have no diminishing effect on pastoral identity, VIPCare moved to accept third-party payments and required that full-time staff become licensed while part-time staff were encouraged to do so.

VIPCare's position eventually resulted in difficulty for trainees in pastoral counseling who did not meet the qualifications needed to enable clients to make use of their insurance benefits when seeing trainees. While the training program was originally designed to generate income adequate to cover training expenses as well as small stipends for trainees, it became clear that it could no longer be self-sustaining because of the lack of clients who paid for services outside of third-party payments. In the early 1990s, the training program was painfully and reluctantly terminated.

Wandering in the Wilderness

With the ending of the full-time residency training and formation program, VIPCare entered its Wilderness Time. Educational training at VIPCare did, however, continue. Two programs–a part-time internship and a part-time Certificate program–carried forward some of the emphasis from the earlier full-time residency program. During this time of transition, training at VIPCare gradually moved in a direction of focusing on academic credit for pastoral counseling students. Wanting to be responsive to the new cultural realities impinging on students, including the need for licensure in order to make a living, VIPCare partnered with the School of Theology at Virginia Union University, a historically African-American seminary, in offering courses for academic credit.

As formation shifted to a stronger focus on academics, there was a concomitant shift away from one of the strongest components of VIPCare's formation tradition, namely that of the individual supervision of students' work with clients. While VIPCare still emphasized the importance of such supervision, many students found it very difficult to locate the additional time and funds to take this important step. Despite VIPCare's efforts to carry forward the emphases from the "immersion model," intensive formation remained missing in the new situation. VIPCare wandered as did the Israelites, with the vision of a Promised Land of pastoral shaping mostly grieved rather than realized.

THE PRESENT MOMENT

Approximately five to six years ago, several factors coalesced to produce both a nadir and the impetus to move forward. As VIPCare continued to evaluate educational programs and offerings, staff members began to make a series of observations. First, we noted that while the pastoral *care* skills track was going great, our pastoral *counseling* track seemed to be attracting students who were less motivated, less capable of competence and less mature than needed. Along with some diminishing of pastoral counselor identity and function, the *numbers* of graduates from our pastoral counseling track was declining and VIPCare staffers noticed our own aging staff. Unless VIPCare found some way to shape yet again another generation of competent, theologically and clinically grounded men and women, the nature, culture and ministry of VIPCare would inexorably change in ways that seemed not at all for the better. That this could happen at a time when persons needed help to make meaning in life and, in the words of a Katrina Hurricane survivor, to "not allow suffering to be wasted" was contrary to VIPCare's belief that suffering is instead to be redeemed into compassionate and graceful acceptance of self and others, the community of God's beloved.

From the perspective of hindsight it can be argued that these providential and sobering realizations and observations arose inevitably because this is part of what Wilderness Wanderings do to folks. The wanderings succeeded in birthing a time of conscious confusion and hunger. Now, the Wanderings were entering the stage of calling forth a time (kairos) of clarity and knowing *what* VIPCare was hungry for in its educational programs.

Several steps assisted in making the way gradually clearer. A group at VIPCare was formed to look into AAPC's vision of formation and to contact other AAPC-approved training centers to learn about changes that had occurred in training and formation across contexts. Strategies were developed to reach seminary students interested in "counseling ministry" near the beginning of their seminary experience rather than later when they often decided to become social workers or professional counselors. The staff members began to remember and speak of their own formation processes as a way of learning from our shared and individual journeys. During one of these discussions, Catherine McCollough, then a staff member at VIPCare, spoke of "being known into being." The phrase found a home in the staff and began to gestate.

The VIPCare Internship Program was revised in an effort to offer a more intensive training experience. Although this effort could not be called very successful, important lessons were learned which found their way into the present Formation Program, including the need for a thorough screening of candidates, a rigorous interview by the full faculty, individual supervision, close monitoring of students' functions, and the need for greater personal engagement between the students and VIPCare staff. We developed a series of meetings for students to focus specifically on the integration process for students and appointed a Formation Coordinator/Mentor to work with the Director of Education in keeping formation in front of us all. To support this work, VIPCare's seminary-educated Director of Development secured small, but immensely helpful grants for this purpose.

Ongoing passionate discussions took place among the staff around the sometimes competing needs to accommodate to the more academically oriented licensure process in Virginia and to reassert a primary educational mission of raising up pastoral counselors for certification in AAPC. Some spoke of formation incarnationally, noting that the engagement and encounters of students with supervisors, clients, peers, and selves occurred best in a challenging and supportive atmosphere, as opposed to expecting it to emerge primarily through the acquisition of knowledge and academically based instruction.

During this period of clarification and creative energy, VIPCare was blessed with two visitations which served to crystallize further the direction and emerging structure of a revised formation emphasis at VIPCare. The first visitor was Bonnasue, a professor at Eastern Mennonite University, Director of their Pastoral Counseling Training Center and an AAPC Diplomate. For one day a week for nine months, Bonna-sue pitched her tent at VIPCare, seeking to come to know of VIPCare's educational program for pastoral counselors. Her contribution to VIPCare was not only a series of videos/DVDs of the VIPCare staff members reflecting on their identity and functions as pastoral counselors, but her presence and helpful nudging brought renewed engagement about formation.

A second visit was with persons representing AAPC in its periodic review of VIPCare as an accredited center. They observed that VIPCare was, metaphorically, "a vigorous specimen of a nearly extinct species" in its commitment to hire theologically trained pastoral counselors who have standing as ministers in their faith groups and who understand their work as a "calling." They affirmed VIPCare's Coordinator of Common Life as a position that nurtures the theological reflection and spiritual development of the staff. However, these visitors were cautionary, also. Their view was that in the midst of these strengths were the seeds of great challenge and that VIPCare's ongoing task was to discover ways to share its model and be generative beyond the work life of the current practitioners. VIPCare felt both supported by the affirmation and deeply challenged to continue to develop ways and means both to develop and share its model of formation.

Four foundational principles guide VIPCare's Formation Process. The intent of the process is to enable a pastoral counseling student to: (1) *integrate* theological, spiritual, clinical, psychological, and administrative aspects of pastoral counseling; (2) solidify the student's identity as a minister and pastoral counselor with an emphasis on the *being* of the student; (3) foster the student's growth in the capacity of *being with* other human beings; and (4) nurture the student's "being known into being," which has become an emphasis on the student's capacity for *openness in community.*

Building on these principles, the Formation Program seeks to enable students to: engage in a process of vocational formation and of *being* a pastoral counselor; acquire knowledge of the theological, spiritual, clinical, psychological, and administrative aspects of pastoral counseling; and become a Certified Pastoral Counselor and/or Fellow in the American Association of Pastoral Counselors. The program assumes that *being precedes doing*, and therefore formation has priority over intellectual acumen and therapeutic skill development. Intellectual acumen and therapeutic skill are highly stressed, but are seen as effective primarily when congruent with the *being* and *becoming* of the pastoral counselor using them. The Program assumes that this congruence is foundational for the personal authenticity and presence of the pastoral counselor with the client.

The VIPCare faculty remains involved in a rigorous and engaging application process. Applicants are carefully screened and must have a graduate degree in divinity, theology, biblical studies, or pastoral counseling. It is expected that each applicant is endorsed as a candidate for ministry by their denomination or judicatory and is eligible for malpractice insurance. Applicants also are required to have psychological testing, a tape and analysis of a counseling session, and a faculty interview prior to being accepted.

Once in the program, students meet monthly in a series of ten meetings with a Formation Mentor and peers. The purpose of these meetings is to assist the student with the integration process of becoming and being a pastoral counselor. Mid-year and end-of-the year interviews with faculty are scheduled for each student. The Mentor also monitors whether various responsibilities of the student are being carried out, including payment of tuition and supervision fees, the writing of weekly reflections, fulfilling of therapy requirements and attending/participating in monthly formation meetings. Additional components include academic coursework, interdisciplinary and small group continuous case conferences, semiannual formation retreats, individual supervision (60 hours over 2 years), at least 375 hours of pastoral counseling, at least 25 hours of personal psychotherapy (at least 12 during the first year), and a final integrative paper.

The syllabus design for the series of monthly meetings lays out three phases arranged to engage students both educationally and theologically. Phase I includes meetings one through five. *Educationally*, the design is that of *experiential learning* in that students are assigned to engage/encounter such things as (1) their four favorite passages from Scripture, (2) three seasoned VIPCare pastoral counselors of their own choosing, and (3) through use of DVD interview, one of the late grandparents in the pastoral counseling movement, William B. Oglesby. Following these encounters, the students reflect individually on their experiences, write about their reflections and have dialogue with their peers and the Formation Mentor during the monthly meetings. *Theologically*, concepts woven into the design of Phase I are (1) Scripture as an authoritative guide to faith and practice, (2) the centrality of incarnational realities, (3) the communion of the saints, and (4) the importance of community. While these concepts are "woven" into the design of Phase I, they may be said to be lying in wait to be brought to life by the mind and soul of the students.

Phase II includes meetings six through eight. Educationally, the design remains similar to Phase I, with the exception that the three experiences laid out for the students to engage are a novel (Margaret Craven's, *I Heard the Owl Call my Name*), a film (*The Mission*) and three formation incidents drawn from the ordinary lives of children. In writing about their reflection on these meetings, the students are asked to compare and contrast their formation processes to those of various persons or characters encountered in the novel, film and incidents. Theological issues introduced for students in these three experiences are suffering, death, trust and broken trust, crucifixion and resurrection, incarnation, power and its uses, grief, acceptance, and community.

Phase III includes meetings nine and ten. In nine, students are led, through engagement with readings and interviewing the Executive Director of VIPCare, to reflect/write/discuss how pastoral identity informs the doing of administration in a pastoral counseling agency. Meeting ten involves students in a process of reflecting on year one of their formation and consideration of what in them required attention in year two of the program.

FORMATION'S EMERGING FUTURE AT VIPCARE: APPROACHING A LAND OF MILK AND HONEY?

It is instructive that after all the wilderness wanderings of the Israelites, when the people *finally* approached "a land flowing with milk and honey" (Joshua 5:6), Joshua, the new leader of the Israelites following the death of Moses, received a message from God which could be viewed as decidedly mixed. On the one hand, God spoke resoundingly of fulfillment of long-made promises and of Presence, saying in the first chapter of Joshua such things as: "Every place that the sole of your feet will touch upon I have given to you, as I promised to Moses"; "No one shall be able to stand against you all the days of your life"; and, "As I was with Moses, so I will be with you; I will not fail you or forsake you." On the other hand, there was another, more ominous or at least reality-laden part of God's message to Joshua as we read: "Be strong and courageous"; "I hereby command you: Be strong and courageous." And if God somehow did not get through to him, the narrator of the story has Joshua hear nearly identical words from several of the tribes of Israel a bit later in the story: "Only be strong and courageous." Apparently, movement into a promised land does not diminish the need for toughness and a brave heart.

Peering into the future, it is true beyond doubt that VIPCare's Model of Formation is indeed a work in progress. It remains to be seen whether it will lead to a new generation of pastoral counselors responsive to the spiritual, emotional and psychological needs of those who suffer. It is not yet clear whether it can shape pastoral counselors for the future who can *be* and *be with* fellow pilgrims. It is still unknown whether the reality of incarnational engagement and encounter can be sustained here beyond the near future. There has not been adequate recent time to determine these things.

But we are hopeful because of the commitment of the faculty and staff to this renaissance in VIPCare's history. We are hopeful because of the deep and growing interest shown in the formation process by present students and those inquiring about the future. We are hopeful because the syllabus for year two of Formation Meetings is being developed as this article is being written. We are hopeful out of a rashness that refuses to believe we have been brought out into the desert to die.

Finally we are hopeful as we trust in the promises from the past–from the far, far past. Trusting, perhaps all necessary for formation at VIPCare to continue is to ". . . only be strong and courageous." Soon enough all will be made clear.

doi:10.1300/J062v08n03_14

Expanding the Context of Care: Formation from the Inside Out and the Outside In

Charles Mendenhall, PhD
Douglas M. Ronsheim, DMin

SUMMARY. Pastoral counseling formation can expand the context of care by moving with and beyond the clinical paradigm to embrace the communal-contextual. By creating new visions and opportunities at the boundaries of community mental health and pastoral counseling, the field is shaped by its engagement with expanded notions of care as well as shaping the cultures around us. The project described in this model is illustrative of such partnerships. doi:10.1300/J062v08n03_15 *[Article copies available for a fee from The Haworth Document Delivery Service: 1-800-HAWORTH. E-mail address: <docdelivery@haworthpress.com> Website: <http://www.HaworthPress.com> © 2006 by The Haworth Press, Inc. All rights reserved.]*

KEYWORDS. Vision, paradigms, clinical, communal-contextual, partnerships

[Haworth co-indexing entry note]: "Expanding the Context of Care: Formation from the Inside Out and the Outside In." Mendenhall, Charles, and Douglas M. Ronsheim. Co-published simultaneously in *American Journal of Pastoral Counseling* (The Haworth Pastoral Press, an imprint of The Haworth Press, Inc.) Vol. 8, No. 3/4, 2006, pp. 209-219; and: *The Formation of Pastoral Counselors: Challenges and Opportunities* (ed: Duane R. Bidwell, and Joretta L. Marshall) The Haworth Pastoral Press, an imprint of The Haworth Press, Inc., 2006, pp. 209-219. Single or multiple copies of this article are available for a fee from The Haworth Document Delivery Service [1-800-HAWORTH, 9:00 a.m. - 5:00 p.m. (EST). E-mail address: docdelivery@haworthpress.com].

The field of pastoral counseling is in transition. Steeped historically in one model of ministry (the clinical pastoral paradigm), pastoral caregivers are now pushed and pulled by another model (the communal-contextual) (Patton, 1993). Thus, clinicians and staff are located in an uneasy, transitory space; we are not comfortable standing where we were, but we are uncertain about where we are moving. Our professional identities are in flux, and we are seeking once again to discover who we are in a new place and time.

We are not, however, standing in unfamiliar territory. Psychologist Donald Winnicott (1971, 1979) spoke of "potential space" (p. 108)–the distance between infant and mother that develops as the child begins to differentiate. By its very nature, this transitional space is threatening, disruptive, and disquieting; at the same time, it is tremendously creative and generative. It is a "liminal" or "threshold" area where one perspective, lifestyle, or theoretical model blends with or crosses over into another. As such, it is a gateway from an established structure to an unsettling unknown, but also a point of potential and possibility. It is the place in which all of us who heed the call of pastoral care and counseling find ourselves in the twenty-first century.

As the context of care expands, pastoral counselors who want to optimize community health will be required to employ old skills and practices in new ways. They need to increase their awareness of their particular context, observe it fully, and act in ways that are a congruent response to what they have perceived. This is well illustrated by Families and Youth 2000, a collaborative health ministry in Pittsburgh, PA, that was heavily influenced by pastoral counselors. This article uses Families and Youth 2000 as a case study to highlight issues of formation that arise within a communal-contextual model as pastoral counselors address the expanding context of care.

CLINICAL PASTORAL PRACTICE IN THE MODERN AGE

Over the past 40 to 50 years, pastoral care and counseling has stood more or less firmly in the modern age. During this time, we all have held a generally agreed upon understanding of what constituted good therapy. Psychoanalytic and psychodynamic theories of psychic development and understandings of human behavior provided an accepted framework around which we ordered our thinking and practice. Although psychoanalytic theory evolved over these years as it was studied and articulated by a variety of teachers and supervisors in the field, the intrapsychic core held.

In the modern era, counseling focused on the emerging, self-aware ego and the psychic forces influencing its development. Care was centered on the individual as a "living human document" (Boisen, 1936) to be engaged, probed, and understood. The plan of therapy was based on the medical model of diagnosis and treatment of a disorder; this necessitated long term, one-on-one therapy, both for the good of the client and the financial stability of the pastoral counseling profession.

CHALLENGES TO THE CLINICAL PASTORAL MODEL

However, as the twentieth century moved into its final decades, financial, theoretical, cultural, regulatory and educational forces were at work to challenge the stability and viability of the clinical pastoral model for care giving. The healthcare crisis that emerged in the late 1980s brought with it managed care. Suddenly, the income from insurance reimbursements, upon which pastoral counselors and counseling centers were beginning to become dependent, became constrictive. Pastoral counselors were forced to join managed care "provider panels," which established policies that began to impact and intrude upon the therapeutic process. Referrals, reimbursements, treatment plans and length of therapy came under the control of these panels. Payments were lowered, therapy shortened, treatment plans tightened, outcomes scrutinized. The medical model for therapy took a stronger hold on the pastoral care process.

Not all of this was bad. Thoughtful reflection upon the models, practices and economics of therapy is necessary and useful. But the result for pastoral counseling was a dramatic shift in the market. An increasing number of schools began to turn out a growing number of master-level marriage and family and professional counselors, license eligible and trained for the managed care climate. Competition for clients grew. Many pastoral counseling centers hired laity, many of whom had little sense of clinical pastoral integration.

At the same time, systems theory and family therapy shifted the focus of therapy from the individual to the relational, focusing attention on what takes place between people. Narrative, solution-focused, cognitive-behavioral, and other therapeutic approaches began to crowd the once-dominant psychodynamic model. Pastoral counseling, which had begun as a white male profession, started expanding through the inclusion of women, African American, Hispanic, Asian, and other inter-cultural therapists. All of these things shook the once-stable clinical pastoral model. But it was postmodernism which began to alter the conceptualization of pastoral counseling practice and service delivery in the last decade of the twentieth century.

THE RISING COMMUNAL-CONTEXTUAL MODEL
IN A POSTMODERN AGE

The inclusion of a number of new voices in the pastoral counseling community began to lift up a new paradigm. Feminist and womanist pastoral theologians refocused pastoral care and counseling from the psyche of the individual to the community. Whereas the clinical pastoral model imagined the individual as the focus and the community as the field, the communal-contextual model moved the community to the fore and the individual to the field. The spotlight was now upon the way cultural and political contexts shape the lives of people. Gender, class, race, economics, privilege, age, sexual orientation, and religious worldview became the important factors influencing behavior and identity. New voices in pastoral counseling began to direct our attention to the complexity of the person in culture.

Whereas the clinical pastoral model focused on Boisen's "living human document," the communal-contextual model concentrated on what Bonnie Miller-McLemore (1993, 1996) identified as "the living human web"–the way we are woven together in our various communities and how our own particular place in the tapestry and the texture of the weave determine who we are and how we act. Particularity and difference–a respect for the knowledge and truth in a variety of voices–began to push against what we had traditionally held as universal diagnostic and treatment procedures. Social location became a key hermeneutic in assessing dysfunction mentally, socially, spiritually, and behaviorally. Issues of justice and the effects of power dynamics gained importance in this human web, where the essential relationality of human beings was the key ingredient of growth and development.

Intercultural influences have also had their impact. The clinical pastoral model promoted "globalization," in which Western pastoral care and counseling was imported to the non-Western world. In contrast, the communal-contextual model promotes "internationalization," a mutual exchange of pastoral care knowledge between Western and non-Western contexts. Emphasis is placed upon authentic participation of all people so that each voice can be heard.

The effects of this paradigm shift have been persistent and progressive. The clinical pastoral model's focus on caring for and developing the self in relationship is foundational to care and counseling in any context. Yet communal-contextual concerns nudge us to expand beyond a focus on ego psychology and long-term therapy. A single therapeutic modality is no longer sufficient; we are beginning to see the need to develop skills and knowledge in a multiplicity of modalities and theoretical perspectives which will provide a variety of approaches for an array of contexts.

In the process, we are being formed and informed, looking beyond our offices and stepping into the community to understand the places where people live and develop and to appreciate the specific needs and struggles they encounter. We are exploring how our particular skills and human resources can be employed in new ways in new settings. Because care and counseling knowledge is multifaceted, we are finding it helpful to collaborate with partners who have skills and knowledge we do not. We are growing more aware of the particularity of our own location on the living human web, and we are looking around to see with whom we are connected and how. We are talking more with diverse groups of people and thus expanding our understanding of ourselves and the world around us. An influx of intercultural students is stretching traditional forms of supervision and training. We are examining boundaries not only to keep issues separate and distinct, but also to see how issues interrelate and come together. In this context, there is a need for a more viable communal and contextual direction.

EXPANDING THE CONTEXT OF CARE: A CASE STUDY

"Families and Youth 2000" (F&Y 2000), a community-based collaborative project in Pittsburgh, illustrates one way that pastoral counselors can address community health while contributing to the economic stability of a pastoral counseling center. The project created a communal-contextual model of care by bringing churches, community residents, schools, a university, grassroots organizations and foundations into relationship for a common purpose. While its formal structure and delivery of services ran from 1994 to 2001, its work continues as part of the larger Faith Based Health Initiative of Greater Pittsburgh. Key elements included the creation of a distinctive and intentional community, a capacity for sustained theological reflection, and an ability to engage in *praxis*.

Participants sought broad community participation because many of the factors that affect the health and well-being of people in communities–poverty, substance abuse, environmental hazards, obesity, and inadequate access to care–cannot be solved by any person, organization, or sector working alone (Lasker and Weiss, 2003). The challenge is to bring the necessary community constituents and partners into a broad-based coalition that is truly collaborative. The interdisciplinary scope of such work creates unusual complexity; while it adds to practical and methodological wisdom, it can also fragment efforts as community members, providers of service and individual practitioners work with researchers from complementary disciplines (Lasker and Weiss, 2003). What has endured is a model of care and service that connects all participants as learners and teachers in a process of ongoing formation.

RESPONDING TO EMERGING NEEDS

The project was a comprehensive health model addressing physical, spiritual, and emotional well-being and social indicators of health in four contiguous neighborhoods in the East End of Pittsburgh. From the beginning, it sought to transform relationships between communities and health care providers as a means of increasing access to health services. Sensitizing healthcare professionals to community needs and assets, and helping them to develop culturally appropriate models of communication and health service, were viewed as ways to enhance community trust and facilitate access to care. The project reached beyond primary care and behavioral health to include pastoral counseling, mentoring, life skills training, family recreation, drug abuse interventions, addiction recovery programs, parenting skills training, peer counseling, biblical counseling, parent support groups, and entrepreneurship and economic development.

A diversity of services were critical, as African American families in the East End of Pittsburgh experienced the "double exposure" (Hartman, 1996) of race and poverty. Among 50 large American cities, "Pittsburgh had the largest percentage of black males age 25-54 not in the labor force (30%) and the largest disparity in labor force participation between black and white males age 25-54 (18%)" (Bangs and Hong, 1995). Social indicators of health in the targeted neighborhoods were declining rather than improving, and unemployment, suicide, academic failure and school suspension plagued African Americans at disproportionately high rates.

In response to this data, the collaborative's coordinated network of providers worked to promote healthy lifestyles and communities by intervening early with trained natural helpers and mentors. These helpers and mentors–youth, college students, graduate students, and professionals–provided health promotion, advocacy for access and a continuum of efforts to address emotional, physical, and spiritual well-being. Community residents educated professionals about the culture of the community and ways to eliminate barriers to effective services.

In order to succeed, project partners found that they had to integrate spirituality, develop a model of care sensitive to the community culture, provide care in community settings rather than in healthcare institutions, recognize and involve congregations, address chronic disease through health promotion and pre-primary prevention, address root causes of poor health through community organizing and policy change, and provide integrated health services regardless of a person's ability to pay. Funding sources sought partnerships between community-based organizations and institutions of higher education, leading Families and Youth 2000 to form working partnerships with the Graduate School of Public Health at the University of Pittsburgh; the University of Pittsburgh Medical School Family Residency Training Program; Shadyside Hospital; and Pittsburgh Theological Seminary.

IMPLICATIONS FOR THE FORMATION
OF PASTORAL COUNSELORS

The project carries two implications for the formation of pastoral counselors. First, pastoral counselors must be trained to use multiple perspectives in community assessment if pastoral actions are to be fully congruent with community needs. Second, pastoral counselors must be able to identify and observe isomorphic patterns that influence the efficacy of service delivery in expanded clinical contexts.

By drawing on multiple perspectives during assessment, pastoral counselors can address the "narrative, contextual, cross-disciplinary and pragmatic aspects" of postmodern pastoral care (Doehring, 2006, p. 165). Pastoral theologian Carrie Doehring (2006) suggests that this might be accomplished through a "trifocal lens" that incorporates pre-modern, modern, and postmodern epistemologies (pp. 2-6). The premodern lens glimpses the sacred "through sacred texts, religious rituals and traditions, and religious and spiritual experiences"; the modern lens draws "upon rational and empirical methods, like biblical critical methods, medical knowledge, and social sciences," while the post-modern lens "brings into focus the contextual and provisional nature of knowledge, including knowledge of God" (Doehring, 2006, p. 2). Each epistemology is distinct but does not stand alone; together, they reveal a greater whole. In order to observe fully, a caregiver needs to view a person or situation through each of these three lenses.

An additional lens used by the partners of Families and Youth 2000 was relationality. By attending carefully to the relationships of its members, the collaborative developed an expanded perspective that guided the project's capacity to monitor and correct its internal functioning in ways that facilitated productive interactions with the broader community. Indeed, the partners of F&Y 2000 were a "living model" of the community within which they worked. The issues and elements "out there" in the community (e.g., race, power, inequality, privilege, gender, etc.) also manifested "in here" in the life of the collaborative, and the ability of partners to respond differently and creatively to these elements "inside" the collaborative had everything to do with the project's health and efficacy and its capacity to offer a congruent response to community needs. The complexity of a community collaborative offers multiple points of observation from which helpful information can be gleaned to ensure the health of a collaborative in service to the health of a community. Multiple lenses are needed.

To address the ways in which community issues played out in the life of the collaborative, participants needed a way to view and understand these systemic interactions. The family therapy concept of isomorphism (Hofstadter, 1979) provided a helpful perspective. Isomorphism relates to the recursive ways in which aspects of complex structures can be "mapped onto" each other–as, for example, the structures of the collaborative partnerships in Families and Youth 2000 unintentionally corresponded with the unjust structures of the broader community. When issues of culture, control, race and trust emerged among the partners, the lens of isomorphism increased the awareness of participants and supported their capacity to teach, learn from and respond to each other. By observing isomorphic patterns, collaborative members could intentionally change their patterns of interaction–and these changes then could be "exported" to the community to enhance community health. This ability to respond rather than react became increasingly important as the collaborative and its members interacted and interfaced with groups and institutions in the broader community outside of the targeted neighborhoods.

We believe that the ability to identify, observe, and influence isomorphic patterns is a skill required of pastoral counselors involved in communal-contextual work. The integrative nature of pastoral counseling allows pastoral counselors to offer unique, corrective means of responding to recursive, isomorphic patterns–but only if they have the ability to notice and reflect on them in the first place. It is especially important that pastoral counselors be able to shape a community model of care that not only addresses isomorphic patterns present in the community, but also in the institutions that can assist in ameliorating the factors which impact the health of communities.

For the ongoing formation of pastoral counselors, then, the movement into an expanded context of care provides the opportunity and necessity to observe more fully, increase awareness, and act congruently. In a collaborative, communal-contextual model of care, the elements of observation, assessment, and action are required at the levels of both provider and client within the context of relationships with the broader community. As each level of observation is expanded–from individual, to dyads, to family, to community–the increasing complexity of patterns of interaction are seen more fully and clearly.

CONCLUSION

Expanding the context of care for pastoral counseling is about providing optimum care. It requires attention not only to the traditional therapeutic relationship, but also to a multiplicity of relationships in the larger community that impacts client care. The degree to which the formation of pastoral counselors equips them for this work will have everything to do with the health of a recipient of care and the broader community.

As illustrated by the Families and Youth 2000 project, the ongoing formation of pastoral counselors in the expanding context of care will involve exposure to practice and training in communal and interdisciplinary contexts. The processes and skills necessary to develop working partnerships in expanded contexts of care are the same skills necessary for service delivery, training and education. As the context of care expands, all professional disciplines are facing similar issues. This shared dilemma creates opportunities for pastoral counselors to develop relationships with other educational, training and service delivery institutions. Doing so will enhance the well being of individuals, families and communities.

Thus, pastoral counselors today stand at a threshold where the clinical pastoral model touches the communal-contextual model. We are in the process of being formed anew–crossing from "what is" to "what is not yet." It is a place of confusion and trial, where we make tentative steps toward new and expanded methods of caring. But it is also a place where we remember and carry forward our precious possessions–the best of what we are–as we move from our familiar clinical pastoral home to the new one which we are constructing.

In describing this sort of "in-between place," health ministry leader Gary Gunderson (2004) uses the ecological image of wetlands, where salt water and fresh water come together. In wetlands, there is no line of demarcation where salt water ends and fresh water begins. Instead, there are vast estuaries full of beauty and incredibly rich and complex life forms where fresh and salt water clash, engage each other, and engender a new creative process. In this boundary zone, life must adapt and adjust to fields of relationship and power which are seldom, if ever, clear, stable, or certain. These boundary zones can be places of conflict, where the powerful try to protect what they have from what they fear. But these boundary zones can also be places of courage, innovation, flexibility, adaptability–of newness and creative growth.

As pastoral caregivers in formation, we are roaming these boundary zones–struggling with those parts of ourselves which would protect our clinical pastoral "home" while at the same time scanning the horizon for new opportunities to connect with those in need and others who care. Our new caregiving takes on an experimental nature; projects are more likely to be research and development operations–opportunities to test and shape ideas–than well-planned and carefully executed ministries. As we engage in these experiments, we are constantly seeking and saying "yes" to what matters most–giving meaning and value and understanding to the incremental steps that we discern are the "next right things." Along the way, new structures begin to take form, structures which incorporate the best of what we have been with the most relevant and meaningful aspects of what we are embracing. This pastoral formative process is one which can excite, energize, and mobilize us and others for the changing world around us. Its rewards can be great. It is made for living betwixt and between–where we can grow and matter and make a difference. Yet, even as we step with fear, trembling, and courage into this liminal, sacred, transitional boundary zone, it is important for us to know that we are not alone. For it is these "sacred spaces" in which God's spirit tickles, calls, enlivens, empowers, connects and invites us to play with new forms of caring.

REFERENCES

Bangs, R.L., and Hong, J.H. (1995). *Black and white economic conditions in the city of Pittsburgh*. Pittsburh, PA.: University of Pittsburgh.

Boisen, A. T. (1936). *The exploration of the inner world: A study of mental disorder and religious experience*. Chicago, New York: Willett, Clark, and Co.

Couture, P. D. and Hunter, R. J. (Eds.). (1995). *Pastoral care and social conflict*. Nashville, TN: Abingdon Press.

Doehring, C. (2006). *The practice of pastoral care: A postmodern approach*. Louisville, KY: Westminster John Knox Press.

Graham, L. K. (1995). From relational humanness to relational justice: Reconceiving pastoral care and counseling. In P. D. Couture and R. J. Hunter (Eds.), *Pastoral care and social conflict* (pp. 220-234). Nashville: Abingdon.

Gunderson, G. (2004). *Boundary leaders: Leadership skills for people of faith*. Minneapolis: Augsburg Fortress Publishers.

Hartman, C. (Ed.). (1996). *Poverty and race in America*. Armonk, NY: M.E. Sharpe, Inc.

Hofstadter, D. (1979). *Godel, Escher, Bach: An eternal golden braid*. New York: Basic Books.

hooks, b. (1990). *Yearning: Race, gender, and cultural politics*. Boston: South End Press.

Lasker, R., and Weiss, E. (2003). Broadening participation in community problem solving: A multidisciplinary model to support collaborative practice and research. *Journal of urban health: Bulletin of the New York Academy of Medicine, 80*, 1, March 30, 2003,1-47.

Miller-McLemore, B. (1993). The human web: Reflections on the state of pastoral theology. *Christian Century*, April 7, 366-369.

Miller-McLemore, B. (1996). The living human web: Pastoral theology at the turn of the century. In J. Stevenson-Moessner (Ed.). *Through the eyes of women: Insights for pastoral care* (pp. 9-26). Minneapolis, MN: Fortress Press.

Patton, John (1993). *Pastoral care in context: An introduction to pastoral care*. Louisville, KY: Westminster/John Knox Press.

Ramsay, Nancy J. (Ed.). (2004). *Pastoral care and counseling: Redefining the paradigms*. Nashville, TN: Abingdon Press.

Winnicott, Donald. (1971, 1979). *Playing and reality*. New York, NY: Basic Books.

doi:10.1300/J062v08n03_15

Index

adventure as a theological concept, 24
African American Episcopal Church,
    94
African Catholic Church, 104
African Methodist Episcopal Church
    (AME), 93,128
Aggett, P., 145
Albers, Robert H., 193n3
Ali Watkins, Carroll, 53,94
American Association of Pastoral
    Counselors (AAPC), xxiii,
    xxiv,1-2,6,17,30,33,36-37,
    39-40,75,108,114,158,168,
    171-172,190,199-200,
    203-204
    Body of Knowledge, 17,172
American Baptist Church, 30
American Indian, 103
Andrews, Dale P., 95
Appiah-Kubi, K., 103
Aron, L., 64n2
Ashbrook, Jim, 200
Ashby, Homer, 92
Association of Clinical Pastoral
    Education (ACPE), 1,75,
    113n5,186,193n5,199-200
Association of Professional Chaplains
    (APC), 1
Auburn University, 75
Augustine of Hippo, 151

Bangor Theological Seminary, 194n6
Bangs, R. L., 214
Baptist Church, 128
Bass, Dorothy C., 84
Bateson, G., 30
Beasley-Topliffe, Keith, 4

Beaumont, Hunter, 193n3
Behan, C.P., 144,146,148
Benedictine Monasteries, 162,164
Benedictine Spirituality, 155,
    156,162-165
Benson, Herbert, 80
Berea College, 194n6
Berg, S., 146
Bidwell, Duane R., xxiv,78,129
Bion, Wilfred, 61-62
bio-psycho-social-spiritual model, 170
blending, 22,104
Bob, S.R., 144,146
Bohler, Carolyn J. Stahl, 193n3
Boisen, Anton, 64n3,211-212
Bollas, Christopher, 60
Bonhoeffer, Dietrich, 19
Bonnasue, 203-204
Boston University School of Theology,
    194n6
Bowen, M., 30
Brite Divinity School, 194n6
Bronfenbrenn, U., 31
Browning, Don, 52
Buber, Martin, 52
Butler, Judith, 64n8,117-118

California, 54,71,182,185
Carlson, T.D., 144,146
Carnegie Foundation for The
    Advancement of Teaching,
    26n2,75
Carver School of Medicine, University
    of Iowa, 194n6
Casement, Patrick, 49,59
Catholic Church, 114,128,137
Celebrating the Disciplines, 84

BOOK ORDER FORM!

Order a copy of this book with this form or online at:
http://www.HaworthPress.com/store/product.asp?sku= 6022

The Formation of Pastoral Counselors
Challenges and Opportunities

____ in softbound at $48.00 ISBN-13: 978-0-7890-3296-6 / ISBN-10: 0-7890-3296-1.
____ in hardbound at $65.00 ISBN-13: 978-0-7890-3295-9 / ISBN-10: 0-7890-3295-3.

COST OF BOOKS _____

POSTAGE & HANDLING _____
US: $4.00 for first book & $1.50
for each additional book
Outside US: $5.00 for first book
& $2.00 for each additional book.

SUBTOTAL _____

In Canada: add 6% GST. _____

STATE TAX _____
CA, IL, IN, MN, NJ, NY, OH, PA & SD residents
please add appropriate local sales tax.

FINAL TOTAL _____
If paying in Canadian funds, convert
using the current exchange rate,
UNESCO coupons welcome.

❑ BILL ME LATER:
Bill-me option is good on US/Canada/
Mexico orders only; not good to jobbers,
wholesalers, or subscription agencies.

❑ Signature _____

❑ Payment Enclosed: $_____

❑ PLEASE CHARGE TO MY CREDIT CARD:

❑ Visa ❑ MasterCard ❑ AmEx ❑ Discover
❑ Diner's Club ❑ Eurocard ❑ JCB

Account #_____

Exp Date_____

Signature_____
(Prices in US dollars and subject to change without notice.)

PLEASE PRINT ALL INFORMATION OR ATTACH YOUR BUSINESS CARD

Name

Address

City   State/Province   Zip/Postal Code

Country

Tel   Fax

E-Mail

May we use your e-mail address for confirmations and other types of information? ❑Yes ❑No We appreciate receiving
your e-mail address. Haworth would like to e-mail special discount offers to you, as a preferred customer.
We will never share, rent, or exchange your e-mail address. We regard such actions as an invasion of your privacy.

Order from your **local bookstore** or directly from
The Haworth Press, Inc. 10 Alice Street, Binghamton, New York 13904-1580 • USA
Call our toll-free number (1-800-429-6784) / Outside US/Canada: (607) 722-5857
Fax: 1-800-895-0582 / Outside US/Canada: (607) 771-0012
E-mail your order to us: orders@HaworthPress.com

For orders outside US and Canada, you may wish to order through your local
sales representative, distributor, or bookseller.
For information, see http://HaworthPress.com/distributors

(Discounts are available for individual orders in US and Canada only, not booksellers/distributors.)

Please photocopy this form for your personal use.
www.HaworthPress.com

BOF07